DAVID LEFFMAN is a travel writer and photographer who first visited China in 1985. Since then he has clocked up over six years in the country, researching guidebooks for Rough Guides and Dorling Kindersley and writing articles on Chinese history and culture for the *South China Morning Post* and *The Diplomat*.

He has also authored *The Mercenary Mandarin*, a biography of the nineteenth-century British adventurer in China, William Mesny; and *Paper Horses*, about traditional woodblock prints of Chinese folk gods.

A Murder In Yunnan

The Unsolved Killing of a British Diplomat on China's Southwestern Frontier

David Leffman

BLACKSMITH BOOKS

A MURDER IN YUNNAN

ISBN 978-988-76749-1-7

Published by Blacksmith Books
Unit 26, 19/F, Block B, Wah Lok Industrial Centre,
37-41 Shan Mei Street, Fo Tan, Hong Kong
Tel: (+852) 2877 7899
www.blacksmithbooks.com

Edited by Paul Christensen

Contents

History is not what you thought. *It is what you can remember.*

– Sellar and Yeatman, *1066 and All That*

Acknowledgements

First thanks as ever to Narrell, not least for company and support on many trips to Yunnan. Also to the late Keith Stevens for giving me his copy of Fletcher's *Tengyueh: Route Book of Travels in the Neighbourhood*. Elsewhere, archive.org provided easy access to out-of-print books, ditto JSTOR and Academia for academic papers; staff at the National Archives, Kew were always helpful; Helen Yang shared family stories about her great-great-great grandfather Yang Yuke; Ms Jiang, a taxi driver in Lijiang town and descendant of Jiang Zonghan, took me to see the bridge her ancestor had built over the Yangzi; Mr Lee Maoqing and Ms Bi Xiaoyi tracked down background information from Chinese sources and translated from classical Chinese; while Rachel Silberstein, Nick Shaw and Simon Lewis provided invaluable feedback. Thanks too to Laszlo Montgomery of the splendid China History Podcast; and not forgetting Pete Spurrier, who once again has agreed to publish me.

In memory of my good friend Paul Tomic, who I hope would have enjoyed this book.

Notes on names

Much of this story takes place in a border region awash with ethnic groups and languages. Many places – and even individuals – have multiple names, depending on whether sources are using English, Burmese, Chinese or Shan terms. For example, the Chinese city of Tengyue was also called by its Shan name, Momien; Burma's Kachin people are the Jingpo in China; and one of the key players in Margary's story, a Sino-Burmese named Moung Yu, was known in Chinese as Li Tongshi, allowing the British of the time to confuse him with another Sino-Burmese man surnamed Li.

Complicating this are the various transliteration systems used for these languages, each of which creates a different spelling in English. Some variations are fairly familiar – Pekin or Peking for modern Beijing – others less so: for example the town of Mangyun appears in various texts as Manwine, Mangwyn or Manwaing.

And then many places have been renamed since the nineteenth century: Tengyue is now Tengchong, Yongchang is Baoshan, Mengmao is Ruili, Sanda is Yingjiang and so on. Several of these changes carry political overtones, such as Burma – favoured in colonial times – against today's Myanmar.

To reduce confusion names have been standardised throughout. Chinese is written using modern *pinyin* transliteration, and for other languages I've chosen arbitrarily what I feel is the most useful British spelling. Just be aware that these names are not necessarily those found in original sources.

The Glossary on pp.223-237 includes alternative names for people and places, with short biographies of the important players.

Apology

The attitudes of historic sources towards nationalities and ethnic groups given here do not reflect my personal opinions or experiences.

Please get in touch at davidleffman.com.

Preface

On 21 February 1875, the dead body of British diplomat Augustus Raymond Margary lay on the ground at Mangyun, a remote Chinese town near the frontier with Burma. He had been murdered. That much is certain.

Margary may have been beheaded. Or not. Perhaps he shot one of his attackers before being killed, though this same man – or somebody that officials claimed was the same man – later denied it. Margary's Chinese servants all died alongside him, or were picked off elsewhere, or one of them escaped. The attack happened inside Mangyun at a banquet, outside the town on the way to some hot springs, or up in the far-off hills. His killers were regular Chinese soldiers, lawless bandits, tribal "savages", former Muslim rebels or a civil militia; they might have been led by a warlord, were acting independently, were under orders from the Chinese provincial governor, or were obeying the wishes of the Burmese king. The men arrested for the crime all confessed their guilt, or they were innocent villagers whose admissions were fabricated by a court interpreter. It's possible the interpreter himself was the murderer.

So whose version of events to believe? The choice of sources includes reports from both Chinese and British investigators, some high-profile, others undercover, who each spent months interviewing the players but managed to arrive at completely different conclusions. Private observers with local experience wrote down their own suspicions in journals and diaries. And then there were the English-language newspapers in China, Britain and India, who trumpeted the often biased, badly-informed, outraged popular opinions of the day.

When you look beyond what happened and who might have been to blame, other aspects of what reports of the time dubbed "The Margary

Affair" seem equally intriguing. Just *why* was Margary, a well-respected but obscure civil servant based thousands of kilometres away on the other side of China, even at Mangyun in the first place to get himself killed? And what on earth could he have possibly done to make so many different suspects want him dead?

The answers to all these questions have their roots in a centuries-old struggle between European powers for control of East Asia's wealthy trade networks, a long story involving colonial arrogance, invasions, wars, drug dealing, unaccountable international corporations, phantom railways, mistaken identities, mutual cultural incomprehension and the foundation of the Chinese embassy in London. There are even several tigers and a parade of elephants.

But in the end it was all about money.

Setting the Stage

In fact there's no mystery behind why Margary was murdered in 1875: it's because he was British. And if you want to know why the British were so unpopular along the China-Burma border during the late nineteenth century – and why they came to be there at all – you need to go right back to the medieval global trade in spices.

Native to India and south-east Asia, exotic spices such as cinnamon, pepper and ginger have been used in European cooking and medicine for thousands of years, traded from their sources via the Arabian Gulf and the Middle East. Over time all sorts of people were involved in this traffic, but by the Middle Ages – given that the Islamic world then stretched from Morocco right through to China – the trade had become concentrated in Muslim hands. It was a valuable trade too: during the fifteenth century a pound of peppercorns (one of the cheaper spices) would have cost a skilled British craftsman around two days' wages. Resenting the fortunes being made by Islamic wholesalers, a race began amongst European maritime nations to trace the origins of these spices for themselves and put the profits into Christian pockets.

Following in the footsteps of independent merchant-explorers from the Italian city-states of Venice and Genoa, who had reached India (and beyond) during the thirteenth century, this race was won in 1498 by the Portuguese, when an expedition led by the navigator Vasco da Gama made landfall on India's west coast. Da Gama was granted limited trading rights by the local king, but the long-established Muslim community here rejected the idea of European competition and had him thrown out of the country. Undeterred, the Portuguese returned home the following year with enough stories of wealth – if only token amounts of spices – to convince their government to send out an annual trading fleet.

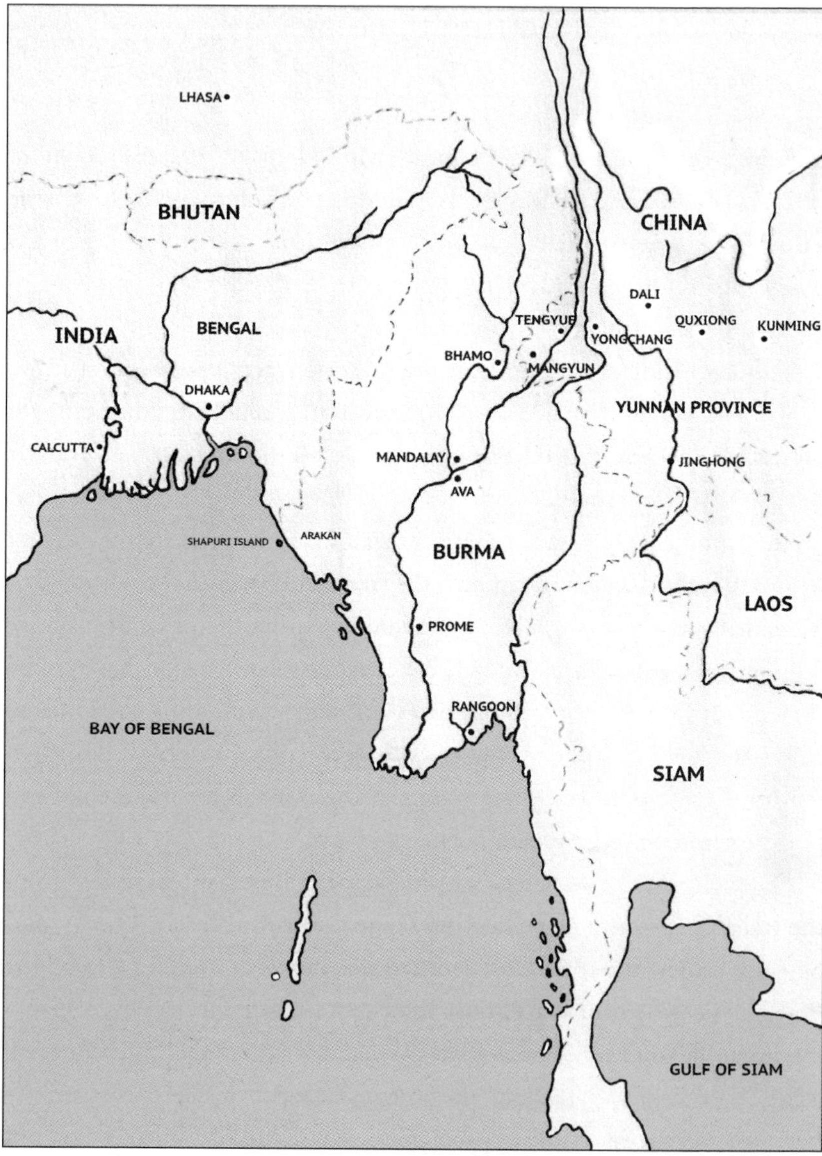

Setting the stage

Within a decade the Portuguese had managed to establish themselves as the first European power in India. Under the piratical viceroy Afonso de Albuquerque their ships soon dominated the Indian Ocean's sea lanes, forcing local states to accept, in the name of the Portuguese king, Albuquerque's "protection". And it was on Albuquerque's orders that in 1512 a Portuguese fleet traced the source of the entire world supply of nutmeg and cloves to Maluku, a remote island group in eastern Indonesia, where they bought these spices for about one thousandth of their resale value in Europe.

Spain was the next country to pick over the region. Beginning in 1519, a Spanish expedition led by the Portuguese explorer Ferdinand Magellan spent three years undertaking the first ever recorded global circumnavigation: his fleet of five ships rounded the tip of South America, crossed the Pacific to the Philippines, stopped at Maluku to stock up with spices, and from there sailed around Africa and back to Spain. Magellan himself was killed in the Philippines, and just one battered hulk with eighteen emaciated crew made it home – out of the 270 sailors who had begun the voyage – but the twenty-six tons of cloves and cinnamon they brought back must have gone some way to recompensing Magellan's sponsors for the enormous cost of equipping the expedition.

By the late sixteenth century, religious and political tensions in Europe saw Catholic Spain, backed by their ally Portugal, at war with Protestant England and the newly-established Dutch Republic (which had just broken free from two centuries of Spanish rule). Their animosity extended from battlefields to trade, with Dutch merchants in particular targeting their Portuguese rivals in south-east Asia. In 1599 the Dutch arrived in Maluku and, despite efforts by the Portuguese to oust them, managed to establish their own successful trading post. Even after having to work through middlemen, this meant that the Dutch too had access to inexpensive bulk quantities of cloves, nutmeg and mace – the red membrane surrounding the nutmeg seed.

New Year's Eve 1600 proved to be a pivotal moment, marking when the British East India Company (often known simply as "The Company") was founded in London as a joint-stock corporation, with an agenda to develop trade with east Asia. They didn't do too well at first, subverted by Dutch protectionism and the fact that there was little call in the coastal tropics for woollen cloth, one of Britain's major exports. But their efforts did inspire the Dutch to launch their own East India Company two years later, the Vereenigde Oostindische Compagnie (VOC), who by hard-headed business methods and physical force eventually displaced the Portuguese and consolidated the Netherlands' own long-term hold in Indonesia.

Less successful was the French East India Company, founded in 1664 but, like its competitors, with roots running back some decades earlier. Although France garnered a firm toe-hold in China and India – much to British irritation – it wasn't until the nineteenth century, when it annexed Vietnam, Cambodia and Laos as French Indochina, that it made a significant impact on the region.

And so it was left for the British and Dutch to slug it out for naval supremacy in the Anglo-Dutch Wars, which spread from Europe to their Asian possessions. The fighting was brought to a diplomatic end in 1674 (though mutual animosity simmered away for decades) in a settlement notable for the British exchanging their sole possession in Maluku – the tiny, insignificant islet of Rhun – for Dutch-held Manhattan Island, now the core of New York City.

*

So, having abandoned Indonesia and its spices to the Netherlands, the British concentrated on making their mark in India, whose largely Hindu population was coming under the sway of the Islamic Mughal Empire. The Mughals were a warrior clan from central Asia who claimed descent from Timur and Genghis Khan; they had expanded into India during the sixteenth century and were still busy finishing off their conquest of the country. They were ruled from Delhi by an emperor who acquired his vast proverbial wealth through control of land taxes, gathered by local governors or princes.

Despite successful early ventures in pepper, the British soon became besotted with another product entirely: cotton. Indian cotton cloth was extremely fine, and by the mid-seventeenth century Britain was importing hundreds of thousands of pieces annually, seriously undermining its own domestic textile industries and leading to an eventual ban on Indian imports under the Calico Act of 1700.

But what really shifted British attention towards India was the explosive rise to power of the East India Company, sparked in part by the marriage in 1662 of the British king Charles II to a Portuguese princess, Catherine of Braganza. At the time Britain was bankrupt and depressed in the wake of the civil war and Cromwell's oppressive Puritan dictatorship, and the marriage not only unified the two countries against a mutual rival, Spain, but also gifted Charles the Indian port of Bombay, formerly a Portuguese possession, along with immense wealth – Catherine brought along a dowry worth around £500,000 – supported by Portugal's own trading empire.

Events during the recent war with the Netherlands had made it obvious that control of the seas was an essential part of Britain's national security – at one point in the fighting a Dutch fleet had sailed up the Medway to Chatham Dockyard in Kent, where they destroyed thirteen warships and towed away the royal flagship. But besides protecting the British coastline, a strong maritime presence could also be used to dominate trade, both in Europe and beyond. To make sure Britain succeeded in these arenas, Charles not only funded a new Royal Navy, he also threw his support behind the East India Company, which for decades had been floundering around in a sea of indecision and insolvency.

The Company was now given royal permission to raise its own armies, fight its own wars, mint its own money and to govern independently of the crown, and in 1700 parliament voted them a monopoly on all British commerce in east Asia. Prior to this point, the various European nations in India were competing more or less as rival businesses – generally using politics rather than military might to undermine each other's trading rights and gain favoured status with local rulers. But the 1740s saw conflict again breaking out in Europe between Britain and France with the fighting spreading, as before, to their overseas possessions. Both countries now sent out so many troops to defend their interests that there came to be more foreign soldiers than merchants in India. Campaigns flared intermittently, in which the French besieged Britain's fort at Madras and the British targeted the French headquarters, Pondicherry.

Britain's richest Indian holdings were in the northeastern state of Bengal (modern Bangladesh and West Bengal), whose vast wealth had gained it virtual independence from the Mughal throne. This wealth was largely agricultural, all down to fertile soils deposited by the lower reaches of three major rivers – the Brahmaputra, Ganges and Meghna – which emptied through a huge, muddy, mangrove-clad delta into the Bay of Bengal. The British founded a settlement here in 1690, some seventy kilometres upstream from the sea at the hamlet of Calcutta. With the Burmese coast sloping away on one side and eastern India stretching down the other, the town grew rapidly through trade in saltpetre, sugar and textiles, but in every other respect Calcutta was an awful place to live, hemmed in by jungle and low-lying marsh. From March onwards the climate grew fiercely hot and feverish, and a third of new arrivals died within their first year.

In 1756 The Company got into an argument with Bengal's new ruler, Siraj-ud-Daulah, who captured Calcutta after barely token resistance. Initial casualties were light but scores of British prisoners later died after being crammed overnight into a tiny cell – the infamous "Black Hole of Calcutta". The British retaliated the following year with an expeditionary force to oust Siraj and place their own pliable candidate on Bengal's throne. Defeating Siraj and his French allies at the Battle of Plassey, they suddenly realised they were not just king-makers, but in a position to run Bengal for themselves.

Almost overnight The Company's purpose in India changed direction, as they set aside ad-hoc commerce in favour of taking effective control of the country, leaving local princes nominally in charge but commandeering the enormously profitable land taxation system. Military enforcement provoked fierce resistance – especially from the Marathas of central India – but one by one regional governors fell. Britain's merchants gained from the incidental removal of European competitors and the opening up of Indian markets, allowing access to 183 million customers, one fifth of the world's entire population. Calcutta, grown into a city flooded with migrants eager to "shake the pagoda tree" and make their fortunes, became the seat of British rule in India, a position it held until 1911.

So, with its European rivals quashed, trade blossoming and profits pouring in, The Company looked around to see if the methods which had succeeded in India could be applied elsewhere, and found another monolithic empire with enormous commercial potential just next door: China.

*

In fact Chinese textiles had reached the Mediterranean in Roman times, ferried overland through central Asia along the Silk Road, and by the eighteenth century Europeans were already dealing directly with China. Once again the Portuguese had been first in 1557, leasing the gateway port of Macau, a small, rocky peninsula on the southern Chinese coast at the mouth of the Pearl River. Here they built a fortified town, which over the next eighty years flourished by exporting Chinese silk to Japan. And it was the Portuguese who began sending small quantities of Indian opium into China, where it had been used since the seventh century as an aphrodisiac and anti-malarial. While expensive, these new Portuguese imports made opium widely accessible, and for the first time it caught on in a small way as a recreational drug amongst China's moneyed classes.

It was around this time that Europe also discovered a stimulating Chinese herb: tea. The Dutch introduced it in 1606, though there was little initial interest in this medicinally bitter brew. But as with opium in China, tea drinking slowly became fashionable amongst the European aristocracy – including the wife of King Charles II, Catherine of Braganza – from where it filtered out into the wider population. In September 1658, a London coffee house published the earliest known advert for "The Excellent, and by all Physitians approved, *China* Drink, called by the *Chineans*, *Tcha*, by other Nations *Tay alias Tee*", and just six years later the East India Company fulfilled its first order, for one hundred pounds of leaf, shipped from China via middlemen in Java. As the beverage became part of British life the government imposed enormous import duties, but this simply fuelled a healthy smuggling industry accounting for almost half the tea consumed.

With tea came an interest in Chinese porcelain to drink it from. The secrets of porcelain manufacture were unknown in Europe until 1712, but examples had certainly arrived from China by the sixteenth century – two blue-and-white Ming porcelain bowls feature in the Italian Giovanni Bellini's 1514 painting *Feast of the Gods* – and being brighter, lighter and stronger than most European ceramics, porcelain was much sought after.

Although opium, silk, tea and porcelain would become the cornerstones of Britain's future dealings with China, establishing that trade proved difficult. China's ruling Ming dynasty was beginning to fall apart, and being fully occupied with quelling popular uprisings had no time or interest in developing export markets. Britain made its first attempt at direct contact in 1637, when a fleet of four ships under Captain John Weddell moored off Macau, but they were repulsed empty-handed by both the Chinese and Portuguese.

Seven years later the Ming dynasty finally fell; the last Ming emperor committed suicide and a rebel force stormed the Chinese capital, Beijing. But then a foreign army, the Manchus, gatecrashed through the Great Wall from their northeastern homelands, chased out the rebels and took Beijing for themselves. Within fifty years the Manchu Qing dynasty had pacified the entire country, crushing dissent and putting the majority Han Chinese population under a much-resented alien rule.

Being foreigners themselves, the Manchus were perhaps more open-minded about contact with the outside world than the previous administration. At any rate, in 1715 the British East India Company was finally allowed to open a trading post just up the Pearl River from Macau, outside the great walled city of Guangzhou (then known to the British as Canton). Not that this meant that they had access to the rest of China. Guangzhou is far down on China's southern fringes, over two thousand kilometres from Beijing; even the local dialect, Cantonese, was incomprehensible to speakers of Mandarin Chinese, the language of the Imperial court. Foreigners were confined to their enclaves and forbidden to enter Guangzhou city, let alone to travel further afield. As it was illegal for Chinese to teach foreigners their language, all business had to be conducted through Chinese middlemen, adding to the expense.

And there was another problem. The Chinese government approved of taking foreign silver in exchange for silk, porcelain and tea – annual tea exports topped two million kilograms by the 1750s – but proved reluctant to buy anything that Britain had to sell. China's rulers scorned foreign trade as demeaning and there was a good political lesson here too; by keeping in mind the motto to "value nothing that comes from afar" and producing all its own wares, China retained the upper hand in negotiations with foreign powers, being impossible to pressure through sanctions or debt manipulation.

By the late eighteenth century Britain's Industrial Revolution was in full swing: one-time cottage industries were becoming fully mechanised and expanding to fill factories, whole cities were being built to accommodate the new workforce and the country was busy weaving more finished cottons and woollens than it could ever hope to sell domestically. By 1790 Britain was importing over eleven million kilos of raw cotton a year to feed the industry; this quantity doubled over the next decade, by which time almost two thirds of the cloth produced in British factories was being exported.

So Britain no longer considered itself primarily a customer for exotic foreign goods, but as a major manufacturing power seeking overseas markets for its own wares. Having spent years buying Chinese products, it seemed only fair to British minds that China – with a population of three hundred million potential customers – should start buying something from Britain too. Yet the Chinese government continued to insist that their country already had everything it needed, and had no interest in imports (though in fact there was a limited demand for British woollen cloth, prized by China's elite for its warmth and water-resistant qualities).

In 1792 the East India Company sponsored a diplomatic mission to the Chinese court, headed by George Macartney and including artists, scientists, a military escort and all the secretaries and civil servants needed for such an enterprise. By appealing directly to the long-lived emperor Qianlong, the mission hoped to secure improved trading rights for British merchants, open up ports to foreign trade and establish a permanent embassy at Beijing. But after Macartney refused to kowtow – to kneel and touch his head to the floor in submission – these requests were rejected by Qianlong, who was unimpressed with the mission's "tribute gifts" of clocks and scientific instruments, dismissing them as utilitarian trifles.

The Company was not to be discouraged. Where honest diplomacy hadn't worked, perhaps more underhand methods might succeed. Thanks to those Portuguese imports, opium had become an increasingly popular recreational drug in China, leading to the first of many ineffectual bans on the trade in 1729. Now the British joined in too, sourcing opium cheaply from their fertile Bengal holdings. As direct sales into China were prohibited, the opium was trafficked via Calcutta to the British trading posts at Guangzhou, from where it was distributed across the country by Chinese go-betweens, often with the connivance of corrupt authorities. Substantial quantities were also smuggled directly by freelancers through other Chinese ports. The Company's profits from opium sales funded ongoing military operations in India.

In 1834 the East India Company lost their monopoly on eastern trade and began a rapid decline. But far from ending opium sales, this meant that anyone could dabble in the traffic. The subsequent unregulated boom saw opium become so inexpensive in China that everyone, rich and poor alike, could afford it. Demand and usage soared: within four years, the annual importation of the drug into China reached forty thousand chests, around 2500 tons, spurring an alarming flow of silver out of the country. British opium-trading firms reaped the benefits.

The Chinese government again attempted to deal with the problem, appointing the incorruptible commissioner Lin Zexu to shut the pernicious trade down for good. Having unsuccessfully appealed to the British authorities to halt it themselves on moral grounds, in 1839 Lin barricaded British merchants into their warehouses at Guangzhou and destroyed the entire stock of opium.

Britain immediately opened hostilities with the Qing empire, Lin Zexu was exiled to China's far north-west, and for the next twenty years the two nations battled through the two Opium Wars. It was never much of a contest. China's military was armed largely with a medieval assortment of swords, pole weapons, bows and badly-cast cannon, while the British had a battle-hardened army and the world's strongest navy, both bristling with modern firearms. After years of skirmishes, ineffectual negotiations and the shelling of Chinese coastal cities – the term "gunboat diplomacy" was coined to describe British tactics – the Opium Wars ended in 1860 with the flight of the Chinese emperor into Manchuria and the occupation of Beijing by an Anglo-French force.

For having the nerve to fight Britain, China was forced to sign the Treaty of Nanking in 1842, the Treaty of Tientsin in 1858, and the Convention of Peking in 1860. These three humiliating "Unequal Treaties" legalised the opium trade, ceded Chinese territory to Britain, demanded colossal indemnities (including a fine of four million ounces of silver for destroying the British opium), established foreign legations at Beijing, allowed Christian missionaries to preach their alien religion, and – the whole point of the exercise from the British perspective – saw selected Chinese cities forced open as Treaty Ports, where foreign merchants could live and conduct business. France, Germany, Russia, the United States and other Western powers demanded similar concessions.

Government failure to protect China from these aggressive foreigners saw the Chinese population lose faith in their Manchu rulers, exacerbated by the huge increase in taxes needed to pay off the war indemnities. Resentment and poverty bred dissent, and dissent erupted into civil war. In 1850, a failed civil-service exam candidate and Christian convert named Hong Xiuquan launched the Taiping Uprising, an unlikely attempt to overthrow the Manchu Qing dynasty and reinstate ethnic Chinese rule. Claiming he was the younger brother of Jesus Christ and promising equality for all in his "Taiping Heavenly Kingdom", Hong rallied a vast peasant army which stormed eastwards through central China, sweeping aside the Imperial forces sent against them and taking the enormous walled city of Nanjing as their capital.

Bogged down in the Opium Wars with Britain, the Chinese government had few resources available to quell Hong Xiuquan's insurrection. By the time the Taipings were finally defeated in 1864, the death toll from their rebellion was estimated at over twenty million and eastern China was in ruins, making the Taiping Uprising the most destructive civil war in world history. Inspired by the Taipings' anti-Manchu message, similar localised conflicts – far smaller but still involving millions of deaths – persisted for a decade or more afterwards, which the destabilised Qing dynasty found equally difficult to suppress.

No wonder then if these drug-pushing foreigners and their divisive Christian religion found themselves unwelcome in China. Still, with the Taipings gone a relative stability settled over the country, and newly-established British merchants tried to calculate the profits they could make from the vast population – now standing at four hundred and thirty million, according to the official census.

And yet the China trade consistently failed to reach its imagined potential. While brisk enough in the coastal settlements, it remained prohibitively expensive to ship goods all the way from Britain to the coastal ports of Shanghai and Hong Kong, and then cart them hundreds of miles inland to where the bulk of China's population actually lived. Even major roads were often in appalling condition, seldom paved and often little more than dirt tracks, impassable in wet weather; most of the time there was no chance of using carts, so goods had to be carried by pack animal or porter, both expensive and slow. Where feasible, boats offered a cheaper and faster alternative, especially in the maze of inland rivers and waterways covering eastern and southern China, though piracy was always a problem – as were bandits by land.

On top of this goods were subject to transport tax, *lijin*, paid at any number of customs posts along the way. Although a ticketing system was eventually set up so that foreign-registered firms could pay *lijin* in advance and simply display the receipt where needed along the road – hence avoiding having to cough up the additional "tea money" inevitably demanded by local officials – all this meant that the further you shipped goods away from the coast and into the interior, the more expensive they became, and the less likely anyone would want to buy them.

So the British began looking for a back door into China's landlocked, remote, heavily populated southwestern provinces. Sandwiched between Britain's emerging empire in India and southwestern China lay just one country, Burma, and cross-border trade was already well-established: Chinese gold and silk flowed into Burma, while the Burmese sent back rich green jade and enormous quantities of raw cotton fibre. The British wanted their cut of this lucrative business; if China was buying cotton, they felt it should be theirs. Why not move British goods directly overland from India into China, through Burma?

*

Burma's core stretches along the Chindwin and Irrawaddy rivers, two lengthy systems which flow south from the foothills of the Himalayas through the centre of the country, finally disgorging themselves through a complex of deltas into the tropical Andaman Sea. The north-west frontier buffered up against various states, beyond which the coast of India stretched for over two thousand kilometres around the Bay of Bengal. East through Shan territory lay the Chinese province of Yunnan; while south-east were the various Siamese kingdoms which make up modern Thailand.

Compared with neighbouring India and China – both of whose written records went back for thousands of years – Burmese history was fairly brief. Around 800 AD the majority Burman ethnic group, after which the country was named, moved south from the Tibetan borderlands to found the Pagan kingdom. Within two centuries Pagan controlled the length of the Irrawaddy valley, plus coastal Arakan (modern Rakhine, on the frontier with Bengal) and the Shan states to the east, including border regions with Siam. Even though these boundaries would be contested vigorously over time, from now on they formed the basis for the country's long-term historic borders. And it was also under the Pagan that Theravada Buddhism, introduced from India centuries earlier, became Burma's state religion, with the king as patron of the church.

Over the following centuries the Pagan kingdom was replaced by a succession of dynasties with ever-shifting capitals, visited by the first European adventurers – including Italians Hieronimo di Santo Stefano and Caesar Frederike, and the Londoner Ralph Fitch. They brought back reports of white elephants kept in royal stables, golden pagodas, wealth in rubies and precious stones, and the king's jealous monopoly on trade.

In 1617 the British East India Company, recently established in India, sent agents to Burma to reclaim goods left by a deceased British merchant. Though they failed in their mission, they did arrive back in India with a letter from the Burmese king offering friendship and free trade for British merchants.

Yet for a good while The Company was less interested in establishing a long-term presence in Burma, than they were in intriguing to keep their European rivals out – especially the French. True, British merchants sailed in and out of Burmese ports all the time, but these were freelancers which the East India Company tolerated as long as they only conducted local coastal trade, and didn't undermine their monopoly by sending goods back to Britain. The few times The Company *did* attempt to establish themselves, sending embassies to the king, signing treaties and setting up trading posts, either profits were so slight that they lost interest, or they managed to offend the authorities and get themselves expelled, sometimes violently.

It wasn't until after the British became masters of Bengal in 1757 that they began to consider their relationship with Burma more seriously. The two territories were separated only by the independent state of Arakan – a sliver of coast, almost cut off from the rest of Burma by a mountain range to the east – and Burma was now ruled by the expansionist Konbaung dynasty. By the 1780s the Konbaung had annexed Arakan, gone to war with Siam and fought four campaigns with China for control of the Shan states that buffered their mutual border, and which both countries claimed as their own (for their part, the Shans saw themselves as independent). The first three of these campaigns saw Qing forces beaten – it's believed that China lost 70,000 troops – while the fourth was fought to a standstill and ended in a truce. From here on, however, China considered Burma as a vassal state, and indeed Burma began sending a tribute to Beijing every ten years – which, whoever had "won" the Sino-Burmese conflicts, was probably cheaper than going to war again.

By this point The Company's Indian dockyards had become dependent on Burmese teak for shipbuilding. Rather than relying on buying the timber through agents, they wanted to save costs by founding their own base in Burma, from where they could also promote sales of British cloth. Though their request was rejected by King Bodawpaya, the British were granted very favourable trading terms: they would be charged low customs duties; they could travel and trade without restriction inside Burma; and were allowed to appoint a full-time Resident to oversee their affairs at the southern port of Rangoon, around forty kilometres upstream from the coast along the Rangoon river.

Yet there was soon a breakdown in trust, not least over Arakan, that buffer state with Bengal. As The Company spread its rule over an ever-increasing chunk of India, the Governor-General, Lord Richard Wellesley (older brother of the famous Duke of Wellington) wanted to define firmly the country's frontiers. British maps marked the Bengal-Arakan border as the River Naf, but the Burmese saw the frontier as far more nebulous, extending west beyond this river and well into what the British considered to be their territory.

In addition, ongoing resistance to Burmese rule within Arakan often saw rebels staging uprisings and then fleeing into Bengal to escape reprisals. Britain's routine refusal to hand them back angered Bodawpaya, who wrote to the East India Company demanding that all Arakanese in Bengal were rounded up and returned or else "powerful forces will be despatched both by sea and land... for the purpose of storming, capturing and destroying the whole of the English possessions".

It was all bluff. Bodawpaya didn't want to fight Britain: he was already struggling to contain internal resistance to heightened taxation and conscription for the war with Siam, which was not going well. But a decade later the Arakan issue was still festering and now Bodawpaya's ambitious grandson Bagyidaw was on the throne. Convinced of Burma's moral and military superiority, he considered the consequences of confronting the British: a war would mean the loss of trade with India, the king's largest source of personal income, but this would be easily surpassed by new revenue from Bengal, should Burma conquer it.

The flashpoint came in 1824 during a seemingly trivial squabble over tiny Shapuree island off the Arakan-Bengal coast, which the British had occupied. Burmese troops sent to evict the British were mistaken for an invasion force heading to Bengal, and suddenly the First Anglo-Burmese War had erupted: British warships captured Rangoon and the Burmese army was defeated nearby at the Battle of Danubyu, where their heroic commander Maha Bandula was killed. As the British advanced up-country towards the royal city of Ava almost unopposed, district heads submitted to the invaders rather than risk having their villages destroyed by fighting. When news got out that Britain was considering an alliance with their old enemy Siam, Burma sued for peace.

The war had cost the British dearly in both men and money, and the terms of the 1826 Treaty of Yandabo were harsh, including Burma ceding Arakan and the adjacent territories of Assam and Manipur, and a crippling indemnity of twenty million rupees (later reduced to ten million). Resentment at this land grab, the humiliating imposition of a British Resident at Ava, and the financial burden – which bankrupted the country – was taken out on British traders, who suddenly found themselves facing bureaucratic obstruction and extortion from local authorities.

The situation came to a head in 1852 when two British captains at Rangoon were charged with murder, but then released after paying a fine equivalent to some £990. The captains protested their innocence and appealed to the British administration at Calcutta for compensation. A small fleet under Commodore Lambert duly arrived at Rangoon to investigate the claims, but when Lambert was refused an audience with the governor because he was asleep, he seized the king of Burma's private ship. Rangoon's governor, facing likely execution if he lost the imperial vessel, pleaded unsuccessfully with the hot-headed Lambert and then shelled the British in desperation. The fleet returned fire, killing three hundred Burmese and kicking off the Second Anglo-Burmese War.

British-language newspapers all pitched in to supported the conflict, disparaging the Burmese king as "vindictive and imbecile" and reporting the minor diplomatic causes as if they were major outrages against British prestige. *The Friend of India* offered a typically bombastic editorial: "The second war with the Burmese has commenced. They have fired the first shot; they have thrown down the gauntlet, and we must take it up and pursue the conflict till it ends in their complete submission". Others, such as the *Bombay Gazette*, were quick to suggest using the war as an excuse to occupy Burmese territory: "To enter upon a second Burmese war without a determination to annex the maritime provinces would be an act of inconceivable impolicy...It requires only a small exercise of moral courage to make [all of coastal Burma] British."

To balance all this raucous jingoism, Manchester manufacturer and Liberal politician Richard Cobden penned *How Wars are Got Up in India: The Origin of the Burmese War*, a level-headed summary of the case and Lambert's extraordinary over-reaction to the Rangoon governor's mild snub. *The Times* later summed up the facts succinctly: "England went to war with Burmah, and annihilated its political existence, for the non-payment of a disputed demand of £990."

As in China, where an antiquated military had faced modern weapons and tactics, the Second Anglo-Burmese War could have only one outcome. On 20 December 1852, after Burmese forces had been routed (and which saw the death of Rear Admiral Charles Austen, brother of novelist Jane), Britain formally annexed coastal "Lower" Burma, giving them control of Rangoon and the Irrawaddy and Salween deltas, so cutting off Burmese access to the sea and restricting the king's rule to interior "Upper" Burma. King Mindon Min – newly raised to power during a palace coup – refused to sign a treaty to officially end the war, which the Governor-General of India, Lord Dalhousie, shrugged off pragmatically with "our real treaty is our military power".

Dalhousie's glib confidence was soon put to the test, but not in Burma. In 1857 a major uprising broke out against British rule in India: the Indian Mutiny, also known as The First War of Independence. Suppressed the following year after immense brutality and slaughter by both sides, the conflict heralded a complete change of government in India as The Company was stripped of power and replaced at Calcutta by the crown, who instituted direct rule – the British Raj.

The Mutiny also highlighted that the British presence in India, Burma and China was insignificant compared with the numbers of people they were attempting to control. From fear of future risings – and perhaps a need to soothe their conscience – the conquerors began to portray those they dominated as inferior and the occupation of their lands as a moral duty: British rule in return for modernity, stability, civilization. But as Dalhousie realised, it wasn't modern policies or "superior" culture which actually enforced the British presence, but fear of the military. If awe of British firepower was undermined, their rule was finished; a bold front, backed by an overwhelming response to any challenge, was vital to maintaining British prestige.

*

Public disobedience and armed opposition to the occupation of Lower Burma smouldered away for years, but as a cash economy replaced feudalism the population boomed and trade revenues tripled. King Mindon forged an uneasy working relationship with his British neighbours, who were rapidly developing Rangoon as their administrative capital (complete with hotels, government offices, metalled roads, and church spires poking skywards), but was well aware of their expansionist tendencies and remained steadfast in protecting his authority in Upper Burma.

In 1857 Mindon founded a new capital, Mandalay, on a plain just upstream along the Irrawaddy from Ava; extensive palm-thatched suburbs surrounded a walled city of royal residences about a mile square, where the king gave audiences to ministers, supplicants, officials and a few foreigners who requested the privilege. Rather than be forced to conduct international business solely through Lower Burma's British-held ports, Mindon – "a short, stout, pleasant [and] exceeding crafty-looking gentleman" with a fine moustache – now began to look increasingly eastwards and overland towards China.

The British had also been busy investigating potential Burma-China trade routes. In 1862, the Indian Army officer Arthur Phayre was brought in to negotiate a treaty with the Burmese king about opening a non-specific "commercial highway" between India and China. This would allow the widespread free passage of goods across each other's territory, in return for the British abolishing customs duties levied on Burmese products.

But having surrendered their border taxes, the British found themselves unable to break into markets already controlled by Burmese and Chinese businessmen. In fact, many goods became more expensive in British-occupied Lower Burma, where duties and taxes were still levied, than in the king's territory, which had effectively become a duty-free enclave. Even more galling was that this windfall largely benefited the Burmese king personally, who could simply declare himself the sole permitted trader of any popular goods – rice, cotton, coal, amber, gold, gemstones and so on – taxing them at a rate he decided himself.

In 1866, an attempted revolution broke out at Mandalay headed by two of Mindon's sons, but the British supported the king and the rebels were defeated. Feeling that the king now owed Britain a favour, Phayre attempted to renegotiate the treaty, asking Mindon to renounce his monopolies. After some wrangling he agreed, but this didn't seem to improve British profits in Burma; the London *Times* commented sourly that Mindon did "in fact, manage, in spite of his treaty concessions to us, purchased by us at an enormous price [the loss of border taxes], to maintain his position as the chief and only wholesaler in his dominions."

The paper was especially nettled that the Burmese king appeared to still control all trade with neighbouring Yunnan province in China, incidentally ensuring that the British were unable to muscle in on any profits. "In this he is cordially seconded by his partners the guild of Yunnan merchants, who, as shortsighted as their patron, cannot see that in opening out the trade to the world, the lion's share of the profits would still be theirs" – though anyone aware of the history of the British in India would doubt this statement.

*

But if Mindon controlled the existing Burma–China trade, perhaps Britain could forge its own routes. Initially, the most promising target seemed to be the town of Jinghong, capital of a small Thai-speaking kingdom which lay on the Mekong river in the vague borderlands between southern China, Siam, and Laos: the British believed Jinghong to be a Siamese tributary state of Burma, the Chinese that it lay inside their territory on the boundaries of Yunnan province. Jinghong had already been visited by the Indian Army soldier and surveyor Captain William Couperus Macleod in 1837, "in view to opening out commercial intercourse between the Chinese traders, who were in the habit of visiting the towns of Siamese Laos near our [Burmese] frontier". Macleod was refused permission to continue into China proper, but reported that Jinghong's merchants were all keen for the British to open up a "gold and silver road" to the sea.

Macleod's appearance alarmed Chinese on both sides of the border, who rightly saw the British as potential business rivals. This was before the Opium Wars, but any educated Chinese would have been aware how the British had arrived in India as merchants, and then used their own squabbles as an excuse to import armies and gradually take over the entire country. A similar pattern had been repeated in Burma, and now here were the British again claiming to be traders, banging on China's own doors. Iribu, the governor of China's Yunnan province, reprimanded the Burmese court for allowing the British to explore the region, comparing them to a parasitic strangler fig which smothers its host tree and kills it.

The first person to propose opening up Jinghong to regular traffic was Captain Richard Sprye, a retired Indian Army veteran of the first Anglo-Burmese War. Now a notorious "armchair general" living in London, in 1858 Sprye had simply looked at a map, joined Rangoon to Jinghong by a straight 500-mile-long line, seen that half of this lay within British-controlled territory, and declared it to be a viable route. By banging on about his idea to anyone who would listen, and writing "interminable letters to every Government office in any way concerned", Sprye eventually managed to convince others that a railway could be built, which would bring the wealth and commerce of southwestern China down to the British at Rangoon.

Surveys by the Indian Government in 1867 didn't find any insurmountable engineering barriers to Sprye's idea, but they doubted that trade with Jinghong alone would repay the expense of construction, and advised extending the line four hundred kilometres north to Kunming, capital of Yunnan province. Unfortunately, railway construction inside China was a major issue. Quite apart from the fact that a Rangoon–Kunming line would obviously cart profits out of China and into the pockets of British traders, railways were feared as an alien technology which would extend foreign influence beyond the Treaty Ports. There was also no way to build them any distance in China without desecrating the graves scattered around every village – utterly repellent to Confucianism's respect-for-the-ancestors ethics – and no railways had yet been approved for construction. The idea of a trade route via Jinghong was abandoned.

So where next? Just as politics and expense were demolishing Captain Sprye's hobby-horse, alarming news came through of a major French expedition into the region. Having failed to neutralise British expansionism in India or gain long-term holdings in Siam and Burma, France had maintained a fairly low profile in most of south-east Asia, but they had made headway in Vietnam. French missionaries had been preaching there since the seventeenth century, until their growing influence provoked the Vietnamese government to ban Christianity and execute the missionaries and their converts. France sent in troops to protect them, war broke out, and in 1863 it had annexed Vietnam's Mekong delta region, the southern part of the country, as Cochinchina.

Starting in June 1866 from their new base in Vietnam, the French Lagrée Expedition set off up the Mekong river for what would become a two year, six-thousand-kilometre-long journey to explore and map unknown territory in Cambodia, Laos, Siam, Burma and China. It looked as if France, Britain's long-time economic rival, would find the coveted back door to inland China first.

Right at this moment the British discovered it was possible to get a steamer fifteen hundred kilometres up the Irrawaddy river from Rangoon to Bhamo, a prosperous town close to the border with China's Yunnan province. A centuries-old caravan route for cotton, silk and gold ran from Bhamo east over jungle-clad hills to the Chinese city of Tengyue in Yunnan, just two weeks away. But for some reason, commercial traffic – previously estimated to be worth nearly half a million pounds annually – had almost completely dried up over the previous decade.

So at the beginning of 1868, as Lagrée's expedition was approaching the Yangzi river on the final leg of their journey downstream to Shanghai, the British authorities in India hastily dispatched an expedition to Bhamo, with instructions to explore and map out the road to Tengyue, investigate whether the local ethnic groups were friendly and why trade had ceased, and, if possible, to press on beyond Tengyue to the important city of Dali. They even managed to persuade the Burmese king, Mindon Min, to write letters of introduction to Bhamo's governor and several of the village chiefs along the way.

There was just one problem: another civil war.

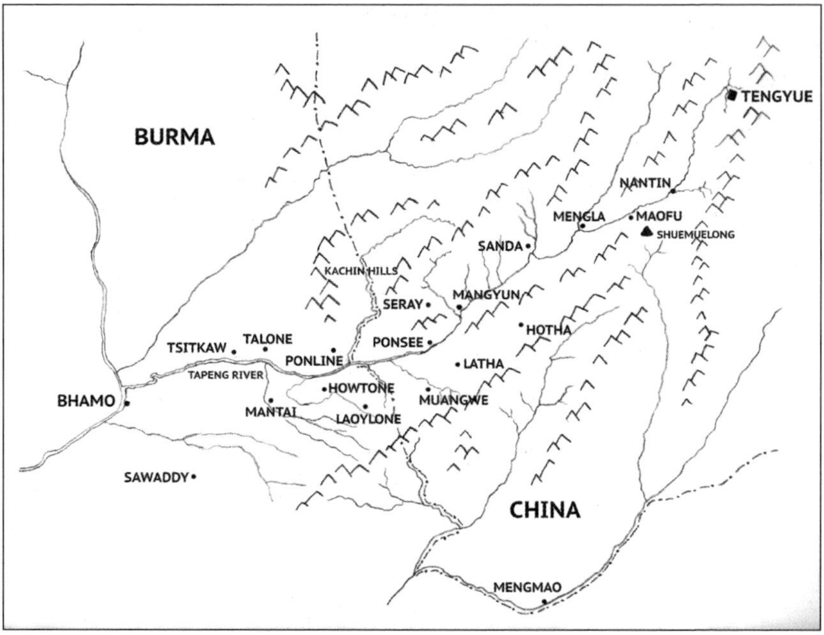

Bhamo to Tengyue

First attempt: the Sladen Expedition

One of the consequences of the Taiping Uprising in eastern China was that it inspired people in other regions, equally impoverished or unhappy with the government, to rebel. Perhaps the most serious of these knock-on conflicts was the Muslim Uprising of 1856-1873 in Yunnan, which devastated the province and caused the deaths of over a million people.

Yunnan is set way down on China's southwestern frontier; its name means "South of the Clouds", giving some idea of just how remote it was considered by the rest of the country. Although the Han dynasty laid claim to the region two thousand years ago, initial attempts to conquer Yunnan were abandoned as too expensive, and in truth the province remained largely independent, with two local kingdoms – the Nanzhao and its successor, the Dali – taking full control between 737 and 1253. Yunnan was only drawn under direct Chinese rule in the thirteenth century, during the Mongol-run Yuan dynasty.

Not surprisingly Yunnan's provincial capital, Kunming, was in the more accessible eastern side of the province; the further into Yunnan you travelled from here, the less "Chinese" the landscape and people became. Westwards lay a tightly bunched string of snow-ridged mountain ranges and enormously deep, parallel north-south valleys, through which flowed the upper reaches of three of Asia's most important rivers: the Yangzi, the Salween (known as the Nü in China) and the Mekong (Lancang). Cut off from the rest of China by this extreme geography, the inhabitants of western Yunnan often had closer ties to neighbouring countries: Tibet to the north, Burma to the west, Laos and Vietnam to the south.

Not that the area was totally isolated. Post roads – some stretches flagged in worn stone slabs and hand-laid cobbles, with simple rutted earth tracks elsewhere – ran south-west between Kunming and Burma via the walled garrison towns of Dali, Yongchang and Tengyue. Mule trains made the difficult journey in a month, crossing mountain passes, thick jungle and settled valley basins terraced in rich green paddy fields. In addition to the Han Chinese, at least sixteen ethnic minority groups inhabited this remote corner of the empire – including substantial communities of Muslims.

Islam had reached China as early as the eighth century, when Arab merchants plying the "Maritime Silk Road" to Asia settled in several of the south-coast cities, building mosques, minarets and tombs which survive to this day. But the religion first arrived in Yunnan during the early days of the Yuan dynasty (1271–1368), when Muslim soldiers from central Asia were deliberately settled in the province to help enforce the Mongol invaders' alien rule. Some ended up in the provincial administration – one Sayyid Ajall, originally from Bokhara in today's Uzbekistan, was appointed governor of Yunnan in 1274 – and Muslim scientists even served at the Imperial court. Known as the Hui, over generations these Muslims gradually became influenced by Chinese culture, though still retaining their own religion, customs and shared sense of history.

By the early Qing dynasty (1644-1912) the Hui were spread all over Yunnan, with a definite concentration in the west of the province along the Dali-Yongchang-Tengyue-Burma trade route. Sometimes feared for their tempers, they were also considered good businessmen, generally working as merchants or with the regional caravans and mule teams (today, many are in the trucking industry). Although official Qing policy towards ethnic minorities was rarely sympathetic and occasionally uncaringly antagonistic, Muslims were theoretically allowed religious freedom and left to themselves as long as they caused the Chinese administration no trouble. But this wasn't how Yunnan's wider population saw things.

While speaking Chinese and often visually indistinguishable from the majority Han population, the Hui kept themselves apart: in cities their communities centred around a mosque, and in the countryside, in all-Muslim villages. One of the causes for this cultural separation was because

Muslims don't eat pork, the Chinese staple meat. As many Chinese social interactions revolve around food, from festival celebrations to simple gossiping in a teahouse, the Hui found it difficult to mix with the broader community.

Religion too was an issue. Chinese folk belief, encompassing thousands of deities and with a wealth of imagery, disgusted Muslims as pagan idolatry; while the Islamic idea of a single god who couldn't even be visualised, far less illustrated, struck the Chinese as baffling and ridiculous.

The Hui, being merchants in control of regional transport infrastructure, also tended to dominate western Yunnan's economy; while they accumulated steady profits, the fortunes of the settled Chinese farmers around them rose and fell alongside seasonal drought, flood and famine. This alone caused resentment, but in bad years farmers were sometimes forced to sell their land to a wealthy Muslim for ready cash, and then rent it back. Nobody likes a landlord.

*

By the nineteenth century then, Yunnan's Han and Hui communities simply didn't get along. For all the reasons given above, the Han saw the Hui as clannish outsiders and resented them for their superior business acumen.

The general situation in Yunnan was also deteriorating. Increased migration into the region from an overpopulated eastern China put pressure on resources; between 1750 and 1800 several of Yunnan's cities quadrupled their populations. This led to direct competition between some of these recent arrivals, such as merchants from Sichuan province, and the Hui, who had long monopolised regional commerce.

One of Yunnan's biggest industries, copper mining, was also in trouble. For years there had been little government investment, and any merchants who privately funded operations were always taking a risk that if the mine failed they would lose their money. The miners themselves formed independent communities, often fighting each other over mining rights and resources such as water. This general volatility created a floating population of impoverished labourers who often turned to banditry to survive, spreading unrest and lawlessness.

The fact that this was a frontier zone remote from the eastern Chinese heartlands made western Yunnan a difficult place to police; the province also tended to get lumbered with second-rate officials who lacked the political skills and personal contacts to get themselves appointed to somewhere more rewarding. Even when this wasn't the case, to avoid corruption officials were never allowed to serve in their native regions, and so had no prior understanding of local situations or politics in the places to which they were posted. This made them reliant on the opinions of the resident gentry class, an informal social elite of wealthy merchants, guild heads and successful candidates in the imperial exams who had retired from office and settled back in their home towns. The gentry's working connections with government officials gave them considerable influence over the local population.

Where disputes between Han Chinese and Hui were concerned, both officials and gentry would almost inevitably assume that the Muslims, as a notoriously troublesome ethnic minority, were in the wrong. So Hui communities, feeling abandoned by the authorities, began to organise private militias to protect themselves.

*

Against this unpromising background, violence finally flared in October 1845 at Yongchang, a busy caravan town along the Dali-Burma road. There had been particularly bad feeling here for a couple of years, ever since Chinese celebrants at the annual "Five Gods" festival had been jeered at by Hui and pelted with rubbish as their procession passed the city's mosque. Now a minor argument between Han and Hui youths in a nearby village escalated into mutual bloodshed which swiftly spread out into the countryside.

The small Chinese government force sent to stop the unrest was annihilated by a Hui militia, who then advanced towards Yongchang. Fearing that the rebels outside would ally with Muslims inside the city, Yongchang's Han Chinese torched the mosque and spent the following two days butchering the Hui population. Some four thousand are believed to have been killed.

One Muslim who escaped from Yongchang was a young man named Du Wenxiu. Born nearby in 1823, Du was either a Chinese orphan adopted into a Muslim household or the son of a Chinese convert to Islam. Either way, he was something of a scholar and had passed the initial exams for the Chinese civil service. Respected despite his youth, he now joined other community leaders in making the long journey to Beijing to petition the Chinese court for justice over the Yongchang massacre.

The resulting investigation was fairly even-handed. Yongchang's officials were demoted or banished for failing to prevent the crisis, while ringleaders on both sides – considerately labelled by the authorities as "bandits" rather than the far more incendiary term "revolutionaries" – were executed as a warning to others. But Muslims returning to Yongchang afterwards found that their land and property had been appropriated by Han Chinese; Hui militias regrouped, and trouble continued to rumble on over the next few years.

In early 1848 an Imperial commission under Lin Zexu – the same man who had been blamed for precipitating the Opium Wars six years earlier – was sent to look into the situation. He reported that both sides were at fault, and that the unrest would only end once authorities stamped out banditry and dealt impartially with both Han and Hui. To this end, Lin ordered ten more Han participants in the Yongchang massacre to be sent to the provincial capital for trial. But the convoy transporting them was attacked by sympathisers who then stormed Yongchang, took the governor and magistrates hostage, raided the armoury, and instigated a second slaughter of the city's Muslims.

Lin Zexu gathered troops and descended on Yongchang in force. The rebels caved in immediately, handing over their leaders in return for lighter sentences. After another round of executions Lin, feeling that Yongchang's Han and Hui were never going to resolve their differences, had the entire Muslim population uprooted and resettled at a new township about fifty miles away.

*

The situation at Yongchang left both Han and Hui across Yunnan embittered, their simmering mutual antagonism often sparking violence. In late 1855, an incident broke out Quxiong in central Yunnan, where Hui and Han workers at a silver mine came to blows. Not long afterwards, some of the Han involved in this squabble stopped at a village south-east of the provincial capital, Kunming. Out for revenge, Muslims from the city plundered the village, burned it down, then held a big parade through Kunming's streets to celebrate their victory.

Kunming's magistrate immediately had the Hui ringleaders arrested, and attempted to calm outraged citizens by issuing a proclamation saying that justice had been done, and that any further troublemakers would also be put to the sword. Unfortunately, his poorly-worded appeal against mob violence was interpreted by Chinese vigilantes as an official sanction to get rid of the Hui. On 19 May 1856 they locked the city gates and, in a replay of events at Yongchang, massacred Kunming's Muslim population.

Hui right across Yunnan rose in rebellion. Led by the fearsome, battle-scarred warlord Ma Rulong, they stormed Kunming in July 1857, destroying everything outside the city's tall, well-defended stone walls: "The rebels burnt the suburbs of the capital city and almost annihilated the inhabitants, but the viceroy [Hengchun] bravely led his troops to the attack". Forced to retreat inside the city's fortifications and appalled by the loss of life – over seventy percent of Kunming had been destroyed – Hengchun and his wife committed suicide. The city spent the next eight months under siege; so many people died of starvation and disease that by the end there weren't enough citizens left alive to bury all the corpses.

Over in western Yunnan, the Chinese governor of Heqing town called out the local garrison, inflicted the usual atrocities on Heqing's Muslims, and marched south intending to repeat his performance at the next major settlement, Dali. Before Dali's authorities could act either way, the Muslim population decided to take charge of the situation and called in nine hundred mercenaries under Du Wenxiu – the scholar from Yongchang, now turned fighter.

Du's men made short work of the Heqing rabble, Dali's officials were either cut down or fled, and Du declared Dali as the capital of the independent Islamic state of Pingnan Guo, "Southern Land of Peace", with himself as its sultan. The Chinese named these Muslim Hui rebels "The White Flags", while the British called them "Panthays" and Du Wenxiu's rebellion the Panthay Uprising, after the Burmese word for Chinese Muslims, *pansee*.

*

In March 1859 a Chinese campaign to retake Dali failed to even reach the city, after the leader of government forces was killed in a battle with Ma Rulong just seventy miles west of Kunming.

Amongst the Chinese troops who witnessed this defeat was Cen Yuying, a thirty-year-old scholar with a talent for military affairs. Born in neighbouring Guangxi province, Cen was from an ethnic Zhuang family who had once been hereditary chiefs. As a youth he came first in the local government literary exams, but his father – not wanting to raise a mere bookworm – also had him trained in martial arts. Unimpressed with the official provincial forces, Cen organised his own militia and led them into battle, zeal that got him appointed as an acting prefect.

Meanwhile, Ma Rulong was losing his enthusiasm for the war; he didn't accept Du Wenxiu's leadership of the Muslim cause, or believe in the likely long-term success of the Panthay state at Dali. So he renewed his attack on Kunming, hoping to force the Chinese government to sue for peace, and in 1862 Cen Yuying was chosen to negotiate the terms of

Ma's surrender. In return for switching sides, Ma's troops were granted an amnesty, while Ma himself was made a general in the Chinese forces and put in charge of military affairs at Kunming. For his role in the negotiations, Cen was elevated to acting lieutenant-governor of all Yunnan, a huge promotion.

By now, Du Wenxiu's rule at Dali had extended its influence over all of western Yunnan, as far as the border with Burma: Yongchang – where the root of the uprising had begun – fell in July 1861, and Tengyue, the last Chinese city in that direction, in October. This left Yunnan split into two camps: in the west, the Panthay leader Du Wenxiu ruled his Islamic state from Dali; while in the east, the former rebel warrior Ma Rulong governed for the Chinese at Kunming.

In 1867, Du Wenxiu dispatched a 200,000-strong army from Dali in a final attempt to take control of eastern Yunnan. The recently-installed replacement governor at Kunming, Zhang Kaisong, followed his predecessor's example and hanged himself in panic. With Ma Rulong badly outnumbered, Cen Yuying was posted back to the capital as acting provincial governor.

*

So this was the situation in Yunnan when, on 13 January 1868, the British expedition departed from Mandalay aboard the Burmese king's own steamer, the *Yaynan-Sekin*, bound for Bhamo. The *North-China Herald*, China's most respected English-language paper, spelled out the expedition's aims: they were to explore "the old trade route from Bhamo... to Talifoo [Dali], the capital of the Mussulman Pansees, who have wrested Western Yunan from the Chinese ... From Bhamo the route runs north-east over the Kachin hills, then through the Shan States to Momien [Tengyue] on the border of Yunnan, thence to Yongchang, the centre of its trade, and finally to Dali, the Pansee capital." The paper added optimistically, "The Kachin and Shan have implored us for years to revive this trade, and now that the Pansees have fairly settled down in independence, all is favourable".

Leading the expedition was Major Edward Bosc Sladen of the Indian Army, an experienced Anglo-Burmese War veteran who for the previous two years had served as the British Resident at Mandalay. Sladen's deputy was engineer Captain J.M. Williams, whose job was to photograph and survey their route. Nobody doubted Williams' credentials: he had organised the draining of Rangoon's marshland so that the British could build their settlement, designed Rangoon's Holy Trinity Church and been one of the surveyors of Sprye's imagined railway. Even so, Williams was later described as an "unwilling and, to say the least, luke-warm" member of the party.

The expedition's medic and zoologist was Dr John Anderson, later Sladen's *de facto* second-in-command. Born into a Scottish banking family, Anderson had studied medicine in Edinburgh and seemed settled into a career there when, in 1865, he had accepted a posting to India as curator of the new Calcutta museum, and almost immediately been seconded to the expedition. Both Anderson and Sladen were to write detailed accounts which differed over details – probably because Anderson's version was aimed at the public, while Sladen's report was for official eyes only.

The two other Europeans were Captain Bowers of the Royal Navy Reserve as the main commercial agent, "his varied knowledge and experience of special utility to the expedition", with a Mr. T. Stewart representing the Rangoon Chamber of Commerce. Protecting the expedition was a police guard of fifty Burmese and Indian Muslim troops under an inspector and three sergeants; and the chief interpreter was a Burmese named Moungshuay-Ya, who had travelled to Tengyue several times and had been loaned to the expedition by the Burmese king himself.

What Sladen's party didn't know was that the French Lagrée Expedition was well ahead of their attempt to penetrate the region, having already struggled up the Mekong river to Jinghong, the first Westerners to visit the town since Captain Macleod thirty years earlier. But unlike Macleod, the French managed to wrangle their way onwards into Yunnan, despite the ongoing Panthay Uprising. Cutting up along the Red River valley, they reached Kunming just before Christmas 1867, where they met the rebel-turned-military governor Ma Rulong and negotiated permission to visit Dali – seat of the rebel Muslim sultanate.

*

On January 21 Sladen's expedition reached Bhamo (known to the Chinese as Xinjie, "Newmarket"), set above the left bank of the Irrawaddy some five hundred kilometres upstream from Mandalay. The British had been here before: in 1835 Captain Simon Fraser Hannay visited, noting that local business was entirely in the hands of the Chinese, who "have always been vigilant in trying to prevent any interference with their monopoly". Hannay was impressed with the town:

> *"With the exception of Ava and Rangoon it is the largest place that I have seen in Burmah... The people I saw were Chinese from the province of Yunnan, and Shans from the Shan provinces subject to China. Bhamo is said to contain 1,500 houses, but including several villages which join it, I should say it contained 2,000 at least, 200 of which are inhabited by Chinese. Besides the permanent population of Bhamo, there are always a great number of strangers there... The inhabitants of this district live in large, comfortable houses, which are thatched with grass, and have walls made of reeds."*

Bhamo's temples and larger homes were solidly constructed in blue brick, the streets were paved and overall Hannay found Bhamo a wealthy, busy place: "If appearance of comfort may be taken as proof of prosperity, the inhabitants of Bhamo show it in their dress and houses. I have seen more gold and silver ornaments worn here than in any town in Burmah."

But now Sladen found Bhamo a beaten-down "ruin of former prosperity", brought low by banditry, a recent fire and a mighty decline in trade since the Muslim Uprising had begun across the border in Yunnan twelve years before. The long mule trains exporting Burmese cotton eastwards into China, once numbering hundreds of animals and normally working even through the hot, sodden, disease-ridden tropical summers, had almost completely stopped running. As the cash dried up, Bhamo's fortunes had sunk so low that the town centre had become little more than a swamp, its religious buildings were dilapidated and nobody even bothered to repair the settlement's protective palisade; one night during Sladen's stay a woman was killed by a tiger outside her own house.

Aside from the Burmese administration Bhamo's population was mostly Shan, whose homelands spread from the Shan States in eastern Burma all the way to Tengyue in Yunnan. A Tai-speaking people, the Chinese name for the Shan was Dai, possibly to avoid confusion with the disparaging Chinese term *shan ye ren*, "wild men from the hills", haphazardly applied to all sorts of country dwellers. Like the Burmese, Shan were Buddhist and lived as traders and businessmen in villages or towns; the women stood out because of their huge turbans, worn like an inverted blue cloth pyramid, and the fact that – unlike Chinese women – they smoked tobacco in public.

Bhamo's markets were also busy with Kachin, slash-and-burn agriculturalists who occupied the high, forested Kachin Hills that the expedition was to traverse between Bhamo and Mangyun, where they grew rice and hunted small game with crossbows and spears. "Kachin" is an umbrella term for at least five clans – they were also known in China as the Jingpo, after their own name for themselves, Jingpaw – and the different villages along the expedition's route were reported to be "not only independent of each other, but jealous to a degree of any advantage obtained by a neighbour, either in the form of political influence or material profit".

Kachin folklore held that when the gods distributed gifts to various nations, they missed out on all the desirable things like firearms, precious stones or fine clothing, and only received an abundance of *nats*, troublesome spirits who needed constant appeasing. In addition the hills were full of wild animals which ate their rice and the few pigs and chickens they tried to raise, so the gods had allowed them to take whatever they lacked from others, as long as they didn't get caught. This perhaps explained the nineteenth-century Chinese view that the Kachin were "blood-thirsty, treacherous savages, lurking in dense jungle, and killing wayfarers and villagers with their poisoned arrows for the sake of their clothes". Bhamo's citizens didn't like them either, and they were banned from staying in town overnight in case they stole children to take as slaves. The expedition actually freed a young Hindu man from India who had been captured by the Kachin ten years previously.

But Kachin were also famously hospitable, and their enormous clan longhouses – up to seventy metres in length – always had a special guest room for travellers. Anderson, the expedition medic, felt that the Kachin's bad behaviour at Bhamo was largely a reaction to the discrimination they faced from the townsfolk; elsewhere he found them friendly enough, though easily offended and prone to bear grudges.

Both Shan and Kachin were led by hereditary chiefs. Not always greatly respected by their own people and nominally answering to the Burmese or Chinese authorities, these chiefs governed their own districts, raising taxes, extorting tolls from wayfarers and – as the expedition was to discover – often exercising considerable local power.

*

Sladen was disheartened to discover that Bhamo's governor had been killed in a recent skirmish with the neighbouring district and that, until his replacement was appointed, nobody was willing to take responsibility for negotiating safe passage with the Kachin chiefs whose territories they would have to cross on the way into China. The townsfolk, initially friendly, suddenly became unhelpful; Sladen was told they had been beaten and threatened by the authorities for aiding the expedition. It was clear that, despite the apparent support of King Mindon Min, Bhamo's Burmese administration was against the British expedition from setting out.

Even so, Sladen gathered enough information to start planning their journey. Thanks to Hannay he already knew that the first town in China, named Momien in Burmese or Tengyue in Chinese, lay at least two weeks to the east across the Kachin Hills. But now he discovered there were three possible routes to get him there. The most direct at around 170 kilometres long was the Northern route, which followed the Tapeng river right through to Tengyue; this was the most frequented trail but could be tough going, as paths completely ignored gradients in favour of following the shortest way between two points. Then there was the even harder Embassy route (traditionally followed by caravans bearing tribute gifts to the Chinese court) which climbed into the hills south of the Tapeng before joining the Northern route around halfway along; this hadn't been used for years and was in a doubtful condition. Finally, the much longer but least severe Southern route avoided the hills altogether and joined the Northern route about fifty kilometres short of Tengyue.

Needing to complete the journey before the monsoons began – and already realising that the longer the journey took, the more people he'd have to negotiate with for permission to cross their lands – Sladen decided to plump for the relatively straightforward Northern route.

*

Meanwhile Bhamo's temporary authorities remained outwardly hospitable, but spent all their meetings with Sladen explaining patiently why his expedition was unlikely to succeed. They depicted the Kachins along the way as endlessly argumentative, duplicitous and protective of their territory, taking every opportunity to fight with others or amongst themselves. And once through the Kachin Hills, the Chinese borderlands would be no better, roamed by bandits and marauders of all descriptions.

Sladen wanted the relevant chiefs to be invited to Bhamo so that he could state his case and negotiate on his own behalf, but the authorities claimed that no Kachin were allowed into the town, as resident Shans would shoot them on sight. Anyway, the chiefs would think that they were being lured into a trap; and even if some *did* turn up and agreed to let the expedition through, they wouldn't be able to make guarantees for the others, who would doubtless attack the expedition if they could. Sladen was wasting his time; he had better give up and go back to Mandalay.

Given the history of Anglo-Burmese relations the British must have expected some resistance to their mission, but Sladen was becoming exasperated at the degree of obstruction he was facing. What he didn't know was that King Mindon Min himself wanted the expedition to fail, as Yunnan's Panthays, isolated from the rest of China and desperate themselves for business with the outside world, had pioneered an alternative trade route from their capital at Dali direct to the court at Mandalay. If Sladen succeeded in reopening the road between Bhamo and Tengyue, this Dali-Mandalay route would be undermined and the Burmese court, already cut off from the sea by the British, would lose yet another source of revenue – not to mention supplies – to British merchants.

Bhamo's Chinese businessmen were also working against the expedition. Some feared that the British would support the rebel Panthays at Tengyue, but most were more generally worried that if the British muscled in on local trade, their own profits would be compromised. Like the Burmese, they did their best to persuade the expedition to turn back by pitching alarming tales of the dangers ahead; when that didn't work they wrote to the chiefs along the route telling them not to let the British through.

The Chinese also contacted Li Zhenguo, a pro-Chinese warlord fighting the Muslims between the border and Tengyue. British accounts usually name him as Li Xietai after his title (*xietai* meaning colonel or military governor); Sladen referred to him scathingly as a "robber chief", but Li Zhenguo deserved better than that. Born at Tengyue into a part-Chinese, part-Burmese family, at the outbreak of the Panthay Uprising Li had gathered together a private army and gone to war, refusing to surrender even after his wife and seven children were taken hostage by the Muslims. He worked closely with both Chinese and Burmese officials against the rebels, and in 1866 had headed a deputation to petition the Burmese king on behalf of the local Shan chiefs, who wanted protection against the Panthays. Anderson later described Li as "a little but broad-shouldered and powerful man, with a large head, an unusually wide mouth, with thick and protruding lips. In conversation he looks straight at the interlocutor, in marked contrast to the usually downcast or shifting glance of other Chinese".

Li's headquarters, a hill fort known as Maofu, overlooked the road the expedition planned to take, and there was no doubt that he would pose a serious threat should he decide to attack them. Undeterred, Sladen cunningly undermined the merchants' intrigues by secretly writing to the chiefs along the way himself, pointing out how much more taxable traffic would be passing through their territories if the British succeeded in reviving trade between Burma and China. He also sent off letters with two trusted Kachin scouts to the rebel Muslim authorities at Tengyue, outlining the expedition's aims and asking for their protection against Li Zhenguo.

*

After ten days of wrangling, Sladen managed to arrange a meeting with the head of Ponline, a key village part-way along the Northern route. It didn't go well. Intimidated by Bhamo's officials, the chieftain appeared hostile to the idea of a foreign expedition hiking over his lands, a situation made worse by the interpreter, who instead of translating went off on his own long diatribes against the British.

With the formal meeting over Sladen managed to privately corner Ponline's chief and found him far more tractable; he eventually agreed to allow the expedition safe passage through his own territory, though as predicted he wouldn't guarantee what might happen to them afterwards. After more haggling, the chief promised to provide mules between Tsitkaw, some thirty miles along the trail, to Mangyun, the first town on the far side of the Kachin Hills, about halfway to Tengyue. But he also admitted his own loyalties to the Chinese traders, who paid him a regular fee not to have their wares molested, and might have him ousted if he was discovered to have helped the British. To conceal his involvement the chief made it conditional on Bhamo's authorities providing the expedition with a Burmese escort, so it would appear that the British had official backing. He left town the next day, promising to organise the mules and make all preparations for the expedition's departure in another ten days time.

The ten days had come and gone when, on February 20, Bhamo's new governor arrived and sent Sladen a message promising to help the expedition in any way he could. In fact he did as little as possible. When Sladen finally obtained an interview after four days of being fobbed off, the governor rejected the idea of a Burmese escort and browbeat Ponline's chief for suggesting it. But when Sladen pointed out that the expedition had the support of the Burmese king, the chief regained confidence and, despite obvious disapproval from the governor, again agreed to conduct the expedition to Mangyun. But he was still clearly worried about his standing with Bhamo's Chinese community.

Sladen also asked the governor to supply Kachin and Shan interpreters; after the usual procrastination two were promised, but only if they joined the expedition after it had left town. And then Sladen was mysteriously unable to find anyone willing to change the mission's Indian currency for silver, the unit of trade from here on: the Chinese claimed to be too poor, the governor pleaded that his treasury was empty, and even Bhamo's aristocrats seemed suddenly to have fallen on hard times.

*

With no funds, no ready interpreters, and knowing that most of the local population – Burmese, Shan, Chinese and Kachin – were all hoping that they would fail, Sladen's expedition set off from Bhamo on 26 February 1868, after securing the help of a reluctant official to act as their guide to Tsitkaw, the first stop. Having been continually stonewalled and obstructed since their arrival, Sladen commented gloomily that if the British met with some disaster, the local authorities could in all honesty tell their superiors at Mandalay that everything in their power had been done to dissuade them from setting out on such a dangerous mission.

It took just a day to reach Tsitkaw, right at the edge of Bhamo's jurisdiction, and – now they were distant from Burmese intimidation – several Kachin village heads or their deputies turned up to meet the expedition, along with the interpreter, Moung Mo. Most of the territory between here and Mangyun belonged to the chieftains of Ponline, Ponsee and Seray, all of whom now promised the expedition safe passage.

Next morning the expedition got their first taste of what was going to become a chaotic daily ritual: loading the pack animals. Having hired a hundred mules through Ponline's chief, it now turned out that the animals belonged to many different owners, each loudly demanding to negotiate their own case. As Shan and Kachin began shouting in their own languages, Sladen found himself completely out of his depth and had to hand all the luggage to Ponline's bilingual headman and trust him to get the business sorted out. But it soon became clear that too many animals had been secured, and the surplus muleteers – who wouldn't be paid – started arguing with those that, they felt, had taken too much baggage and could easily spare them some. Many of the muleteers were drunk, all of them were armed with *dha*, metre-long swords, and every argument seemed about to boil over into bloodshed.

In the end things never escalated beyond a lot of shouting and grandstanding, and in any case all the ruckus was for nothing, as it turned out that Kachin superstition forbade travel over the following few days. During the enforced delay, the expedition's patience with the chiefs wore thin after the inebriated Ponline headman relieved himself in their room; only the fact that they needed his goodwill stopped the British from kicking him out of the house. To be fair, he kept the other district heads in line and openly abused the chief of Talone, who wanted the expedition pay a "tax" to compensate his muleteers for not getting as much business as they were hoping for. More seriously, Ponline's chief privately told Sladen that the interpreter Moungshuay-Ya, sent by the Burmese king, was secretly colluding with the Chinese and plotting against the expedition.

*

On March 2 all seemed ready, though an early departure was stalled by the usual muleteer arguments, alongside a more serious dispute. Back at Bhamo, Sladen had presented Ponline's head with a musket as a gift, and now all the other chiefs wanted one too. But Sladen didn't have any more to hand out and the men, already drunk, became surly and mutinous, refusing to help and openly eyeing up the expedition's valuables.

It was afternoon before they left Tsitkaw behind in a disordered tangle, everybody setting off as they thought fit. There was gunfire ahead as the trail finally began the climb into the Kachin Hills, apparently caused by a party of disgruntled locals being driven away. But it seemed more likely that it was the expedition's own drunken muleteers who were to blame – perhaps hoping that the British would run away in fright, leaving them to plunder the luggage.

At Talone they were asked to dismount – it was considered rude to ride through a Kachin village – but they reached Ponline that evening without further trouble. Here the British had a whole longhouse set aside for them; it was built off the ground on short piles with a corridor running the full length on one side, rooms on the other. The hospitable villagers provided plenty of beer, boiled rice, eggs and geese for the expedition's larder, but the next morning they discovered that their cash box and eight mules had been detained by Talone's chief. They were eventually recovered, but the loads had been rifled and several items stolen.

Sladen now assembled all the village heads and handed out presents. Ponline's leader exhorted everyone to help the expedition, but then took Sladen aside and told him that the local spirits disapproved of the British and would need paying off. A suitable ceremony was arranged to placate them, and Sladen paid the officiating shaman a modest amount to ensure the *nats'* goodwill.

But with the British about to leave his jurisdiction, Ponline's chief demanded that they paid him six hundred rupees – half for allowing them to cross his territory, half to protect their cash box until Mangyun. Sladen compromised by paying him three hundred rupees as a transit tax, and then getting rid of the box and dividing the cash amongst their Indian guards.

And so they set out along the trail to Ponsee, the last predominantly Kachin settlement along their route, descending to the river along a precipitous, boulder-strewn track with treacherously sharp hairpin bends. Fording the fast-flowing Nanpeng near its junction with the Tapeng, they climbed up into the hills again to spend a night camped out in the jungle. Ponsee was reached the following day, Sladen having been warned by Ponline's headman that the local chief was still offended over the musket affair, and he should watch out for treachery. But the villagers seemed friendly, and Ponsee was only about sixteen kilometres from Mangyun, the halfway point to Tengyue, so the British settled down comfortably enough – not realising that they would be stuck here for over two months.

Trouble began the next morning when the muleteers suddenly abandoned the expedition, unloading the baggage and streaming out of camp with their animals – either in a dispute over pay, or because they had been threatened by the other chieftains. The Chinese interpreter Moungshuay-Ya had also vanished, and was rumoured to be heading back to Bhamo; an informant told Sladen that he had been encouraging the Kachin chiefs to wipe out the expedition and steal their money and trade goods. Sladen summed up: "So much for a man who was specially [ordered to assist us] by the king of Burma".

Then the Ponline chief began piling up objections to the expedition continuing to Mangyun, clearly wanting to milk them for everything he could get. He warned them that a large Kachin war party was waiting for them on the road ahead, but hinted that they might be bought off for two thousand rupees. Then he demanded compensation for five houses burnt down at Ponline, which he claimed was caused by one of the expedition's camp fires (an issue quickly settled with a bottle of whiskey) and for more money to ensure safe passage to Mangyun. And then the expedition heard that the head of Seray, the next village along, had refused the British permission to enter his district.

Sladen resisted forcing a showdown – progress would be impossible unless he kept on good terms with the chieftains – but tension was building amongst his own men from the unexpected delays: "A has boils, B is not in good spirits, C is silent and anxious". Still, their camp was secure, they were still being supplied with ample food and drink, and nobody in the village was threatening them.

Next a Burmese official appeared from nowhere, calling the chiefs to a conference at Bhamo; immediately afterwards compensation for the burnt houses was brought up again, and the head of Ponline made it clear that the expedition would not be going anywhere until he was paid three hundred rupees for the fire and six hundred rupees to protect them on the road ahead. Clearly, the official was pressuring everyone to derail the expedition. Sladen stood firm, refusing to be blamed for the fire or any other mishap which might coincidentally occur while the British were here, but after some haggling agreed to pay any reasonable fee needed to pass through Kachin territory. Ponline's chief backed down, asking only for one hundred rupees to settle the fire dispute. Sladen paid up.

Just as they were finalising things two Kachin appeared, splendidly dressed as Chinese officials, who Sladen eventually recognised as the scouts he had sent secretly ahead to Tengyue weeks earlier to petition the Muslim governor. They handed over a very official-looking document, covered in red and blue seals and written in Arabic and Chinese scripts – which, unfortunately, nobody could read in full. But the messengers assured Sladen that Tengyue's Panthay rebels were keen to welcome the expedition; indeed, one of their officials had come back with them.

Even though these messengers had travelled freely along the road, meeting no resistance, the expedition was warned that the Chinese warlord Li Zhenguo was planning to ambush them from his mountain stronghold near Tengyue, and advised not to move beyond Mangyun for the time being. The British were expected to have travelled via the Embassy route, which is where Tengyue's officials had made preparations for their safe passage. This would have avoided the Kachin Hills and Li Zhenguo's fort, and Sladen realised that the Bhamo authorities had only allowed them to take the Northern route because they knew how difficult it would be, and how badly local politics would bog down the expedition's progress.

And now they became embroiled in fresh negotiations with multiple chiefs over mule hire; inevitably, the burnt houses business resurfaced too. Sladen didn't have the amount of money that was being demanded, and anyway knew that if he gave in too easily all the chiefs along their route would start "squeezing" them for outrageous bribes. Ponline's head was clearly stirring things up, creating new problems every time it looked as if everyone might reach an agreement, but finally became so troublesome that even the other chieftains lost patience with him. The meeting ended abruptly when two shots passed through the tent, and that night Ponline's chief fled back west to his village after a violent argument with the head of Seray. Grasping to the last, he looted presents earmarked for the authorities at Mangyun, and also took the interpreter Moung Mo with him.

Despite the loss of the interpreter everyone was relieved to see the back of this avaricious chief, who – despite sometimes valuable service – clearly planned to bleed the expedition dry and then abandon them; though Sladen charitably believed that, without prompting from the Burmese to cause trouble, he would have been happy to have escorted the British through to Mangyun.

Not long afterwards an armed party of fifty more Burmese arrived from Bhamo, claiming that they planned to reopen some long-abandoned, worked-out silver mines. Sladen suspected that they had actually come to harass the villagers and stop them from helping the expedition. Sure enough, the Burmese attempted to bribe a Kachin into stealing their horses, sent runners to Mangyun and beyond to slander the British, and arrested the wife of Sladen's last remaining interpreter as a hostage to stop him working for the expedition. For good measure, they spread a rumour that the expedition planned to torch Ponsee and slaughter the inhabitants.

Then two Chinese were seen passing through the village, heading for Seray. Not surprisingly the Seray chief soon reappeared, with a story that he could no longer help the expedition because he had fallen out with the head of Ponsee. Even worse, the chiefs of Mangyun and Sanda – an important town part-way between Mangyun and Tengyue –emphatically refused permission for the expedition to cross their territories, while the influential chief of another town, Mengla, declared himself "their greatest enemy". In reality all this anti-British posturing by regional leaders was most likely to avoid reprisals from the Chinese warlord Li Zhenguo, now that his enemies, Tengyue's Muslims, had given the expedition their stamp of approval.

Rumour reached Sladen of a planned attack on the British camp, which he forestalled by having the armed escort demonstrate their prowess with breech-loading rifles and colt pistols. The noise and accuracy of these modern weapons shocked and astounded the chieftains; the head of Ponsee sheepishly visited Sladen afterwards, admitting that the Burmese had been pressuring him to obstruct the British, but now he had consulted the *nat* spirits and they were in favour of their expedition proceeding. This didn't surprise Sladen, who had become friends with the shaman and had bribed him to deliver a favourable oracle.

Unexpectedly, the abducted interpreter Moung Mo suddenly reappeared, eager to help the British if they would guarantee his safety. He poured out a catalogue of Burmese plots to frustrate the expedition:

Bhamo's magistrates had been under royal orders to obstruct them from the start; working the silver mines was indeed a ploy, to spy on the expedition and spread rumours about them; that Li Zhenguo has sworn to stop the British on the road between Mangyun and Tengyue; that several Shan and Burmese wanted to help the expedition but were being threatened by the Bhamo authorities; and that Sladen should not send messages back to Burma as they were being intercepted along the way.

Despite everything Ponsee's villagers had remained friendly, seeing the British as a welcome source of income and supplying them with plentiful tobacco, tea, rice and beer. But the expedition was still stuck, their planned five-month journey likely to be extended indefinitely with over a hundred people to provide for. Needing to reduce costs, Sladen asked for volunteers to return to Bhamo. The engineer Captain Williams, unable to complete his surveying work now that the heavy monsoon rains had set in, was the first to put his hand up; with him went the business representative Stewart.

Williams later received considerable official flak for his decision to "abandon" the expedition. While Sladen never questioned his competence, Williams had apparently been against the Bhamo option from the start, favouring instead Captain Sprye's Rangoon to Jinghong route, and Sladen felt this had made him a reluctant team member, "seedy and down in the mouth", always suggesting turning back whenever they ran into difficulties.

But what really annoyed Sladen was that Williams took the expedition's cameras with him, despite Sladen offering to buy them out of his own pocket. And then, on his way back to Burma, Williams met a courier with 10,000 rupees, sent by the government to relieve the expedition's financial difficulties – and yet, despite the expedition being in funds again, Williams still declined to rejoin it. He had taken a vital chronometer and sextant with him too, refusing to return them even when Sladen sent a direct order to do so. The final official verdict was that "Captain J. M. Williams has shown himself to be altogether unfitted to accompany any expedition of this description, and his services will doubtless never be availed of by the Government again in any such capacity".

*

Suddenly good news arrived at the village: Li Zhenguo had been defeated and chased out of his stronghold at Maofu, and consequently all chieftains along the route to Tengyue had decided to side with the Muslims and would no longer oppose the expedition. The Panthay governor at Tengyue also sent a letter promising to compensate Ponsee's chief for any expenses incurred in helping the British; he immediately began arranging transport and found them a Chinese interpreter.

But nothing could be resolved without a good argument. Ponsee's head wanted payment in silver for his hospitality, and rounded up all available mules to prevent them being hired by the expedition until his price was met. Then the chief and his four deputies (it was usual to have just one, but these four were all brothers) fell out over the final fee to be handed over when the expedition made it safely through to Mangyun. It turned out that Ponsee's chief was in trouble at Mangyun for killing a Shan and couldn't accompany the expedition there in case he was arrested, so the British decided to deal directly with his deputies instead. This alienated the chief, and though his patronage was no great loss – he wielded very little authority – the deputies could only assemble six mules and sixty men as porters, far short of the number needed.

An advance deputation of Shan bigwigs now arrived from Mangyun, confirming Li Zhenguo's defeat and the defection of the town to the Muslim cause. They cross-examined Sladen about the expedition's purpose, as letters incriminating the British had reached them from Bhamo – didn't Britain have treaties with China, and if so, wouldn't they aid her in defeating the Panthays? Weren't they really political spies, laying groundwork for a full-scale British invasion?

Sladen pointed out that the Panthay's enemy, the Chinese-backed warlord Li Zhenguo, has sworn to stop the British himself, so they could hardly be in league with the Chinese government. He promised to go alone to Mangyun or Tengyue and speak to the authorities, and that if they were unsatisfied with this proposal the expedition would turn back. This convinced the envoys, but Sladen was still unable to find transport until a party of Muslim officials turned up to escort them, at which point all obstructions finally melted away. The necessary mules were rustled up, and at last the expedition departed Ponsee on May 11, leaving the nominally Burmese Kachin Hills for Chinese-Shan territory.

After an easy journey they arrived at Mangyun, set on a slight rise to the north of the Tapeng river. A huge, intensely curious and slightly hostile crowd had come to meet them, and they needed the help of officials to clear a path through the mass of humanity. A low adobe wall surrounded the town, with two gates: one led through to the market area, the other to a wide courtyard containing a Buddhist monastery, a wooden affair raised on brick piles, whose deeply bowed roof was covered in heavy tiles. As was common in China, the visitors were invited to set up camp inside the temple's grounds.

The Mangyun district's population stood at around five thousand, probably recently swollen by refugees fleeing the Chinese-Muslim conflicts further east. The town itself was divided into a crowded, functional, filthy Chinese district alive with free-roaming pigs, and a much neater, cleaner Shan quarter with detached houses and penned livestock. Shan residents were relatively wealthy, as they didn't have to pay many taxes; the market was busy and the Kachin present seemed very relaxed, in contrast to their generally hostile attitude in Burmese territory, where nobody trusted them.

An invitation arrived for the British to meet the *sabwa-gadaw*, the widow of Mangyun's previous ruler, a small stout self-possessed woman in her fifties who lived in a relatively large house with two courtyards. Being Shan, she appeared wearing a high turban and puffing away at a long tobacco pipe. Sladen explained the purpose of the expedition and she promised to support any attempt to reopen the trade routes into Burma, asking if Doctor Anderson could visit her daughter, a nun, who was ill.

The *sabwa-gadaw*'s approval of the British broke the ice with Mangyun's townsfolk – Shan, Kachin, Chinese and all – though the unabashed scrutiny of the expedition members continued, with no privacy given to the British whether eating, sleeping, reading, undressing, or even going to the toilet.

Three days later a crowd of thousands turned out to watch them leave Mangyun, the Shan officials riding ahead, saddles piled high with red cloth. As the party followed a narrow mule track along the river's north bank, shots were fired at them from the far side; clearly, not everybody had been won over to the British cause. But the main road was safe, with guard posts at regular intervals and villages along the way blandly hospitable, their markets awash with happy, inebriated throngs, stalls lining the road offering everything from daily necessities to meat and quack cures. The only disappointment was that nothing of British manufacture was for sale beyond a few buttons, pins and the occasional piece of cloth.

They arrived at Sanda in the late afternoon to find the town itself "poor and insignificant" behind an imposingly thick, six-foot-high defensive wall. Panthay forces had sacked the place five years earlier and it was yet to recover, with the dismal ruins of houses temporarily patched up and made habitable with flimsy bamboo slats. Sanda had long been governed by the powerful Dao clan, and the incumbent chieftain was a nervous, intelligent-looking Shan who left most of the talking to his underlings. Sladen emphasised their mission had no military intent and hoped to bring peace and stability to the region by re-establishing trade, to the benefit of all. This seemed to make a positive impact and the British were asked to plead with the Muslim authorities at Tengyue not to attack Sanda again; furthermore, Sladen was asked to adopt the chief's young heir, after local shamans had predicted that he would soon die without the protection of the British government. The expedition was provisioned with rice, firewood, ducks, eggs and salt-cured goose as a sign of the town's goodwill, and Sanda's head politely appeared outside his compound to see them off the next day.

Now the route forded a broad, shallow Tapeng river and continued to the next walled market town, Mengla, a busy settlement at the junction of the Tapeng and Tahe with plenty of Lisu and Bulang hill-people jostling amongst the Shan and Chinese majority. Away from the long, straight main road, which acted as the town's marketplace, houses were laid out haphazardly, with no formal street plan. Being a relatively wealthy town, Mengla's many temples – both Shan and Chinese – were built in stone, and sported elaborate statuary trimmed with gold leaf. The party was befriended by a group of respected Buddhist nuns who had travelled widely in Burma and been impressed by British rule. Sladen hoped they would prove a powerful advocate for the expedition, at least amongst the local Shan.

Mengla's chief was a boy of fifteen whose elderly mother acted as regent. The town itself was under Muslim protection, but the next stage of their journey would take the expedition into the hills where, until recently, Li Zhenguo had been based. This unsettled area was said to be still thick with bandits – only a few days earlier a mule train had been raided and several people killed – and Mengla's young ruler was understandably nervous about what might happen to him should the expedition suffer a similar attack.

As Sladen debated whether to push on regardless, a huge caravan appeared from Hotha, a village some days to the south. It was led by Hotha's chief, a man of great status who had been charged by the governor of Tengyue with protecting the British for the rest of their journey. He sent men on ahead to check out the road, as he too had heard rumours that Li Zhenguo's men were regrouping in force, getting ready to ambush the expedition.

At this point Sladen was startled by the re-appearance of his duplicitous Chinese interpreter Moungshuay-Ya, last heard of fleeing back to Bhamo in early March. In fact he had somehow managed to reach Tengyue ahead of them and had just returned from there, bringing along Panthay officers and large military escort. Sladen's view – likely correct – was that Moungshuay-Ya had originally gone to Tengyue on behalf of his Burmese masters to undermine the expedition, but finding that the Muslim authorities wanted to meet the British, saw a bigger financial reward in switching sides. At any rate, Sladen found his services invaluable from here on.

And they had hardly left Mengla behind when they heard that three hundred Chinese were blocking the road ahead, determined to stop the expedition. Climbing cautiously up the narrowing valley – a perfect place for an ambush – they found the body of a travelling merchant who had been robbed and badly cut about by bandits. He died shortly afterwards.

Up on the heights, Li Zhenguo's former stronghold of Maofu revealed itself as a dilapidated, overgrown ruin of a place set on a level basin above a deep river gorge, manned by a few ruffianly-looking soldiers. According to their guard, Tengyue's Muslim governor himself had led a force of five thousand to besiege Maofu, and most of the defenders eventually surrendered or were killed trying to break out. Anderson doubted this story; Maofu seemed so completely deserted he couldn't believe that Li Zhenguo's forces had been driven away only six weeks earlier. Sladen's account contradicts him and described putrefying corpses strewn about the area. Either way, Li and his surviving followers had retreated further up onto Shuemuelong mountain at the head of the valley, and no longer posed a threat.

The expedition pushed on along the difficult road, watched from the ridges above by Shan and Kachin soldiers. Descending into the next valley, they crossed the Tahe river on a substantial iron-chain suspension bridge before arriving at Nantin, another filthy and poor run-down shell of a town, whose officials rudely tried to search their luggage and demanded a list of the presents they had brought for Tengyue's officials. Nantin's governor later apologised; he had been told that Anderson's collection of preserved reptiles and amphibians were poisonous mythical creatures which the British planned to release unless their demands were met.

On May 26 the British left Nantin on the final stage of their journey, passing noisy thermal springs – a tourist attraction today – whose water was too hot to stay in for more than a few seconds. Shortly afterwards the front of their mule train was attacked by bandits; eight mules were looted and driven off, and two of the Muslim bodyguards from Tengyue were killed. Nervously, they pressed on into the hills beyond, expecting to be attacked in force at any moment, passing abandoned, ruinous villages half-swallowed by tropical vegetation and crossing an arched bridge whose flagstones, polished mirror smooth by centuries of traffic, caused the unshod mules to slip all over the place.

Over one final ridge the road descended past a tight clutch of extinct volcanic cones; around the corner rose the large bald summit of Laifeng Hill, topped by a tapering white *wenbi* pagoda, said to resemble a writing brush. In front of them, surrounded by a rich, heavily cultivated black-loam plain, rose a square Chinese town a kilometre wide, walled in precisely cut black blocks of lava and ringed by the ditches of a now-dry moat. After taking four months to cover just over 170 kilometres, Sladen's expedition had finally reached Tengyue.

*

They were met in style. Tengyue's Muslim governor himself rode out in the full regalia of a top-ranking Chinese official, his enormous military retinue sharply dressed and waving colourful flags, beating gongs and firing guns in welcome. The expedition felt distinctly drab and travel-worn by comparison but Sladen did his best to rise to the occasion, sending the Burmese escort ahead in their green livery, under two large golden umbrellas. Carpets were spread out on the ground with chairs for the expedition members to sit on, and then the governor came forward to greet them formally. The British couldn't possibly have hoped for a more magnificent reception, unexpected and all the more welcome after the frustrations of the road. They were escorted towards the city and settled just outside Tengyue's main gateway at Yaowang Gong, a gourd-shaped temple complex dedicated to ten Chinese medical deities, where they were given ample provisions.

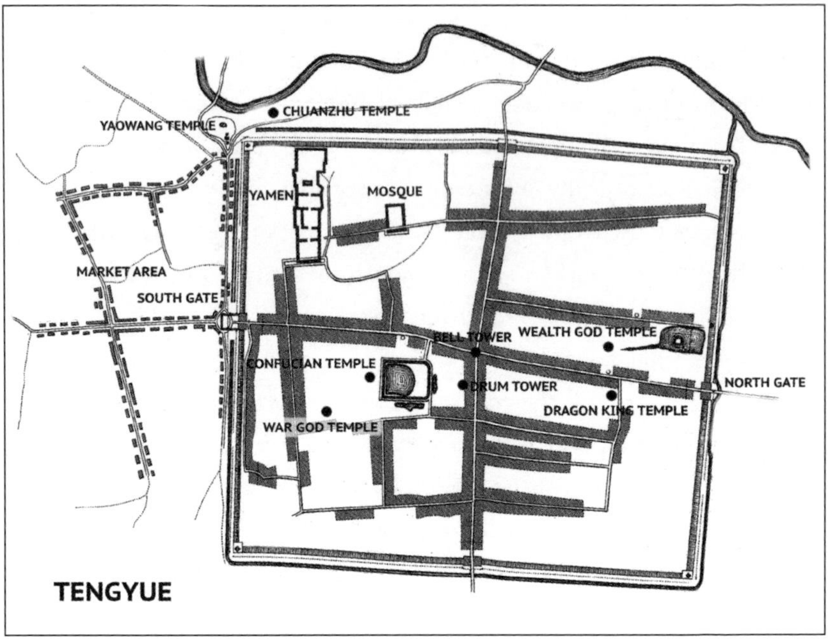

Tengyue in 1868

*

Originally Shan territory, Tengyue district was incorporated into China proper during the thirteenth century, and the city itself was founded as a military outpost in 1382. Tengyue's walls – complete with a gate tower supporting the bronze, one-tonne Houjing bell – went up fifty years later; and in 1638, less than a decade before the Ming dynasty's collapse, the great traveller and diarist Xu Xiake visited the city during the last of his extensive walking tours around China. At the time Tengyue's Chinese population lived inside the walls, while near-naked ethnic minorities "untouched by imperial rule and orthodox culture" inhabited the surrounding countryside. Xu found the minorities' primitive state difficult to square with their fondness for growing garden flowers, something he believed only the civilised Chinese could appreciate.

Tengyue had long profited from its location along the route into China for Burmese cotton, but the city really boomed in the late eighteenth century thanks to the growing market in precious gems, especially jade. The Chinese value this stone for its supposed preservative properties – two thousand years ago nobles were buried in jade suits made from tiny tiles sewn together, and even today southern Chinese wear jade amulets and bangles to preserve their youth and health. The pale translucent *yu* variety had long been mined in China's far north-west, but during the seventeenth century tastes began to shift towards dark green *feicui* jade found in Burma, and Tengyue became one huge marketplace for the raw stone, with a concentration of shops outside the south gate lining what became known as "Hundred Gems Street".

Then came the war. Panthay forces captured Tengyue in late 1861, sparing most of the population but bringing all trade to a halt and cutting the region off from the outside world. Yet despite the Muslim occupation, the British found Tengyue remained a thoroughly Chinese-looking city. The traditional square plan was slightly off-kilter, however, so that the main "south" gate actually faced south-west; there was a defensive crescent embankment in front, and you had to approach the entrance from the side. Once through the thick wooden doors, a tunnel led under the walls, emerging into the usual grid of narrow lanes and grubby streets. Not far along was the governor's *yamen*, a courtyard complex containing the courthouse and official buildings, surrounded by another low wall and rectangular stone gateway. Tengyue's main road ran right through the centre of town; wealthier Chinese patronised the few eating houses here, while everyone else ate at street stalls or bought snacks from hawkers. The market district lay outside the south gate, a broad street lined with booths selling fresh produce, clothing, jewellery, pipes and other daily necessities, where Shan, Kachin and Lisu villagers came to stock up.

Much of the northern end of the city was abandoned and overgrown, as were most temples to Chinese gods and the Shan's Buddhist shrines – all of which had been deliberately vandalised as heathen idolatry by the monotheistic Panthays. Tengyue's old mosque had also been destroyed at some point – probably by Chinese in the disturbances leading up to the Panthay Uprising – and by 1868 the city's Muslims worshipped in a Chinese-style building. The expedition's own Muslim escort were unimpressed with the local interpretation of Islam, but their shared religion saw friendships form on both sides and probably helped towards the British being accepted by Tengyue's authorities.

With trade almost at a halt the city was no longer wealthy. Tengyue's citizens dressed in ragged, Shan-style blue cotton clothes, and many had large goitres which they put down to the local river water. Almost the entire male Muslim population were enrolled in the military and lived inside the walls; Chinese traders and merchants stayed in the market area, separately walled and guarded, outside the south gate. But despite the downbeat atmosphere, the Muslim administration gave the impression of being fair, if tough. Criminals were tried before the governor, and those judged guilty were marched straight to the marketplace and decapitated. Bandits were executed immediately wherever they were caught and their heads hung on the city walls as a warning to others. Justice was utterly impartial as to race, and the expedition witnessed the execution of several Muslim criminals, as well as Chinese and Shan.

Meanwhile, fighting continued across the district. During the expedition's stay, troops from Tengyue defeated a Chinese force which had been threatening a town to the north-west, returning with three hundred Chinese ears as trophies. Muslim losses amounted to forty men killed.

*

A couple of days after their arrival, Sladen took Doctor Anderson and Bowers along for his first official meeting with Tengyue's Muslim governor. British accounts call him Tasakone, a transliteration of his official title, *da sikong*, something like Duke; his actual name was Li Guolun. Li was a very tall, contained, determined and extensively scarred man – including a dent in his forehead where a spent bullet had hit him between his eyes – with four wives; his military commander was a man named by the British as Tahzyungyee (possibly a transliteration of *da xiangyi*, an archaic title for "minister").

Once formal greetings were out the way, Sladen handed over the expedition's presents, which included carpets, velvet drapes, shotguns and pistols, ammunition, binoculars and a telescope. Li Guolun appeared receptive to the idea of re-opening the trade route to Burma – or as he put it, the "gold and silver road" – though this was something he put aside to discuss later. Sladen asked about the possibility of continuing to the Panthay capital, Dali; Li replied that the Muslim leader Du Wenxiu had approved a visit, and if they insisted on going he would of course provide them with an armed escort. But he advised against it, warning that bandits along the Dali had been picking off and robbing two out of three of their own messengers, and that they were extremely unlikely to get through safely. This was unlikely to be a stalling tactic by Li; the origins of Panthay Uprising had begun at Yongchang, part-way between Tengyue and Dali, and the area had now been in lawless chaos for twenty years.

Promising to follow Li's advice, Sladen mentioned that he would ask the British government to provide for the families of the two guards who died protecting them from bandits just outside town. This was met with surprised approval from Li, and when Bowers spontaneously presented the Muslim governor with his own rifle as a gift, Li handed over a dagger in return, a highly ornamented affair with a golden handle and scabbard.

Sladen might have made more of an effort about pressing on beyond Tengyue had he known that on March 2, the very day that he left Tsitkaw, the Lagrée expedition had reached Dali with the unlikely help of Father Leguilcher, a French Catholic priest who had spent fourteen years in China and was tolerated by the Muslim authorities. The French expedition didn't stay long at Dali and failed to secure an audience with the now-reclusive Du Wenxiu – following a punch-up with his guards they were lucky to leave alive – but it's possible that Du later regretted this missed opportunity of connecting with the outside world, and was genuinely interested in meeting with the British. His son would later travel to London on a mission to seek support for the Panthay cause.

The next few days were spent in meetings with Chinese traders to discuss business. Typically, these merchants all claimed that they didn't care who was in power as long as they made a profit, but also complained bitterly about how trade had stalled since the Uprising began and hinted that they would welcome the return of Chinese rule. Their main concern was to get the route to Burma reopened, which they believed would bring prosperity and peace.

Li Guolun returned the British visit, bringing gifts of cattle, confectionery and cash, which Sladen distributed amongst the expedition's escort and followers. Though the meeting was brief, Li suggested that Sladen could call on him informally whenever he wanted, a high honour. After this, Li took to dropping by in plain clothes and without his usual retinue, genuinely seeming to enjoy the foreigners' company; he laid on various entertainments, promised to send an ambassador to Rangoon in November to discuss the resumption of trade, and told them he was arranging for their safe passage back to Burma via the central Embassy route. But he didn't want the British to leave just yet, as he was waiting for even more gifts to arrive from Dali – though after these were looted by bandits, he promised to send replacements along with the embassy to Rangoon.

Li also revealed that his campaign against Li Zhenguo at Maofu was undertaken specifically to protect the expedition. (Sladen afterwards wrote that Li Zhenguo's defeat marked the first step towards peace returning to the region, and that the British expedition, by precipitating it, had done some real good. But if true, this wouldn't have helped Britain's standing with China later on, after the Chinese had returned to power at Tengyue). Li Guolun presented Sladen with another dagger, along with three gold rings which he personally put on Sladen's fingers as a mark of friendship. Sladen was genuinely touched.

By now the rainy season had truly taken hold, with enormous downpours daily. Despite the weather and ever-present danger of banditry

– thirty mules belonging to Li Guolun's nephew were stolen one day, right outside the town – the British took time to explore what they could of the surrounding countryside. They visited small Dieshuihe waterfall, climbed grave-strewn Laifeng Hill (today covered in woodland but then with fine views from the summit), and made a day-trip to Heshun – a large, formerly wealthy walled village whose Han Chinese population had recently been massacred after attempting to revolt against Panthay rule.

News arrived from the east: the Panthays had recently stormed Kunming, the provincial capital, with so little trouble that the Chinese armies reportedly had been smashed like "an egg tossed against a stone". A jubilant Li Guolun posted a proclamation about the victory on Tengyue's walls, full of circumstantial details about towns captured and the numbers of Chinese killed. (In truth, although Muslim forces recaptured Kunming's suburban districts, they were again unable to break through into the walled city and would abandon their siege that November). They also claimed to have routed Chinese forces led by Cen Yuying, and the proclamation ended confidently, "I pity those who must still perish. All are hereby warned that death awaits them if they give ear to the words of our enemies".

Li Guolun had passed on garbled news of the Lagrée expedition, which he believed had suffered severe losses while traversing Burma's Shan States. Sladen, not having heard anything of Lagrée's progress since leaving Mandalay months earlier, felt the story might be based on truth but doubted its accuracy. But he was really taken aback when Li calmly told him about a huge shipment of cotton sent by the Burmese king from Mandalay to Kunming as a present for the Chinese government. Li asked Sladen why, if Mindon Min truly supported the British expedition to Tengyue, was he simultaneously sending presents to their enemies? Clearly, this was another attempt by the Burmese to undermine Sladen's efforts; if Li Guolun hadn't been so astute, and if the British hadn't already won his confidence, this affair would have caused them serious trouble.

By early July the rains were drawing to an end. The British had achieved everything possible given the circumstances: they had reached Tengyue, met and befriended the Muslim administration, and investigated the state of trade. As there was no chance of pressing further on to Dali and the rest of China, it was time to head back. Li suggested using porters for their return journey – not just because they were cheaper than mules, but also because men were easier to assemble in secret, so bandits along the road would be less likely to hear about their imminent departure. However, the plan backfired as the secrecy prevented them from finding enough porters at such short notice.

There was just time for one final interview with Li Guolun. Sladen presented Li with copies of the British treaty with Burma and with two of his own seals; in return he received a long letter professing the Muslim desire to establish official trading relations with Britain, and the promise to send an embassy to Rangoon later that year.

Li Guolun was delighted when Sladen proposed that goods from China into Burma would pay only one percent duty, but doubted that the Burmese would approve. Even so, he was prepared to test the promise the following cool season by sending a caravan from Dali to Bhamo, instead of to Mandalay – exactly what the Burmese king, Mindon Min, had feared would happen. Li only cared that all their goods could be sold, and that they loaded enough cotton at Bhamo to make the return journey profitable; Bhamo was far closer to Tengyue than Mandalay, and so it might be possible to run three trading missions a year, instead of one. For his part, Li glossed over whether any tariffs would be levied on British goods sold in Yunnan, but did promise free passage for merchants continuing along the road to Yongchang and Dali.

The expedition received generous parting gifts: full official robes for Sladen, silk jackets for the other Europeans, white coats, hats and finely worked daggers and spears for their men. The British appreciated the efforts that had been made to treat them well, despite the city's poverty; Sladen's one regret was that had their surveyor, Williams, still been with them, they might have found out more about the route to Yongchang and Dali.

*

On July 13 the British began their return journey along a wet, slippery road. It wasn't long before they passed two fresh corpses, apparently thieves caught by their advance guards; they were warned that this stretch was notorious for bandits who hid in long grass by the roadside, firing at passers-by and then rushing out to slit their throats. They overnighted once again at Nantin, where they had hoped to meet up with the influential chieftain of Hotha, a village along the central Embassy route they planned to follow back to Bhamo. But he didn't show, and the Nantin to Hotha road came dangerously close to Li Zhenguo's new stronghold on Shuemuelong mountain, not something they wanted to tackle without extra protection. It seemed more prudent in the circumstances to press on back the way they came as far as Mangyun, from where there was an alternative, safer track to Hotha.

The next morning they found that boxes containing powder and cartridges had failed to turn up; rather uncharitably, considering how well they had been treated at Tengyue, they blamed Li Guolun for having them pilfered. All three horses had also been stolen right under the noses of the night guard, and most of the porters had taken off too, so they only managed to leave after renting animals and impressing unwilling locals to carry their gear for the next stage. The day passed climbing up and down muddy hills in the rain, slipping and sliding their way past Li Zhenguo's old stronghold of Maofu.

At Mengla they were met by fifty Burmese guards led by Robert Gordon, an energetic engineer with the Indian civil service who had been sent to replace Captain Williams. He had travelled along the Northern route unhindered, largely because the Burmese government had heard of their successful reception at Tengyue and decided it was pointless to obstruct the mission any further. Gordon was loaded with extra funds, keen for them all to head back to Tengyue and, with their hundred-strong armed force, attempt to open a trail right across China. But Sladen calmed him down; quite apart from the hazards involved crossing Yunnan during a civil war, Gordon's plan would be considered a serious breach of trust by Tengyue's Muslims, and almost certainly seen as an invasion once they reached Chinese-controlled territory.

On July 20 they took boats over the Tapeng and entered the valley, most of which had been flooded for irrigation and by the seasonal rains; the fields were a vivid rich green, in contrast to the dark, encircling mountains. Further on they had to swim the swollen river at a ford they had waded over easily just weeks before, and arrived at Sanda wet and exhausted, happy to spend the next few days settled into a temple, drying themselves out and waiting to hear from Hotha. Sanda's chieftain came to visit, along with other heads from villages they passed through on their outward journey; none of them wanted the British to tackle the Embassy road in case they found it preferable to the Northern route, and they lost out on any future trade.

Anderson tried shooting in the hills above Sanda but was asked to stop; this was where an invading Chinese force entrenched in 1767, and ever since had been inhabited by a cantankerous *nat* spirit which if angered took the form of a tiger and carried off children. One night a silver-mounted spear presented to them by Li Guolun was stolen from Sladen's room while he slept, clearly with inside help – they suspected one of the temple's monks, acting on orders from Sanda's chief. The culprit was later caught and kicked out of the priesthood, but the spear couldn't be recovered.

A message now arrived from Hotha's errant head, who as suspected wanted to meet up with them at Mangyun. So despite continuing heavy rains the party set out, reaching Mangyun on August 4 to learn that the chief was still delayed, bogged down in deep mud on the far side of the engorged Tapeng river. He eventually arrived and immediately tried to dissuade them from travelling through his territory, but finding the British determined took it in good part and went back to prepare the way. But he warned them that the district between Mangyun and Hotha considered itself independent; to get through they would need a local escort. Mengla's ruler, the man who once declared himself their "greatest enemy", immediately volunteered, asking Sladen to provide him with a stamped certificate proving their friendship.

Before they left Mangyun, the British had a sad encounter with an old woman, born hundreds of miles away to the west in Manipur, north-east India, who was captured by the Kachins as a young girl. Sold as a slave and then traded from village to village, she eventually ended up at Mangyun, and could still speak a few words of her native language.

*

At last, on August 9, the expedition made a start on the track southwards to Hotha and the Embassy route. It was slow going; once over the river they spent an exhausting few hours wading through deep, thick, slimy, sucking mud flats which almost engulfed the horses. A stiff climb into the hills followed, slowed again by lagging porters, the heat, and having to pay a toll at each Kachin village they passed through. Admiring the views from a high ridge, they bumped into a party of Lisu carrying a deer carcase, which the hunters refused to sell. As a fitting end to a tiring day, they were mistakenly directed along the direct path to Hotha, instead of branching off it to a village in which they could have spent the night. Caught short at dusk, they made do with a rural Buddhist temple whose Shan monks refused them food or bedding.

They reached Hotha the next morning. Set in a temperate highland valley and renowned then as now for its expert swordsmiths, the village sported some splendid Buddhist temples but was otherwise semi-ruinous in the wake of an attempted rebellion a year earlier. The chief welcomed the British in his official regalia, but it was clear that the local population were none too happy to have the foreigners around; all sorts of rumours were being spread that the expedition carried noxious spirits and bad luck in their wake, partly owing to the unusually heavy seasonal rains causing landslides along their earlier route, which had killed dozens and buried whole villages.

Despite this they enjoyed their stay. The head proved an entertaining, intelligent man who looked forward to the resumption of unrestricted trade and showed great interest in gas, railways, steamships and other modern inventions; he wanted to visit Rangoon but with the local situation so unstable planned to send his thirteen-year-old son instead. He was also disarmingly pragmatic: peace might be a fine thing, but trade had to involve making a profit; it was just as easy to pay outlaws and bandits protection money to allow their goods through, as it would be to fork out for government transit taxes.

The chief also revealed that the Embassy route had been almost unused for five years, a situation which had nothing to do with the Muslim Uprising. Seven local Kachin had been killed by a drunken Burmese official at Bhamo and, as the authorities refused to compensate the families of the victims, word went out to kill anyone from Bhamo who came this way. But now they planned to forget their vendetta and reopen the road; it was two days faster than the Northern route, and five days faster than the Southern one. As Hotha's leader was on good terms with most of the other villages along the way, he felt that regular income from renewed traffic and the appointment of a British resident at Bhamo would end all the feuding going on at the moment, and restore friendship between the Shan, Burmese and Kachin peoples.

Making the most of opportunities, Sladen dispatched a small party to Mengmao, a key border town on the Southern route, with instructions to survey the road from here back west to Bhamo. As Mengmao's population were believed to be hostile to foreigners, the party comprised a Burmese assistant surveyor named Moung Thazanoo, dressed up as a Shan, a Kachin-speaking Shan local guide, and Sladen's own Kachin-speaking Shan interpreter. Their instructions were to travel fast, only making a rough map of the terrain. If he considered it safe, Moung Thazanoo would be allowed to let chiefs along the way know that the British were looking for the best trade route between Bhamo and Tengyue, and that they stood to make a profit if their road was chosen. The easy, "broad beaten track, passing for the most part over undulating country" that they found, and the positive response given by the local rulers to their proposals, most likely later influenced the 1875 British expedition in their attempts to reach Tengyue this way.

Back at Hotha, the British witnessed the Shan's annual Fire Festival, one of four similar events through year to placate unpredictable elemental spirits, and involving the slaughter of cattle and a night-time torch parade. Shortly afterwards the head of Mantai district arrived, as a messenger from the Bhamo authorities, to escort them the rest of the way.

On August 27 they departed Hotha amidst goodwill from everyone. The track headed south-west through hills clustered tightly amongst forest; the next substantial settlement, Latha, had a feud with Hotha and the chief here was said to be "old, imbecile and superstitious", so they skirted around the village. Cultivated, well-watered country descended to the Namsa river, beyond which they climbed up into the hills again to Namboke, whose hospitable Kachin population detained them for a day – spent arguing with their muleteers over pay.

The next stretch crested the southern edge of the Tapeng valley to tiny Ashan village, the route so overgrown that the Kachins had to cut a fresh track with their *dhas*. Views along the way dropped down to the Tapeng across virgin rainforest, a sea of dome-shaped hills in every direction, some estimated by the expedition at over two thousand metres high. The direct route continued via Howtone village, but they detoured at the request of other local chiefs who wanted the chance to pledge their hospitality to the British; Sladen, now months behind schedule, moaned about this constant "procrastination".

The detour over, they made an extremely steep descent from Ashan down a slippery path, pack animals and people sliding and falling alike, to the dangerously engorged Namkong river, which they crossed with difficulty. Then it was into the mountains once more, up and down across countless ridges, to Muangwye, surrounded by giant granite boulders. Here the hospitable, wealthy Kachin chief poured rice spirits down their throats and put them up in his fifty-metre longhouse, whose porch was decorated with pig and buffalo skulls.

Another day brought them to Loaylone, a large village with ruins of a Chinese garrison post on the heights above. The chieftain's brother, ruler of nearby Mutthin, impressed the party for his manners, intelligence and fluency in Chinese, Kachin and Shan. He also seemed eager for the Burma-Yunnan trade routes to be reopened, especially if they came through his village. In contrast to their experiences along the Northern route, the expedition got on extremely well with the local Kachin, and Sladen wished that they had been able to bring a Burmese escort along from the start to smooth their way with village heads, so that they could have done the journey in four months instead of eight. The Embassy route had also taken them out of the range of Li Zhenguo's troublesome allies, the cause of so much delay on their outward journey to Tengyue.

After the usual porterage disputes they departed Loaylone, passing a long mule train laden with cotton and salt and enduring a tiring and unnecessarily lengthy journey via Mutthin. Here Mutthin's chieftain occupied a veritable palace, laid out in a series of Chinese-style courtyards and full of ornate woodwork. Back on the main trail, they stopped overnight at Howtone, where Sladen unintentionally set off a furious quarrel between the ruler and one of his relatives, resulting in a flood of insults, reminders of unpaid debts and threats of violence to everyone present. The muleteers took the opportunity to stage another strike, but after an hour or so of recriminations everyone had burned off their anger.

Mantai, reached after the by-now-routine stiff hike, offered fabulous views into Burma and a welcoming string of young women bringing spirits. Their journey nearly over, Sladen was finally enjoying himself: "It teaches us that a people who love money, drink beer, and fire salutes in honour of European travellers, are neither dead to enterprise nor dangerously opposed to friendly intercourse." Well-watered, they made a shaky descent through bamboo groves to yet another fierce seasonal torrent of a river, bridged by a flimsy bamboo span.

And so they arrived at the Tapeng once more, crossed the next morning on rafts to find a party of downcast Burmese officials from Bhamo waiting for them, depressed that the British had managed to return intact, despite their "profound belief in the certainty of our annihilation". Burmese war boats towed their raft to Tsitkaw, where they were royally received by villagers.

Accompanied by thirty-one Kachin chiefs and their two hundred followers the British made the final leg of their journey downstream to Bhamo on September 5. The Kachin hoped to persuade Sladen to settle at Bhamo permanently, where he could represent their interests to the hostile Burmese government and help reopen the trade routes; even though he declined, they laid on a ceremony promising eternal goodwill to the British, and to protect them should they ever return. Bhamo's townsfolk, already aghast at their town being flooded by so many despised Kachin, were further outraged when they sacrificed buffaloes for their ceremony right outside the gates of the governor's house. The Burmese, being Buddhist, abhorred taking life, and the unfortunate event still rankled in local memory many years later.

*

Sladen's instructions had been to investigate why the Bhamo-Tengyue trade had stopped, to encourage its resumption, and to gain insights into the borderland's ethnic groups. In general terms, the expedition had covered all these points. But in specifics, they had achieved little beyond mapping routes through this difficult area. Sladen's extensive official report (his account of the journey runs to over two hundred and fifty pages, with another two hundred pages of notes) cites almost no hard data: for instance, he states in slightly baffling terms that "goods" in Yunnan cost "between 50 to 100 per cent below English rates", while never saying what these goods actually were or whether anyone would want to buy them, however cheaply. Nowhere does he provide figures, charts, quantities.

Even so, he believed that commerce would blossom the moment obstructions to trade were removed. He favoured establishing the hilly Embassy route as the main highway, having been so well treated by its chiefs, but if new roads needed to be built, Gordon, the backup engineer, proposed following the less challenging northern or southern options instead. Either way, Sladen believed "it is now a significant and important truth that 130 miles of road or railway on the most practicable line between Bhamo and Tengyue would effectually tap the resources of Yunnan, and put us into direct communication with the wealth and resources of South Western China."

The British had also gained instructive insights into the complex politics and conflicting loyalties of the region's ethnic groups. The Burmese and Chinese were both firmly against their presence, seeing Britain as a dangerous commercial rival, and Sladen put all his problems in getting through to Tengyue down to the machinations of Bhamo's Burmese authorities, working alongside the pro-Chinese warlord Li Zhenguo. Sladen also realised that while the Shan and Kachin both understood the benefit to themselves if the trade routes reopened, they were only friendly to the British because they shared a common cause; if the Burmese or Chinese reopened these routes themselves, the tribes might well become hostile towards the British again, especially if pressured to be so.

Burmese concerns went beyond losing trade to a new rival: "What Burma has always dreaded [following the British occupation of Lower Burma] is that British interests would not be confined to British possessions, but that contingencies might arise which would give the foreigner the right of extending his influence to Upper Burma and to a point above and beyond the limits of the present Burmese Capital." If Bhamo opened up to foreigners, the Burmese feared a flotilla of British vessels cruising up and down the Irrawaddy, perhaps using the protecting of river traffic as an excuse to expand their territory and influence.

What isn't clear is if the expedition realised the implications of their meeting and befriending the Muslim Panthay rebels at Tengyue, and how this might be seen at the time – and remembered long after – by the region's Chinese authorities. The mission would be later described by British commentators as "ill-timed and impolitic", and it's perhaps no coincidence that soon afterwards the Chinese military in Yunnan began systematically suppressing the Panthay Uprising, possibly spurred on by the thought of Britain uniting with the Muslim cause. This wasn't just paranoia: Sladen brought back a shopping list from Li Guolun which included three hundred muskets, twenty revolvers, fifty shotguns, three hundred and sixty pounds of gunpowder and fifty thousand rounds of ammunition – not enough to win a war, but perhaps a gesture of further support to come. Sladen also suggested that Britain should side politically with the Panthays in their negotiations with Beijing, either to end the conflict in the Muslims' favour, or to engineer an honourable surrender for them.

There was one tangible result: on Sladen's recommendation, in 1869 the British appointed a Resident at Bhamo to represent their interests and demonstrate that they were serious about re-opening the trade routes through to China. Until now the main obstacle to this happening had been the Panthay occupation of western Yunnan, but Li Guolun had entrusted Sladen with a letter to "The English Ruler", declaring his regard for the British and his desire "to encourage commercial relations with other Governments". A Resident could also maintain friendships with local chieftains, and arrange for an engineer to make a full survey of the routes and decide along which a road or railway should be built. Most likely any opposition would come from the Burmese king, who wanted to keep the Bhamo option shut so he could make sure none of the China trade into Upper Burma fell into British hands.

So whatever its limitations, and perhaps only dimly aware of its wider implications, Sladen's expedition from Bhamo to Tengyue had given the British a tantalising glimpse of the rich potential of the region, and a platform for future exploration. Sladen summed up: "Finally I record with deliberation my firm conviction that the [British Government in Burma]... has in its power at the present time almost without effort and in spite of present Yunnan disturbances to open an immediate trade with

Bhamo, not only with Yunnan itself but probably also under suitable arrangements with other of the outlying provinces of South Western China".

Clearly a new, better-prepared expedition should be sent out at the earliest opportunity.

The British Return: Murder in Yunnan

At the same time that Sladen's expedition was cruising downstream from Bhamo, back in eastern Yunnan the Muslim Uprising was heating up. As Li Guolun had reported, Du Wenxiu's forces were laying siege to Kunming, while Ma Rulong and Cen Yuying were struggling to defend the city. At one point some of Ma's own Muslim soldiers inside Kunming decided to go over to the rebels; but Ma stayed loyal, called up Chinese reinforcements, fought ferociously and managed to save the capital, despite being severely wounded. Meeting him a few months earlier, French explorer Francis Garnier – one of the Lagrée expedition – described Ma as already "riddled with wounds, proof of his bravery which he proudly shows off". Ma had turned his house into a private arsenal and firing range, piled high with everything from blunderbusses to modern rifles, and blew his furniture to pieces with daily target practice. Everyone at Kunming was terrified of him.

The Chinese now recruited another Frenchman to their cause, the adventurer and freelance arms dealer Jean Dupuis. For several years Dupuis had been living over in eastern China at the great Yangzi port of Wuhan, where Cen Yuying wrote to him asking for modern "arms, cannons and ammunition of all kinds". Dupuis immediately made his way to Yunnan, arriving in March 1869 to find Kunming at the point of falling to the rebels; one of his escort was shot and killed before they could get inside the city walls.

During his stay at Kunming Dupuis got on well with Cen, describing him as "hardworking, tenacious, tough and very skilful, lacking the habitual distrust of Chinese officials towards Europeans; he was also extremely polite, always calling me 'older brother'. I never had anything but very good relations with him." He agreed to send the arms that Cen needed, along with some European instructors to teach the Chinese soldiers how to use them.

It had taken Dupuis six months to make the long and difficult trek to Kunming from eastern China. But he wondered if it would be possible to transport arms to Kunming in far less time by shipping them from Europe to the northern Vietnamese capital, Hanoi, and then making his way upstream along the Red River directly into Yunnan. He suggested that if peace were restored and Yunnan's rich copper mines reopened, it would become financially viable for him to use this Red River route to supply Cen regularly with weapons, and export copper in return.

*

In late 1869 Cen Yuying and his understudy, a young warlord from the Bai ethnic minority named Yang Yuke, finally managed to clear the rebels from around Kunming, freeing the city. Buoyed by success, Cen and Ma Rulong launched expeditions to stabilise central and southern Yunnan, while Yang Yuke fought his way westwards towards the Panthay capital, systematically retaking rebel strongholds along the way and laying siege to Dali itself in mid-1872.

About the same time, a Burmese embassy led by the king's minister, Kinwun Mingyi, arrived in Britain to request a treaty with Queen Victoria and secure their country's independence. They were toasted by high society, met with royalty and the business community, travelled all over, and did their best to convince disbelieving British politicians that the Burmese king was in fact in favour of reopening trade with China, but that all routes so far suggested were impractical. The embassy was impressed with their treatment and modern technology, but the idea of a treaty was never brought up and they left, disappointed, that November.

Hidden amongst the higher-profile Burmese entourage was Du Wenxiu's adopted son Liu Daohong, known as Prince Hassan, who was in London to enlist British support for the Panthay state. The presence of "three respectable but not ostentatiously-dressed Chinamen at the

Charing Cross Hotel" was barely noticed by the public; few people in Britain had ever heard of Yunnan, let alone the Panthays. Only *The Pall Mall Gazette* bothered with an interview, reporting that Hassan had been living in Beijing as a spy and was busy organising a China-wide Muslim revolt.

Hassan, who had been sent to London by the British administration in Burma after popping up at Rangoon, failed to wrangle support for his father's cause from a desperately embarrassed India Office, nor gain an interview with Queen Victoria. Britain had no interest in seeing the fairly malleable Qing dynasty replaced by an Islamic state, which might create trouble in British India by encouraging Muslims there to rebel. But Hassan's mere presence in London could have seriously upset Sino-British relations; had the Chinese government known about it at the time, they would have believed that the British were negotiating with the son of a notorious rebel – just as Sladen's expedition had courted the Muslim leadership at Tengyue.

In any case, Hassan's mission was too late. On 26 December 1872, the Muslim capital, Dali, surrendered to Yang Yuke after a bloody siege. Du Wenxiu, the former scholar who had survived the first Islamic pogrom at Yongchang before becoming leader of the Panthay Uprising, committed suicide by taking an opium overdose on his way to the execution ground. His corpse was decapitated anyway by the victorious Chinese, and the head sent to Beijing preserved in honey. Cen Yuying arrived at Dali a few days later, invited Du's seventeen remaining generals to a banquet, had them killed as they ate, and then ordered the wholesale massacre of Dali's Muslim population. Ten thousand people died, many of them as they fled the city in panic; reports described Chinese soldiers chasing civilians into nearby Erhai lake where they were cut down in the shallows.

It took another year for Chinese forces to pacify the final pockets of resistance in western Yunnan before the uprising was finally suppressed. Tengyue fell in June 1873 and Li Guolun, the rebel Hui governor who had befriended Sladen's expedition, died the following year – though his son escaped into the Burmese borderlands, where he continued to stir up trouble. The Panthay's seventeen-year-long rebellion was over, having caused the death or displacement of over a million people, perhaps a quarter of Yunnan's entire population.

*

As a reward for spearheading the pacification of Yunnan, Cen Yuying was appointed provincial governor, and for a career soldier with such a brutal record his first act was surprisingly enlightened. With much of the population impoverished by the war, Cen successfully petitioned the throne so that successful government exam candidates from Yunnan could travel to Beijing at public expense to have their results confirmed, rather than having to pay the considerable cost out of their own pockets.

A reopening of trade routes came next. Prior to the war, the Burmese had sent their China tribute overland through Yunnan every ten years, and now Cen wrote a memorial to the Imperial court at Beijing, describing how he had been approached to renew contact:

> *"Last year I led an army against the city of Dali, attacked and took it; and I was thus able to proceed into the prefectures of Yongchang and Tengyue... Subsequently Han Chun-pang, the local prefect, brought a Burmese official to me at the capital of Yunnan, who delivered to me a petition in Burmese and a translation of it in Chinese, in which it was stated that the King of Burma, having heard that hostilities in the province of Yunnan had completely ceased, had ordered the Burmese official to repair thither in order to request that I would give the necessary orders that Burma might again send tribute to His Majesty the Emperor; and that trade might again go on as was formerly the custom."*

And it wasn't just the Chinese who were contemplating a resumption in traffic between Burma and China. Now that Dali was back in Imperial hands, a May 1873 editorial in the Shanghai-based *North-China Herald* suggested that "there ought to be no obstacle to opening communication with Bhamo", and that appointing a British trade representative at Dali – halfway between Tengyue and Kunming – "would certainly be beneficial for both China and British Burmah."

But yet again, it looked as if the British would be beaten by the French. By this point Jean Dupuis had successfully navigated his way up the Red River in northern Vietnam to Kunming, and even though his expedition ended in a complete debacle – the Panthays were already defeated by the time he reached Yunnan, and on his return to Hanoi Dupuis fell out violently with the city's authorities, nearly started a war between northern Vietnam and France, and had to be hauled out of the country in disgrace – the British were naturally alarmed.

Spurred on then by fear of French expansionism and an enthusiasm for profits, The Associated Chambers of Commerce of the United Kingdom now resurrected the plan to survey a railway line between Burma and China. As reported in the *North-China Herald*, the job sounded simple: "at the present moment Great Britain possesses, to the east of the Gulf of Bengal, the [Burmese] provinces of Arracan, Pegu and Tenasserim, which reach within some three hundred miles of the western frontier of China; that adjacent to these three provinces is the Kingdom of Burma, very well disposed to be friendly; and that, finally, along the borders of China are independent tribes who are willing to aid in the work."

Of course, little of this was true: as Sladen had found, nobody in the region, from the local authorities down to the border tribes, had proved to be friendly or in any way willing, unless they saw a good profit in it for themselves. Even so, in late 1873 the Secretary of State for India, Lord Salisbury, and Ashley Eden, Commissioner of British Burma, approved a second Burma-Yunnan expedition, and appointed Colonel Horace Browne to lead it. Then based in Calcutta, where he had made himself an expert in the ongoing French expeditions across Indo-China, Browne was described by one contemporary as "a fine looking man", with a thick, upward-curling moustache. He was also an old Burma hand: he'd been commissioned into the Indian Army in 1852, aged twenty-one, and served in the British administration at Pegu. He would later be the last Resident at the Burmese royal court before the country was annexed by Britain, and in 1907 published *Reminiscences of the Court of Mandalay*, featuring frank diary extracts of his experiences.

Having learned their lesson from Sladen's hastily-assembled expedition of 1868, made without Chinese approval, this time the British decided that care would be taken "to obtain the consent of the Chinese Government, and the mission will not start until the passports, applied for by the Ambassador, have been obtained from Pekin." These passports for travel within China were imposing, poster-sized documents stamped all over with vermilion seals from the British Minister and the Chinese Ministry of Foreign Affairs, but were printed on such flimsy paper that they often fell apart from being unfolded for the benefit of local officials at every town along the way. They were issued under article nine of the 1858 Treaty of Tientsin, which allowed British subjects to travel throughout China for business or pleasure; if the bearer committed an offence under Chinese law, they were not to be punished but should be restrained using minimum force and handed over to the nearest British consul.

The passport issued to the expedition read:

> *Mr. Wade, Her Majesty's Minister at Beijing, has received an intimation from the Viceroy of India to the effect that four officers of His Excellency's Government are about to pass from Burma into China with a certain number of followers. The officers in question may return by the way they came, or may proceed by way of the Yangtse river to Shanghai. This [passport] is to request the Governor-General of Yunnan, and the high authorities of any other provinces through which the above-mentioned may have to pass, to give orders to their subordinates in charge of the frontier passes, or elsewhere, to treat them with civility, and to assist them on their way with all speed. Their names, and the names of their attendants, are given below.*

Wade also sent Browne an introduction to Cen Yuying, though he felt it would be of little use; despite Dupuis' good relationship with Cen, the British believed him to be strongly anti-foreign. In light of the expedition's experiences along the road to Tengyue, Cen's attitude towards the British, and the terms of their passports – or whether they even had them – were to become much-debated issues.

In some ways Browne was an unusual choice to lead an expedition into China from Bhamo, as he was one of the few theorists who still favoured following Sprye's route from Rangoon to Jinghong. That was just 750 kilometres in total, and Browne felt that the British needed a presence at Jinghong to keep an eye on the French in nearby southern Vietnam. Though the north of Vietnam was still independent, if the French got a foothold there it would be a relatively easy matter for them to follow Dupuis' route up the Red River valley and perhaps build a railway through to Kunming, from where they would have access to the rest of southwestern China's markets.

Bhamo, on the other hand, lay fifteen hundred kilometres upriver from Rangoon, with a further 170 kilometres of difficult country to traverse before reaching Tengyue. And in any case Browne considered Tengyue a poor target, a long way from the more mainstream, populated areas of Yunnan. The country between the city and the next important marketplace, Dali, was cut by the tail-end of those three enormous, parallel north-south mountain ranges separating the upper reaches of the Yangzi, Nü and Lancang rivers; even if a railway could be built from Bhamo to Tengyue, the extreme geography beyond here would make continuing the line further into China almost impossible.

But while Sprye's route might have had greater potential, it passed through the volatile Shan States, which the Burmese King Mindon wanted to keep closed to the British in case they encouraged the Shans to rebel against him. Mindon himself suggested that Browne's expedition take the Bhamo-Tengyue option; a Burmese tribute embassy to Beijing was just about to travel along this very route, so it was clearly the best one to follow.

The Viceroy of India, Lord Northbrook, who had approved the expedition only because he was being badgered to do so by Eden and Lord Salisbury, decided not to offend King Mindon. Browne's expedition would travel via Bhamo to Tengyue. Browne accepted this political decision, but was alarmed by the thought of a Burmese embassy running ahead of them:

> *"Though everything looks auspicious for the movements of the mission through both countries, still it can be scarcely anticipated that no difficulties will arise... the circumstance of the Burmese Embassy immediately preceding the British mission is a matter to be seriously taken into account... for slight as may be the influence exerted by Burmah upon the Chinese Government under ordinary circumstances, yet when added to the natural wariness of the local officials, heightened by the prompting of the local merchants, who have vested interest in the Overland trade, [it is almost inevitable there will be at least passive resistance from the locals]".*

Browne went on to warn his superiors that even in the event of a wholly successful expedition, they shouldn't expect a sudden blossoming of trade – only that the groundwork for such trade would have been laid.

*

While Browne fretted that a Burmese embassy moving ahead of the British expedition would have nothing to do but stir up the locals against them, the embassy itself had far weightier concerns: the problems of transporting a shipment of live elephants from Mandalay to Beijing, a distance of over three thousand kilometres.

Elephants are associated with wisdom in Chinese lore – the bodhisattva Puxian, the very embodiment of intelligence, is depicted riding one – and the emperors themselves used them as a symbol of their own sagacity and authority. Life-sized stone carvings of elephants guarded the Imperial tombs while live ones featured in processions, drawing the imperial carriage; they were trained to kneel before the emperor too, and during court a pair guarded the palace gates, linking trunks to bar the entrance once all the participating officials had arrived. They were housed in special stables, the "Tame Elephant Facility", just inside Beijing's Xuanwumen gate (a site occupied today by China's Xinhua News Agency), and exercised on the nearby archery grounds. There was even an official Elephant Washing Day, the sixth of the sixth lunar month, when the beasts were paraded through the streets to a section of Beijing's moat where huge crowds of spectators paid to watch them being scrubbed down and performing tricks.

Once widespread across southern China, by the nineteenth century elephants were only found in the far southwestern borders, so the court often demanded them as tribute from adjoining client states in south-east Asia. In 1791 Burma – where elephants were also venerated – had sent seven of the animals to celebrate the eightieth birthday of emperor Qianlong, and by the beginning of the nineteenth century Beijing's elephant stables were so full that offers of more were actually turned down, as looking after them was draining the treasury. Aside from having to pay a small army of dedicated handlers and staff, each resident elephant (at the time there were thirty-nine) ate three buckets of rice and eighty kilos of straw every day.

But by the late 1860s the last of these elephants had died – from old age said some, though others blamed the keepers for pocketing their feed money and letting the hapless pachyderms starve to death – and the emperor was having to make do with being carried around in a humiliatingly humble sedan chair during his public appearances. So, now that the Muslim Uprising had been crushed and trade routes were reopening, the Imperial Guard Office ordered Cen Yuying to procure replacements. Cen instructed Zhu Baimei and Wu Qiliang, officials in towns along the Burmese border, to organise it.

In 1874 the King of Burma, Mindon Min, dispatched two elephants in advance to Kunming while the main tribute embassy was assembled. This comprised the envoy and his assistants, interpreters, servants and elephant handlers – over fifty people – along with a further five elephants and the tribute gifts: a letter written in gold to the Chinese emperor, a stone statue of the god of longevity, tusks, jade, gold rings, gemstones, textiles, ten thousand sheets of gold foil and silver leaf, sandalwood and peacock feathers. The embassy planned to meet up in early 1875 with the other two elephants at Kunming, and from there make their way north-east across China to the capital.

This was no easy task. Aside from the sheer distance to be covered, involving a change from tropical to temperate climates, the elephants had to cross mountain ranges and ford deep rivers, and local authorities could be fined and even demoted if the journey through their territories took too long. Knowing this, the handlers often deliberately ordered their elephants to go slow unless they were paid hefty bribes, until the Qing court decreed that "no arbitrary delay be allowed", and sent their own officers as escorts to keep an eye on things. Officials along the way were expected to provide all necessary personnel, fodder and stables, to check that boats were sturdy enough to carry the animals over dangerous rivers, or even to build new roads and strengthen bridges. As recorded in the county annals of Huangping in Guizhou province, labourers hired for this work were sometimes cheated of their pay by unscrupulous foremen, leading to lengthy court cases over settlement. If an elephant died in transit, its ivory was sent to the emperor and the escort team was fined.

In short, anyone involved in the elephants' transport across China already had plenty to occupy their time. Spreading malicious rumours about the British expedition was probably the last thing on the embassy's mind.

*

By late 1874 Browne had made his way across from Calcutta to Burma, following the Irrawaddy upcountry to the town of Pome (Pyay). Here he met up with Superintendent Fforde of the local police, who had been appointed to command the expedition's military escort, a fifteen-strong Sikh contingent from the 28th Punjab Native Infantry. Fforde had also found an interpreter for the expedition fluent in English, Chinese and Burmese, named Moung Yu.

In his late thirties, Moung Yu was of mixed parentage, part Burmese and part Chinese; he was also a "nephew" (in reality, just a distant relative) of the warlord Li Zhenguo, the man who was blamed for stirring up trouble against Sladen's expedition seven years earlier. But unlike his uncle, Moung Yu was no fighter and had fled Tengyue to avoid conscription during the Muslim Uprising and settled down as a merchant at Bhamo, where he married and raised a family. Now keen to return home to Tengyue and visit his elderly mother, he was initially reluctant to accompany Browne's expedition as he felt Chinese authorities would prove hostile, but agreed after learning that the British had been issued with official passports from Beijing's Ministry of Foreign Affairs. Moung Yu was unflatteringly described by expedition members as "by no means of prepossessing appearance, and remarkable for a peculiar, loud voice", but also "undoubtedly intelligent, and appears honest". His Chinese name, Li Tongshi, was going to cause a good deal of confusion later on.

On December 23 the three expedition members reached Burma's royal capital, Mandalay, where they had an interesting conversation with expatriate Frenchman Fernand d'Avera. D'Avera had arrived in Burma as a spy for his government but had since gone native; he had a difficult position politically but was otherwise living a comfortable life, growing his own grapes and married to a Burmese woman. Having no axes to grind, he swiftly befriended Browne and let him know that the king was suspicious of the expedition, which claimed to be exploring trade routes into China and yet had no merchants with it. Its real purpose must be to agitate Yunnan's Muslims into another uprising, this time with British backing.

Browne appreciated d'Avera's goodwill in passing on this gossip, but believed that the idea was so ridiculous that nobody would take it seriously unless he went to the trouble of denying it. This was naive: the Burmese knew that Sladen's expedition had made friends with the Muslim leadership at Tengyue, and they might also have known about Prince Hassan's trip to Britain to ask support for the Panthay cause. But at any rate, in meetings with the king Browne found Mindon Min good-humoured, vigorous and apparently sincere in wanting to help the expedition, even offering to lend them his royal barge. He generously attributed difficulties experienced by Sladen's mission to mutual cultural misunderstandings between the British and Burmese.

On 3 January 1875 the expedition departed the city for Bhamo aboard the steamship *Mandalay*. They had been joined by two veterans of the 1868 mission, Dr Anderson and Colonel Sladen, who along with Browne, Fforde, Moung Yu, the armed Sikh escort and various servants and staff, brought the expedition's number to thirty-nine people in all. Their journey upstream along the Irrawaddy was slowed by fog and hidden sandbars, and it took them twelve days to reach Bhamo.

The town had grown since the first expedition, when Bhamo's fortunes had been at a low ebb. Now the disruptive war in China had ended, a British Resident had been installed and Bhamo opened up to regular river traffic, and the annual trade in cotton, tea and copper was valued at £200,000. All this business was in Chinese hands; most were Cantonese traders from southern China or Straits Chinese merchants originally from Singapore or Malaysia, who had made their way here via Rangoon.

The British were greeted by a flotilla of local war boats, led by Bhamo's governor, the *won*, and the Assistant Resident, Captain Cooke, who joined the expedition along with Ney Elias, the expedition's second-in-command and topographer. Elias had already led an adventurous life: having trained in geography and surveying, he reached China in 1866 as a trader for the family firm, but had given up business to explore the historic courses of the Yellow River, then crossed the Gobi desert into Russia – for which he was awarded the Royal Geographical Society's gold medal. Snapped up soon afterwards by the Calcutta foreign office, he mouldered away despondently in "flea and mosquito infested hotels" for several months before his employers decided to make use of his talents and seconded him to the expedition. Elias was not entirely happy with his posting; as a solo traveller he doubted how well he could work in a team, and felt the region offered little in the way of new geographical discoveries.

Like their predecessors, Browne and his companions weighed up the three routes east from Bhamo to Tengyue. Cooke and Elias initially favoured the central Embassy option, as previously Cooke had made friends with the most influential chieftain along the way; but having recently been involved in escorting the Burmese tribute mission as far as the Chinese border, elephants and all, this man now refused to have anything to do with Europeans. It was also likely that, in the wake of such a convoy, no pack animals or carriers would be available for hire. As Browne noted sourly, the Burmese embassy was already causing the expedition problems.

So, as the northern trail had been well mapped out in 1868, Browne decided to follow the southern route (briefly explored by Sladen's scouts during the later stages of his expedition). Although said to be easiest and least mountainous option, the one drawback to the southern route was its length, and the fact that it lay outside the control of Bhamo's *won* – meaning that the expedition itself would have to negotiate directly with local chiefs. But Elias had already approached some and found them amenable, and had even arranged pack animals, along with one hundred and fifty Kachin guides and porters.

As they laid their plans, Browne began to pick up tensions at Bhamo, and realised that by proposing to deal directly with Kachins he was alienating the town's Burmese authorities, who wanted to be consulted over their arrangements too. To counter this he moved from the British Residency at the edge of town to the *won*'s dwelling inside Bhamo, a tactful manoeuvre which was much appreciated. Initially the *won* tried to persuade Browne to take the central Embassy route, where he had more influence over the Kachin chiefs, but when he realised that the expedition was committed to heading south he promised to do everything possible to assist them, and to provide an armed guard as far as the Chinese border.

Kachin guides and porters arrived for the first stage of the journey, but the expedition's baggage – packed for mules – proved too weighty for the bullocks provided, and needed repacking. Heavy rains and local hospitality further slowed arrangements, but at last all was ready to go. They were just waiting for the arrival overland from China of the expedition's main interpreter and troubleshooter, a Mr Augustus Raymond Margary of the China Consular Service.

*

Margary – the name is pronounced with a soft "g" – was born into a military family at Belgaum, India, on 26 May 1846. His father, Major-General Henry Joshua Margary of the Royal Engineers, had begun his army career aged seventeen and seen active service through the 1840s during the Gwalior campaign at the tail-end of Britain's conquest of India's Maratha state, and in the First Afghan War. Margary was one of sixteen children; amazingly his mother, Louisa Jane Layard, lived into her late eighties.

As Du Wenxiu's Muslim Uprising kicked off in Yunnan during the mid-1850s, Margary was beginning his education – first in France, then at various schools in England (including North Walsham Grammar, whose former pupils included Horatio Nelson). In early 1867, having graduated from University College London, he crammed Mandarin Chinese for seven hours a day, passed the civil service exams with honours, and was appointed to Beijing as a student interpreter. Arriving that May, he was sent to live in a temple at the isolated Longwang village fifty kilometres west of the capital for intensive immersion in the language. China is larger than Europe, and Margary soon realised that its population was just as varied, noticing "how pugnacious" the residents of Tianjin city were, compared with the precise, cultured and reserved Beijingers.

Margary's route across China

Training over, he was posted to Shanghai, where outside office hours Margary proved himself an enthusiastic sportsman, taking part in cricket matches as an "exceptional" batsman, along with racket competitions and rowing. Though still rated a lowly third-class assistant interpreter, he must have impressed his superiors; in 1870, after barely three years in the country, Margary was transferred to Taiwan as temporary British Consul at Keelung, on the island's northern tip. Taiwan's arable and accessible west coast had been well-settled by mainland Chinese for several centuries, but the mountainous centre and eastern coastline were still inhabited by hostile aboriginal peoples; neither the British nor Chinese administrations showed much interest in the island's potential, and its once-rich trade in coal and fine tea was at a low ebb.

Even so, Margary managed to stand out. On 9 August 1871, the British schooner *Anne* and French barque *Adele* were wrecked off Keelung during a typhoon. Attempts to reach the stranded crews with a rowing boat foundered, so Margary and a British merchant, John Dodd, swam through the surf with a rope to get men off the *Anne*, and then rescued the *Adele*'s crew – one of whom, the bosun, had broken his leg. Having managed to get everyone ashore, Margary swam out again to save the *Adele*'s cat, just as the ship finally broke apart. After eight hours in the water, battered between rocks and the surf, both men were utterly exhausted and nearly dead from exposure. This heroic episode won both Dodd and Margary the Albert Medal – then the highest British award for saving life outside of war.

By 1873 Margary found himself back on mainland China in charge of the British consulate at Yantai, at the end of the north-easterly Shandong peninsula. He enjoyed the posting as everyone in the office spoke Mandarin rather than the local dialect, which he found difficult to understand at first. But he soon picked it up, seeing fluency as the key to appreciating Chinese culture, through being able to understand "the common talk of the people in the streets, or while engaged in their daily occupations... The country people are always nice, chatty and agreeable". Yet within a few months he was back at Shanghai, playing cricket again, serving as Clerk of Court during a Naval enquiry into the sinking and abandonment of a British steamer, and representing the British authorities on a three day tour of the Zhoushan islands, south-east from the city – the sort of routine work that any junior British diplomat would have expected as part of their job.

So it must have come as a surprise when, on 9 August 1874, Margary received the news that he had been secretly appointed as interpreter to Browne's expedition – not least because Shanghai was literally on the opposite side of the country from the starting point, Bhamo. His instructions arrived a week later along with a Chinese passport, a duplicate of those already sent to the other expedition members in Burma, allowing them to enter China from Bhamo and travel into China as they saw fit. As Margary wrote home to his parents,

> *"These letters direct* [Chinese provincial officials] *to take every care of me, and to issue orders to all their magistrates and officers along my route to protect and help me on. I shall pass over about nine hundred miles of country, of which some five hundred will be new ground. I have to keep an official journal and itinerary, and everything will be published.* [...] *what a glorious opportunity I shall have of seeing this wonderful country, and of bringing to light numerous facts as yet unknown, from regions untrodden by foreigners. It is really splendid; you cannot think how elated I am."*

Still bound to secrecy, on August 22 Margary stole out of Shanghai aboard a Yangzi steamer, late at night, without having been able to say farewell to his friends. His plan was to travel inland by river as far as possible, given that boats were generally faster, cheaper and more reliable than the roads. Accompanying him were his dog and Lu Dalin, aka "Laila" – "Come Along" – a Chinese fixer lent him by one of his superiors, "a sort of confidential rascal, who will do anything, go anywhere, and is never at a loss for an expedient. He knows the greater part of the country through which I am to pass, having been repeatedly sent out in search of golden pheasants and other rare curiosities. [Should anything happen to me], this man will be back to Hankow in a twinkling and bring the news".

A week later he was seven hundred kilometres upstream at Wuhan, the great tripartite capital of Hubei province. The weather had become exceptionally sultry and oppressive, affecting Margary's already shaky health (it sounds as if he might have had something like chronic malaria). Wuhan's British consul helped him recruit the rest of his Chinese staff:

"My party consisted of five, comprising a writer [Yu Dujian, aka Goggles, after his "immense and uncouth-looking" brass-rimmed green spectacles; he had a calm and dignified manner however, and many Chinese thought him a high-ranking official], an official messenger [Lu Dalin/Laila], a cook [Zhou Yuding], and my body servant [Zhang Yongqian, who Margary called Bombazine]". Hunan's acting governor also "helped me through with the most thorough hospitality and friendliness", appointing two officials to accompany Margary to the Burmese border and sending "such weighty instructions along the route that all the mandarins have felt constrained to show me every respect".

One of the problems for travellers in nineteenth-century China was that there was no nationally-recognised currency except for small bronze cash coins. Strung together in their hundreds through a central hole, these strings of cash were fine for buying everyday items, but were worth so little it was physically impossible to carry enough for any serious transactions. Each region produced far more practical silver ingots, *taels*, but the problem here was that weights and purity varied considerably, and getting a fair exchange as you moved between different places – where local traders would claim your silver was impure and underweight – was almost impossible. So finances for Margary's journey were arranged through a Chinese banking firm with agents along his route; he also carried a stash of *jinsha yin*, small silver ingots, to see him through any emergencies.

*

Margary set out again on September 5, but after a day spent battling the current upstream from Wuhan a letter arrived from India, suggesting that he travelled to Burma by sea. Understandably reluctant to return – taking a ship to Burma would have been safer, but would mean the end of his potentially historic trip across unknown China – he moored up at the small customs post of Leshan on the shores of the vast blue spread of shallow Dongting Lake and wrote to the British consulate in

Beijing for further instructions; depending on the reply it would be easy enough to carry on, or swiftly run back downstream with the strong current to Shanghai. But after several weeks without hearing from them he decided to take the initiative and continue, and by late September was at Changde, a busy trading town on the Yuan river in Hunan province.

Here he met Li Pisheng, a high-ranking official and former protege of China's premier statesman, Li Hongzhang. Pisheng's increasingly successful career at Shanghai had been interrupted by illness and a subsequent transfer to relative obscurity at Changde, where he languished under the orders of a local prefect inferior to him in rank – sent there, Pisheng believed, by the intrigues of Li Hongzhang's political rivals, who were nervous that the great man was filling important posts around the country with his loyal supporters. Margary found Pisheng "an extremely agreeable companion" and the two travelled together for several days; Pisheng was desperate to leave Changde and return to power, and was hoping that Margary would recommend him in dispatches to Beijing.

Through early October Margary followed the Yuan river south-west towards the junction town of Huaihua, then moved north up the Wushui and Wuyang rivers into neighbouring Guizhou province. He had fallen ill again, struck down by dysentery, and treated himself with opium – then used as a cure-all for many chronic illnesses – which seems to have worked but left him extremely weak. From here, his diary describes the villages along his route as being more or less hostile, but it could be that he was too ill to deal diplomatically with the usual run of minor daily irritations that afflict all travellers in China.

Not long afterwards news of Browne's expedition was leaked to the public. The *London & China Express* reported how "Mention was made some time ago of the determination to which the India Office has arrived respecting the survey of Captain Sprye's land route from Rangoon to Kiang-hung [Jinghong]... it is now stated that an exploring expedition is being arranged, and will start to complete the survey to the Chinese frontier early next month. The expedition will be accompanied by Colonel Horace Browne, Dr. Anderson, Mr Ney Elias, and by several officials of the China Consular Service". The *North-China Herald* added that Margary had already departed to join the expedition, as had Mr Clement Allen, a backup interpreter sent to Burma by sea in case Margary didn't make it overland.

Despite continuing poor health Margary spent a pleasant day at the small town of Yuping; it had been virtually destroyed in various uprisings but the magistrate, named Qing, was an old friend from Beijing and they spent time together chatting and eating. But then came his first real trouble, showing how easily foreign travellers in nineteenth-century China, even if experienced, tactful and fluent in the language, could still experience real hatred against their presence.

On October 27 Margary reached Zhenyuan, a garrison town strung along either side of a narrow gorge on the lime-blue Wuxi river. The elegant seven-arched Zhusheng bridge, built in stone, connected the two banks; work had begun on it in 1388 but the rival clans funding its construction fell out, and it wasn't completed until 1628. Margary was impressed with the town's setting, but as reported in *The Times*, "On entering [Zhenyuan] town – an extensive and populous one by the way – an armed boat was sent out to attack him. This he succeeded in overawing through the opportune arrival of a friendly official from below, under the escort of a gunboat, and he then landed amid an angry mob." Unable to stay at prepared lodgings, he was put up at the courthouse. He later heard that the situation was possibly caused by the arrogant behaviour of some Christian missionaries who had passed through town recently, and that the magistrate was new to his post and hadn't yet established his authority over the population. Margary left unscathed the next day but the townsfolk took out their anger on the boat crew who had brought him, burning their vessel and beating the captain.

Seasonally shallow water makes river navigation difficult after Zhenyuan, so from here Margary most likely followed the Imperial post road overland, either carried in a litter as befitting his status as a foreign dignitary, or on foot (many Europeans preferred the exercise). At any rate, a week's travel brought him to Guizhou's capital, Guiyang, set in the broad bowl of a river basin and surrounded on three sides by high limestone hills. The population seemed friendly and Margary got on well with the scholarly provincial governor Zeng Biguang, who generously promised to recompense the crew and captain of the boat which had been burned at Zhenyuan. Zeng had overseen the recent suppression of another long-running regional uprising against the Chinese government, this time by Guizhou's Miao ethnic group.

Margary also met Guiyang's French Catholic priests and their bishop, long established in the city, whose splendid new church was being built in a fusion of Chinese and European architectural styles. There had been a Christian presence in China for several hundred years, and as recently as the eighteenth century their scientific knowledge had been greatly valued by the Imperial court at Beijing. Polymath priests such as Ferdinand Verbiest had built modern equipment for Beijing's observatory, improved the calendar's accuracy, predicted eclipses and even produced an enormous woodblock-printed map of the world, complete with pictures of strange animals such as rhinoceros and whales.

But since the first Opium War with Britain, Christianity had been linked in the Chinese mind with the hated foreign invaders; and then of course had come the appallingly bloody Taiping Uprising, with its pseudo-Christian message. As one Chinese pamphlet put it, many people believed that the foreign faith should be eradicated for "deceiving the world and destroying the ancestors", and during the early 1860s Guiyang itself had hosted a massacre of Christians. Now the French bishop had set himself up as a high-ranking Chinese official, blatantly supporting local converts in any legal disputes they might have with their fellow-citizens, another cause of anti-Christian sentiment. There was also a China-wide belief that mission orphanages used infants' body parts for medicine – why else would the church go to the expense of adopting other people's children, unless there was some financial gain for them?

Guiyang had another long-term foreign resident, a British arms instructor and decorated officer in the Chinese military named William Mesny, who had spent six years in the province fighting the Miao insurgency and later married a local merchant's daughter. Margary had apparently written ahead and asked to meet up, but by the time his letter arrived Mesny had left the city to pursue his career in Sichuan province.

*

After another month spent travelling west along the post roads from Guiyang, Margary crossed into Yunnan province and reached its capital, Kunming. Despite its war-ravaged facade (the suburbs outside the walls were still being rebuilt) the city seemed an unpretentious, busy, well-supplied place whose population, living close to the borders with Tibet, Burma, Vietnam and Laos, paid foreign faces very little attention. Kunming's magistrate was so welcoming and helpful that Margary didn't worry that Cen Yuying, now serving as Yunnan's governor, claimed to be too busy to see him – an excuse often used by dignitaries when they wanted to avoid meeting foreigners. A letter from the expedition to *The Times*, presumably based on Margary's reports, gives a potted biography of Cen and describes him as "an officer remarkable for his intelligence and character", crediting Margary's subsequent easy progress through Yunnan as thanks to Cen's "careful arrangements and hospitality".

By now it was late November and Margary, already well behind schedule, was frustrated to learn that it would take another month's travel to reach the Burmese border, and worried that the expedition would start into China before he arrived. The magistrate calmed him down by sending off a fast courier to leave word that Margary was on the way, but he needn't have worried; at this point Browne hadn't even left Rangoon.

Rather more cause for concern were widespread reports that the entire Burmese border area was thick with bandits who robbed just about every traveller attempting to cross the region. This was echoed in a letter the following June to the *North-China Herald* from Father Fenouil, a Catholic priest at Kunming: "...we saw an Englishman [Margary] pass through here, making his way towards Dali to join an English expedition coming from Burma. The mandarins did not seem very satisfied, and persons of high positions assured me that he would be killed on this adventurous expedition, either by savages or the robbers infesting these parts of the country". Fenouil was a respected figure with long China experience, but it's also true that dire and often wholly inaccurate predictions of the dangers of the road ahead were issued as a matter of course by local authorities throughout China; if anything happened to a foreigner within their jurisdiction they would be held responsible – almost certainly demoted, exiled or worse – and so were keen to dissuade them from venturing into regions beyond their immediate control.

With this in mind, Kunming's helpful magistrate appointed Margary with two official escorts named Chow and Yang. Both had taken part in the recapture of Dali from the Muslim Panthays and "described the rebels as fighting with great ferocity; even when wounded lying on the field being actuated with a hatred that fought to the last without seeking quarter". Chow was somewhat effeminate and full of histrionic mannerisms, but Margary found Yang "an honest, blunt soldier, hale and hearty under the weight of sixty-five years, with a deep voice and kindly eye. His face is so dark that he looks like a mechanic, while blackened teeth and rough hands bear out the impression. He takes great care of me, and exerts himself far more than Chow."

On December 3 Margary left Kunming along an incredibly rough road choked by long trains of draft animals – oxen, horses and mules – all carrying salt; the salt trade was a government monopoly and major source of Imperial revenue, with its extraction, sale and transport all tightly regulated. Word had gone ahead and Margary was well received at towns along his route, many of whose officials were from adjacent Sichuan province, a region Margary admired for the intelligence of its citizens. But almost every settlement he saw was in ruins and many fertile valleys abandoned, their once-productive fields overgrown by rank vegetation, reminders of the recent Muslim uprising.

Despite being behind schedule, Margary was keen to make a brief detour to gain a first-hand view of Dali, the former Panthay capital. He reached the outskirts on December 17, but had a tough job winning round the local officials to let him in, as they were initially convinced that the sight of a foreigner would cause a riot amongst the townsfolk; the terrible slaughter of Muslims at the end of the war was very recent in people's minds. In fact he had little trouble during the day or so he spent in the surprisingly small, utterly dishevelled town. The military commander Yang Yuke – that understudy of Cen Yuying whose forces had actually captured Dali – appeared particularly friendly, promising to organise large quarters for Browne's expedition when it arrived.

Even though he enjoyed a good relationship with Cen and had played a major part in bringing the Muslim Uprising to an end, Yang Yuke was widely distrusted by almost everybody else. In part this was because he was from the Bai ethnic minority, enough for many of his Han Chinese contemporaries to sneeringly dismiss him as a greedy, lecherous, bloodthirsty barbarian. But the British pioneer Archibald Little was equally disdainful: "General 'Yang', who commanded the Imperial forces at the time [of Dali's capture], was said to have amassed six million taels – about a million and a quarter sterling – for his own share of the plunder; and we well remember meeting the ruffian, who was returning home by the *Messageries* coasting steamer with six wives, laid out on the cabin table being shampooed by two of them." Some of Yang's funds came from his control of mining operations in the Dali region.

On the other hand, explorer William Gill met Yang just two years after Margary's visit and was favourably impressed, especially after the battle-hardened general walked humbly over to his inn for a visit, instead of insisting Gill call on him: "He is enormously rich and powerful the Chinese government are much afraid of him he keeps 200 soldiers now at his own expense he is almost a hunchback but exceedingly active, so much so that the people here have bestowed on him the soubriquet of "the Monkey" [after the fearless Monkey King of popular legend] – In the war he was always at the head of his men on horseback under fire unlike the other Chinese generals who generally remain in the chair at the rear".

*

The road beyond Dali grew ever more extreme as it crossed south-west over the three high, closely-packed mountain ranges separating the Yangzi, Nü and Lancang river valleys. It took ten days to reach the next sizeable settlement, Yongchang – where the first Muslim massacre had taken place in 1845 – and Margary very nearly didn't make it at all: stalking what he took to be three deer up a hillside armed only with a light breech-loader gun, he discovered that his quarry were, in fact, tigers. Fortunately his bearers ran up in time with hefty sticks, and the tigers took off in surprise.

Margary wrote little about Yongchang, and none of it was good; unusually, he portrayed the city's Chinese administration as "brutes, and gave me trouble", though he didn't say why. Records show that Yongchang's prefect would have been Zhu Baimei, one of the men charged by Cen Yuying with organising the elephant tribute from Burma.

By now the scenery was ever more tropical, flat valley basins planted with vivid green rice fields, the mountains tangled in vine scrub and dark forests. And ahead lay the highest barrier of the entire journey, the Gaoligong range, its bare summits occasionally frosted in winter, which Margary tackled on the last day of December 1874:

> "*On the third stage to Tengyueh, we rested at a little village* [called Hemushu] *nestled high up in a forest-clad mountain. It had been a long stage and full of magnificent scenery. After threading the long gorge, with a torrent dashing below, we entered a wide plain covered with a two-years' jungle growth, and crossed the Mekong River by an elegant suspension bridge. Darkness overtook us just as we mounted up the steep paved path which scaled the opposite mountain. Hastily preparing rough torches of straw, bound in sheaves upwards of 10ft long, we wound our weary way up the interminable staircase for fully two hours, not daring to stop for fear of our lamps not lasting. The latest spark expired as we woke up the village with our shouts.*

> *The valley below, as we zigzagged up the slope, presented a lovely illumination... our Eyrie Rest could only boast of two or three simple huts, and we had missed the way to the temple where they told us quarters could be found. It was fortunate we had, as on visiting the next day I found an open ruin. Chinese officials, however, had to put up in its dilapidated sheds. A fearful wrangling ensued which I put a stop to by taking possession of a hut which turned out to be a newly-erected one. We slept very comfortably, although the walls were only bamboo lathe. Next day being New Year's Day and, curiously enough, our not being able to procure carriers, caused us to stay in this lovely spot, and I resolved to rummage the forest for game."*

Four days later Margary arrived at Tengyue, the walled city where Sladen's expedition had befriended the Muslim administration in 1868. (Strangely, on his journey here Margary had somehow missed crossing paths with the two elephants which had been sent in advance to China by the Burmese king, and which reached Kunming on this same day.) The city was a complete ruin, only recaptured by the Chinese eighteen months earlier. Margary had heard nothing so far about the progress of Browne's expedition and was relieved to find a packet waiting for him from the Political Agent at Bhamo, saying that they didn't expect to be departing before the middle of the month. But having assumed he would meet up with the expedition at Tengyue, Margary was excited to find that they wanted him to continue all the way through to Bhamo and join them there; he sent back an enthusiastic reply with his "confidential rascal" Lu Dalin and then spent a day assembling the necessary mule team for his baggage, and doing the rounds of Tengyue's officials.

> "*The Brigadier commanding the centre division of the Army* [Wu Qiliang, the other man responsible for the elephant tribute] *paid me a long visit and brought his little boy with him. It is customary in China to give presents to children in such cases, and as I am all but cleared out I was obliged to give the little fellow a pair of*

tortoise-shell sleeve links, which seemed to delight him much. I like these military men. They seem devoid of that stuck-up pride of the literary Mandarins.

I called on the General yesterday and had a very civil reception. His name is [Jiang Zonghan] and he is much famed for a daring military feat which brought about the downfall of Dali. I was very curious to meet this intrepid man who scaled the rocky heights behind the great city and dropped down in its rear. He has a calm, sphinx-like countenance with a charming smile. Yet this man slew thousands of Mohammedans on that day without quarter. It was his birthday, and he was giving a fete to the people. A sing-song was progressing in front of the audience dais, and I had my interview in the presence of 200 or 300 citizens who thronged the courtyard."

Both Wu Qiliang and Jiang Zonghan were to play important parts in the events which followed Margary's visit to Tengyue. Not much is known about Wu, but Jiang was born into a poor family in the dry, forested hills north-east of Dali, first appearing in the historic record as a soldier serving under Yang Yuke during the Muslim Uprising, when he proved himself a fierce fighter and clever tactician. After the fall of Dali he was made a military official, awarded *batulu* status – given for bravery – and posted to Tengyue as Acting Brigadier-general.

*

Leaving Tengyue, Margary began the final stage of his journey to the frontier. He was intrigued by the ethnic melange of these borderlands, which he described as "inhabited by a people called Payi [Dai] who are a mixture of Chinese settled here five hundred years ago, and the Shans, or Laotians, who cover the whole country between Burma, Siam, Cambodia and China... Divided into little principalities, they are governed by native hereditary chiefs under Chinese supervision. I have, of course, been the guest of these chiefs, and owing to their sociable disposition, I have a good deal of intimacies with their families. The women are not shy, like the Chinese, nor do they fear to talk with a stranger."

Their clothing also caught his eye, with huge folded black turbans and neat dark blue jackets fastened at the throat with a silver buckle; everything was covered in embroidered panels, even their shoes and puttees. Both men and women wore jewellery and displayed teeth blackened by chewing betelnut, the fruit of a slender-trunked palm. At one market he saw nervous "little semi-savages from the mountains" (perhaps Lisu), whose women also wore traditional clothing, though the men – all carrying spears – dressed in the Chinese style. Inevitably, officials warned Margary that the minorities frequently attacked travellers, but as he had heard this sort of thing many times before, he wasn't too concerned.

On January 12 Margary reached Mangyun, the Shan settlement which more or less marked the notional border between China and Burma. He liked the slightly shambolic town, with its friendly population and muddy, narrow lanes, exchanging presents with his hosts who in turn presented him with a walking stick and chunk of Burmese amber "which is a prized ornament here".

And it was at Mangyun that Margary met Li Zhenguo, the warlord who the British believed was behind all their troubles during the 1868 expedition. Li was in the middle of a meeting when Margary arrived, apparently negotiating an agreement between himself, the gentry of Tengyue and the local ethnic groups, who had been charging the mule caravans moving between here and Bhamo extortionate transit fees. As Sladen's expedition had reported Li to be little more than a licensed bandit, Margary was astounded to be welcomed respectfully by an obviously intelligent man who inspected his passport and then "prostrated himself, and paid me the highest honours. I had a most successful interview. He sent for a few notable townsmen and the chieftain of the savages, and introduced me with the greatest respect... Li told them I had come protected by an Imperial edict, and that they had better take care of me".

At this point Margary had just been joined by an armed bodyguard of forty men sent by Browne from Bhamo, so it was of course in Li's interest to be polite. Margary was also astute enough not to take their seemingly friendly encounter at face value: "I cannot feel certain, however, that I shall not be foiled after all... The Burmese want to thwart our expedition; and Li himself some seven years ago attacked our last expedition and may not be entirely free from enmity."

In fact Tengyue's gentry had already alerted Li to the impending British expedition, naming Margary as their interpreter. According to two letters now in the British National Archives, they believed that Britain was looking for an excuse to occupy the region in order to spy on China, "preach their religion and undermine the local economy". With the Muslim Uprising only recently suppressed, public opinion at Tengyue saw the British expedition as a threat to peace and the gentry wanted it stopped before they reached town. The "central government" – presumably at Kunming – had sent a couple of military advisors to help them; as the British expedition carried passports issued by the Imperial court Chinese troops couldn't openly be used to oppose them and so the gentry had considered using bandits, but decided that they were too untrustworthy. Li Zhenguo was even now mulling over the gentry's request to lend his men to the cause; it's possible that Margary walked right in on these discussions.

Margary later went game shooting outside the town and caused quite a stir coming back through the market shouldering his modern rifle and bag of half a dozen yellow duck. He sent a brace to Li Zhenguo as a present.

*

Five days later, having "floated down the river", Margary joined the rest of the expedition at Bhamo, justly proud to have successfully completed his three thousand kilometre journey across the width of China, along what might well become a major trade route for British goods. "It was one of the most delightful periods of my life to come within sight of a British flag again and soon to be congratulated by a distinguished group of Indian officers on my 'splendid journey'... I am the picture of health, as people tell me, and you may imagine how full of delight I am at the happy result of my journey and the glowing prospect ahead."

For their part, the expedition's other British members – Browne, Elias, Sladen, Dr Anderson and Fforde – were also clearly impressed by Margary, who despite arriving "without shoes or stockings" had not only "solved, single-handed, the problem of the through journey, but he has followed a route across the Central Provinces of the Empire never traversed by Europeans since the days of the Roman Catholic Missionaries at the commencement of the last century." (This of course ignored the French Lagrée expedition of a few years earlier, who had taken a slightly different route but nonetheless made it from the southwestern Chinese borderlands right the way through to Shanghai.)

Aside from his value to the expedition as an interpreter and trouble-shooter, Margary also proved a huge hit with Bhamo's residents, who were amazed at meeting a foreigner able to speak fluent Mandarin and eat with chopsticks. It seemed that every Chinese-speaker in the district wanted to talk to him, and he was invited by the *won* to watch local plays and dances nearly every day.

Inspired by Margary's success, the party now committed to retrace his journey all the way back to eastern China, as their passports allowed them to do – they had previously expected only to reach Dali and then have to return the way they had come. On Margary's advice they converted Indian rupees and most of their gold into the silver ingots, *taels*, widely favoured in China.

*

And yet there were a few disturbing undercurrents simmering away beneath all this apparent goodwill. By now the party had reached "the somewhat formidable number of about 50 persons, exclusive of local hangers-on and bullock drivers", a multicultural mix of Portuguese Indians, Sikhs, Gurkhas, Bengalese, Chinese, Burmese, Shan and Kachin. Bhamo's *won* also came good on a promise to supply soldiers and rounded up one hundred or so "wretched ragamuffins collected from the neighbouring villages" and several capable Burmese officers to guard the expedition until it reached the Chinese border. Most of them were armed only with ancient firearms, which needed a lot of coaxing to work successfully.

A slightly rag-tag assembly then, but not surprisingly the local Chinese and ethnic groups were alarmed at the prospect of such a sizeable foreign armed force tramping through their countryside. In fact the British authorities in India who had organised the expedition had wanted it to travel unescorted, so as not to have been mistaken as invaders, but Browne disagreed; they would be moving through known bandit country, loaded down with presents for Chinese officials – including valuable elephant ivory, rhino horn and two huge Australian "Waler" horses – and it would have been foolish to have dispensed with an armed guard.

Another concern amongst Bhamo's population was the belief that the British had come to begin building a railway to Tengyue. This idea would have upset a lot of people. The regional transport cartels employed thousands of mules and the people needed to handle, raise and look after them, all of whom would have been made redundant by the arrival of rail. Village heads also made a decent income from charging passing merchants a transit tax, which theoretically protected them from robbery or being detained indefinitely along the way, which they would obviously lose if a train whisked these merchants and their goods through unhindered.

The British minister at Beijing, Thomas Wade, had sent instructions with Margary that, although the expedition should collect as much information as possible on trade routes and local situations – including history, resources and geography – they were not to attract suspicion by surveying and map making, or by hunting near towns and cities. Wade also advised them to avoid contact with Roman Catholic missionaries, though it seemed unlikely that they would find any in such a remote spot. But sure enough there was already a French mission at Bhamo, whose two fathers were planning their own explorations north into the remote Tibetan regions along the Burma-Chinese frontier.

*

On January 23 the expedition departed Bhamo and headed a short way downstream to Sawaddy, a ramshackle Kachin village of about thirty houses at the start of the southern route into China. Here they were charged high prices for everything, from fodder to water and firewood, and were deluged in bullocks, ordered as draft animals for the expedition's gear. Nobody would say exactly how many animals had been commandeered – it seemed far more than the hundred and fifty the expedition had ordered – and then the loading procedure became so loud and complicated that Browne reluctantly handed over their luggage to Sawaddy's chieftain and left him to supervise everything. Given that Sladen had suffered exactly the same treatment, it seems likely that this was a time-honoured Kachin tactic for muddying the situation, in the hope of extracting more money. The bullocks carried their loads in baskets, each one of which needed to be hand-woven on the spot to fit its contents exactly, which proved extremely time-consuming.

By the end of the day all activity had bogged down in arguments. First, the bullock handlers claimed that some of the luggage was too heavy for their animals and wanted to open and repack the boxes themselves; but Browne suspected that they were only looking for an opportunity to pilfer the contents. He suggested that anything that couldn't be carried would simply be sent back to Bhamo, and sure enough the handlers immediately dropped their objections. Then the chief revealed that there were over three hundred bullocks, and demanded to be paid for them all. Browne pointed out that they had only contracted for half this number, which the chief reluctantly admitted was true, but then asked full payment for those in advance. Browne laughed this off, promising to pay half up front, but only if the expedition was ready to leave in two days time.

The next day Sawaddy's head reappeared to claim his money, but Browne wasn't convinced that the bullocks would be packed and ready to go as agreed. He believed that the previous expedition had given in too easily to extortion, and that now he needed to stand firm or risk being bankrupted before reaching China. Here he underrated Sladen, who in 1868 had been isolated in completely unknown territory while having to deal with the competing alliances of Shan, Kachin, Chinese and Burmese peoples; and who sat at Ponsee for two months rather than give in to demands and threats.

At any rate, Browne eventually told the chieftain that if the animals weren't loaded by the morning, the expedition would return to Bhamo and try one of the other routes. Far from being intimidated, the man stormed off after telling Browne to negotiate with his underlings, who immediately agreed to start at the promised time if the expedition stumped up a nominal payment for each village along the route. Called back to witness the deal, the chief calmly took the money off the men Browne had paid, pocketed it himself, and walked away grinning and claiming sarcastically that he and Browne were now "brothers".

Next the expedition's Kachin interpreter began stirring up trouble, inciting everyone to ask for higher wages. A group of Kachin tried to carry off some discarded clothes boxes, despite being told not to; Sikh guards stopped them and the Kachin fired off their flintlocks into the air in frustration. Angry at being thwarted, the chief told Browne that he wouldn't accompany them to China and, despite earlier promises, hadn't made any arrangements with other village heads along the route, who remained hostile towards the British and wouldn't let them through. On top of this, the expedition's stores – especially rice and spirits – were being continually pilfered by villagers.

Browne finally lost patience and decided to abandon plans for the southern route, posting Cooke back to Bhamo to see if he could rustle up enough mules for the expedition to set off along the well-trodden northern option instead. He confronted Sawaddy's head with his grievances: they had been there a week and were no closer to leaving;

provisions were being consumed with nothing to show for it; and the chieftain's claims that he arranged safe passage for the expedition was untrue. They were returning to Bhamo and had no intention of paying for the bullocks. Their luggage was duly unloaded and brought back to their camp – minus the considerable amount which had been stolen, either wholesale or by drilling holes in boxes of sugar and the like.

*

Back at Bhamo, the British were touched to find that the *won*, concerned for their safety, had been assembling a flotilla of ships, complete with rusty gingals, to sail downstream to Sawaddy and rescue them. The interpreter Moung Yu was congratulated by his fellow Chinese for returning unscathed, and told him that those who had tried travelling via Sawaddy before had been robbed of everything.

Browne received a secret message from Sawaddy's chief to say that he had a letter sent to him by the Burmese authorities which would explain why he had been so uncooperative – in other words, that the Burmese authorities had been pressuring him to prevent the expedition from setting out. But Browne believed this to be yet more duplicity on the part of the Kachin, an attempt to create bad feeling between the British and Bhamo's administration.

With their return to town, Bhamo was suddenly swamped in new arrivals, including the final expedition member, Clement Allen, the back-up Chinese interpreter sent by sea from Shanghai in case Margary hadn't made it to Burma overland. Then two chiefs from the central Embassy route, who had hosted the first pair of tribute elephants as they passed through their territories, stopped to show off gloriously gilded umbrellas and saddles, rewards from the royal court in Mandalay. (On the same day, the Chinese officials Jiang Zonghan and Wu Qiliang, whom Margary had met just weeks earlier, announced that the main Burmese tribute mission had arrived at Tengyue.) Rather surprisingly, a Russian named something like Levenkov also drifted into town; nobody knew why.

*

And so on 6 February 1875 the expedition packed up their baggage and set off for Tsitkaw, the first stage on the northern route; Browne rode the fifteen miles, crossing the Tapeng river three times. They set up camp at a local temple and enjoyed a few idle days at Tsitkaw, exploring jungle, swimming, shooting wildfowl and socialising with the local Kachins, who brought them groceries and a fermented drink called "sherroo". In contrast with the Chinese, Kachin women were not the slightest bit shy, and wore rattan girdles and belts threaded with cowrie shells, their tubular silver earrings decorated with red cloth. Hints were dropped that royal envoys generally presented red turbans to their guards and Browne, well aware that Tsitkaw's population had been taxed to support the British presence, took up the suggestion.

An assembly was called and Browne began negotiations with the Kachin chiefs along his route: "They are divided into two principal clans, the Lakwons and the Atsees, but the number of *sabwas* [chiefs] is more than a dozen. At the time of the last expedition only three chiefs of note – viz, Ponline, Ponsee, and Seray were met with, but now that trade is reviving the *sabwas* business has been found to be profitable, and some fifteen heads of villages have set up as free and independent *sabwas*, entitled to have their say to all caravans passing between Tsitkaw and Mangyun. The chief *sabwas* of the Lakwons are Ponline, Ponsee, and Seray, and the head of the Atsees is Wonkaw."

Ponline's chief visited to negotiate the price of mule hire, accompanied by a sixty-strong retinue and wearing an old felt hat with a bronze "button" mounted on the top, the insignia of a low-ranking Chinese official. Surly at first, and unimpressed with the expedition's passport, he warmed to them after downing most of a bottle of brandy, and was incredulous when Margary spoke to him in Chinese.

After the usual arguments mules were hired for the journey to Mangyun, but Browne put his foot down at the demand for an additional tax on each load they carried. The Kachins countered that this was the same rate they would charge the emperor of China or the Burmese king, and they didn't see why the Queen of England should get a discount. But they would confer with their agents at Mangyun, so the matter was dropped for now. The other chiefs promised to return in four days to perform a "fidelity oath" ceremony, after which the expedition would be able to set off. As the meeting was winding up, Bhamo's military chief promised to accompany the British with four hundred soldiers.

Browne was exhausted by the long day's negotiations, overwhelmed by what he considered the Kachins' unruly manners and lack of hygiene. A friendly Chinese trader named Wong was far more blunt, describing the Kachin as utterly untrustworthy dogs whom they had to bribe heavily in order not to have their mule trains plundered on the road between Bhamo and Tengyue. He recalled the days when Tengyue's Chinese authorities, angry at the mischief the Kachin were causing, had buried four of them alive at the city gates. For a long while afterwards no Kachin dared rob a Chinese, but with the recent lawlessness of the Muslim Uprising, they had returned to their old ways. Wong also revealed that the usual rate of protection money levied per load by was one *tical*, a fraction of what the Kachin were demanding from Browne.

After this the Chinese at Tsitkaw warmed to the British, confessing that they had originally seen them as friends of the Muslim rebels, here to stir up trouble; but now saw them as allies in re-establishing the old trade routes between Bhamo and Tengyue, restoring their former wealth. The Chinese considered the Kachin as the main obstacle, but warned the British that the Burmese too, though outwardly friendly, had no wish for the British to succeed, fearing that if the Chinese and British cooperated, they would lose their hold on the region. The Burmese were secretly encouraging the Kachin to delay and fleece the expedition; but if the British stood firm, the Kachin would eventually give in. "Do not give them too much money, or you will spoil our business". One Chinese, freshly arrived from Mangyun, reported that the Shan authorities there had been ordered by the Tengyue governor to prepare a formal reception for the British – a piece of casual misinformation that was to have fatal consequences.

Bhamo's *won* arrived on February 12 and called a fresh conference in which all the chieftains pledged to protect the expedition as it passed through their territories – as long as the British gave them plenty of presents. Browne agreed, though it was understood that any gifts would only be handed over once they had all arrived safely at Mangyun. A contract was duly drawn up in Burmese and signed by all, but the *won* remarked cynically to Browne that "Kachin words in the plains and their acts in the hills are often widely different." Inevitably, boundaries were soon being tested as the chieftains began demanding full payment for the mule hire in advance. When Browne refused they asked for half the money upfront, and then just for presents that they could show off to villagers along the way.

Rounding off the agreement – and probably seen as more binding by locals than signing of any contract – was the Kachin "fidelity oath" ceremony, involving a buffalo sacrifice. Aware of the offence that this taking of life caused to the local Buddhist population at the end of the first expedition, Browne was determined to forbid the sacrifice itself from going ahead, or at least to have it performed in some out-of-the-way location. As he believed that the main attraction was the feast afterwards, he intended to soothe Kachin feelings by giving them money to buy pork.

But the next day Browne awoke to find that the ceremony, sacrifice and all, had gone ahead right outside the temple where the expedition was camped, and that one of the building's posts had been desecrated with a freshly-severed buffalo head. He was furious at this insult to Buddhist sensitivities – intentional or otherwise – but the damage had been done. That evening he handed out the small advance payment, which all the Kachin present insisted should be given direct to the head of Ponline. Having solemnly promised Browne that no more financial demands would be made on the expedition before they reach Mangyun, the chief then grabbed the silver "like a tiger pouncing on his prey".

*

At this point the expedition divided in two: Cooke headed back to Sawaddy to see the document that the chief claimed would explain his actions against the British, and Browne sent Elias with him, with instructions for the two men – unencumbered by valuables and equipment – to make another attempt at the southern route. It was a good plan: if successful, it would mean that the British would have explored all three trails between Bhamo and Tengyue, Elias was experienced at this type of independent exploration, and with nothing obvious to steal and little profit to be made by detaining them, Browne believed that he and Cooke would be left alone by villagers along the way. The two parties agreed to meet up again at Tengyue.

On February 16, Browne and the main expedition roused themselves for an early start but spent most of the morning fending off renewed Kachin demands for full payment up front. Having learned not to argue in these circumstances – which solved nothing and stirred everyone up – Browne didn't even bother responding, and soon enough the mules were being loaded. Then he was conned into handing over ropes to secure the pack-saddles with; but instead of using it for this, the Kachin simply stole the rope and used leather thongs that they had brought along for the purpose. When Browne realised what has happened and dug the rope out of the thief's baggage, the man was furious – in Kachin terms, a successful thief owned what he had stolen, and the original owner had no right to take his property back.

Then a rumour went around that the Ponline chieftain had pocketed the wages he was given to look after for everyone; Browne hauled him out to distribute the money fairly, but found that he had already spent it. Nobody was happy and tempers began to fray. The Wonkaw and Ponsee chiefs started arguing; things became heated and *dha* swords were drawn before one of the Burmese bodyguards, known for his martial prowess, stepped in and resolved the situation without bloodshed.

The expedition departed Tsitkaw in the late afternoon through fertile plains and wetlands carpeted with wild strawberries, the valley flanked by a forest well-populated with wildfowl and deer. In light of all the arguments, Margary wrote that pragmatic steps had been taken to secure the expedition's likely success: "The Won has taken hostages from the Kachin chiefs, and we shall in all probability go through their hills without much delay."

They spent the night at Tsihet, at the foot of Kachin Hills, and then ascended a rough but uncomplicated trail straight up into them, via a *sheroo* break at Ponline, following a string of Burmese guard posts. The Wonkaw chief spent the whole journey slandering Ponline's leader, and Browne was glad to find that the Kachin were by no means united, which he saw as extra security for the expedition.

As the party set up camp at the fourth guard post, travellers coming from Tengyue warned them that a sizeable force of Chinese and Shan bandits, tempted by the expedition's wealth, was preparing an ambush between Seray and Mangyun. But remembering the report from the friendly Chinese at Tsitkaw, the general feeling – supported by Margary – was that the "bandits" were probably an honour guard of Chinese soldiers from Tengyue, sent as an escort by the city's officials. If not, Browne confidently boasted that the expedition's fifteen Sikhs, along with their hundred-odd reluctant Burmese soldiers, would be more than a match for any mob of thieves; he was answered by cheers from the soldiers, who swore to annihilate anybody who tried to rob them.

Next morning the expedition heard that the two hostages held at Tsitkaw for the expedition's safety, sons of the Seray and Ponsee chieftains, had escaped. Growing more cautious, they decided to march three miles to the Nanpeng valley and camp at the next guard post there. Along the way they met a Burmese man who cheerfully informed Browne that all was well at Mangyun; but then warned one of the expedition's Burmese soldiers that local cotton merchants were saying Li Zhenguo and Seray's chief had joined forces to stop the British from entering China. A Kachin traveller, also freshly-arrived from Mangyun, elaborated on the rumour:

the Seray chieftain was in league with a Chinese official named Yang to attack the expedition; and that Li Zhenguo had left Mangyun for Mengmao, a border town on the southern route, to halt them there if they tried to go that way instead.

Browne wasn't sure who to believe, but Margary, who had found Li Zhenguo so open and helpful just weeks earlier, doubted there was any real trouble and suggested that he went on ahead to Seray to reconnoitre. If anything was amiss he'd return immediately, but otherwise would continue to Mangyun and wait for them there.

So Margary, accompanied by Goggles, Bombazine, Laila, his cook and a groom, set off for Seray. Guiding him were a Burmese scout named Gna Hmaw, plus one of the local chiefs and his men, all Kachin. Margary was in high spirits, convinced that they were all being ridiculously cautious and predicting that he would have plenty of spare time to write up his journal while he waited for the expedition to catch him up at Mangyun. That evening he sent a note back to say that the roads were clear and the Kachins were laughing at British timidity.

*

On February 20 the expedition made the steep ascent up onto a plateau on the west side of Ponsee Hill. They camped at a flat, circular area about one hundred metres across, with a spur of a hill to the north, past which ran the road to Seray, and a wooded knoll to the north-west. East rose a sharp escarpment, along the top of which ran the Ponsee road. West the land dropped abruptly to the Nanpeng valley, while south along a small stream was the route they had followed from Tsitkaw. Settling in for the night they heard more rumours of an ambush ahead, the number of assailants growing with each report.

The next day Browne, Dr Allen and the Sikh guard marched eight miles to Seray intending, if all was well, to continue to Mangyun. With them were two Chinese-speakers: Browne's interpreter Moung Yu, and one of the doctor's secretaries, named Shi Yutian. They met Seray's chief in his wooden longhouse – a windowless, smoky, tunnel-like affair some seventy metres long. He appeared polite and willing to help, told them Margary had passed through safely, that the road to Mangyun was open, and that he would provide an escort himself if the expedition couldn't persuade their Burmese escort to move. But his somehow evasive manner, whispered conversations with Kachins who drifted in and out, and a warning not to worry if they saw large numbers of Chinese soldiers in the vicinity, convinced the British that something was amiss. Browne's suspicions increased when the headman forgot to ask for any presents, an unheard-of event.

Despite being able to see Mangyun's white cliffs in the distance, the British decided to play safe and return to camp (in retrospect, they were probably only saved from being killed on the spot by their Sikh guard). Before he left, Browne gave the chieftain a letter to deliver to Margary, and asked Moung Yu and Allen's secretary, Shi Yutian, to stay behind and gather information. It would be two years before Browne and Moung Yu saw each other again.

Back at the camp, the expedition was momentarily panicked by the sight of two Chinese watching them from the top of Ponsee Hill, but nothing further happened that day.

*

At eight the next morning, February 22, a "vague report" reached the expedition that Margary and his servants had been killed at Mangyun, alongside the "positive assertion" that four thousand Chinese troops from Tengyue, along with local forces from Seray and Ponsee, were just about to attack. Sure enough, soldiers appeared on the ridge above, encircling the camp, and the expedition took up defensive positions: the Burmese, with their ancient firearms but competent officers, were divided up between the northern spur, wooded knoll and Seray road, with a large group defending the Tsitkaw road; while the Sikhs established a position behind a naturally defensive stone ridge. The Wonkaw chieftain arrived from Ponsee, where he had been held prisoner in case he warned the expedition, confirming that Margary was dead, and that these soldiers were an eight-hundred-strong advance guard sent to annihilate them.

The battle began. Shots came from all directions, stampeding the mules; their handlers ran off after them, shouting abuse at the British as they fled. Tribesmen swarmed from the jungle to the south, waving spears and tridents and shouting to the Burmese in the British camp that they were commanded by the famous Li Shouk-goon; they should flee and leave the foreigners to their fate. But volleys from the Sikhs soon had them diving for cover, and after an hour of desultory pot-shots from behind trees and boulders the attackers suddenly retreated in a rout, leaving one dead behind.

Meanwhile the Chinese soldiers, who had kept well behind cover, were firing away but – perhaps because of poor training and worse weapons – did very little harm, only wounding one Burmese in the neck, and winging a Sikh with a ricochet. Browne remained confident he could hold off their present attackers indefinitely, if only his men didn't run out of ammunition, but knew they would be overwhelmed if they gave the main Chinese force time to arrive.

Then the head of Wonkaw reappeared with the news that his rival at Seray had just offered him five hundred rupees to join the attackers. Browne countered with an offer of ten thousand rupees to fight for the British instead, and – once the man understood that this meant ten baskets of silver – he agreed enthusiastically. With the wind blowing towards the enemy, the Wonkaw men set fire to the tinder-dry undergrowth and the resulting blaze drove off the attackers in panic, the Europeans shooting down stragglers. One Burmese appeared with a Chinese head which he hung up in a tree in triumph. The expedition recovered and loaded some mules, before racing back to their former camp in the Nanpeng valley.

After a fretful night, the Wonkaw men reappeared at dawn with the news that the Chinese had regrouped and were coming in force, and the British needed to abandon their luggage and get going immediately if they wanted to have any chance of escape. The chieftain also showed them a letter from Mangyun's authorities, written on the orders of Chinese officials there, warning him to abandon the Europeans and save himself:

> *"On the 23rd of February you must not remain with the British whom you are escorting: you must either leave them and return or you must stay in some place a mile or two miles from them. If you do not, and if in consequence any of your men are wounded or killed, you must not blame the Chinese... The attack will be made at night on the 23rd. Between 3000 and 4000 men are collecting around you. We think it will be wise for you to retreat."*

Leaving their belongings, the expedition fled along a back road and arrived safely that night at Tsitkaw, after a tough twenty-two mile hike. They remained at Tsitkaw for two days where, significantly, the local Chinese – previously friendly enough towards the foreigners – now took pains to avoid them. But much to everyone's surprise the abandoned luggage turned up, rescued thanks to the efforts of the Wonkaw chieftain and missing only Browne's uniform and most of their stores of liquor – a very small price considering the help the British had been given.

At Tsitkaw Browne intercepted letters sent from the Burmese customs post at Tengyue to one of the Burmese officers accompanying the expedition. These confirmed that Margary and his five assistants reached Mangyun on February 20, and were killed the next day by Chinese; and that three Chinese officials surnamed – according to the writer's transliteration – Bwa, Shoon and Lyu, sent to Mangyun by the governor of Tengyue along with four thousand troops, were to attack the British on the night of the 23rd. The courier himself confirmed the story, saying that on his way to Tsitkaw he had run into Li Shouk-goon – the leader whose name had been shouted out as his men attacked the expedition – whom he described as a Chinese officer.

From these reports it seems that the original plan had been to slaughter the entire expedition when it arrived at Mangyun, but that Margary coming on ahead precipitated events before the full Chinese force could be assembled. His death might well have saved the rest of the expedition, who could never have held out against four thousand attackers.

*

The expedition arrived safely back to Bhamo on February 26, where they found Cooke had returned from his attempt on the southern route, though Elias – whom Cooke had left safely ensconced at Mengmao on the Chinese border – was yet to reappear.

Browne interviewed father Lecomte, one of the French Catholic priests from Bhamo whom they had last heard of heading north along the China-Burma border. Lecomte reported that locals refused entry into their villages until he convinced them that he was not English; they were determined to kill the English "because the king of Burma does not want them in our hills". This belief in Mindon Min's antipathy was eventually traced to a forged letter written by a xenophobic Buddhist priest which had been widely circulated and which implied that the Burmese king had sanctioned the attack on the expedition. The perpetrator was later found guilty by an ecclesiastical court and stripped of his priesthood, but the incident, and the distrust it fostered between the British administration and King Mindon Min, was to have lasting repercussions over the coming months.

More details of the attack dribbled through: reports from the battlefield claimed that the British had killed sixteen Chinese and four Kachin; an official at Tengyue named Yan had punished his officers for not having obliterated the expedition; and that Allen's secretary had been killed at Seray, but there was no news of Browne's interpreter, Moung Yu.

Browne also interviewed a fugitive Burmese cotton agent from Mangyun, Nga Hmoon, whose invaluable first-hand account became the basis of many garbled rumours:

> *"I think it was about 16th Feb that I first heard rumours of Chinamen being collected to go to the hills. On Feb 21st I saw Mr*

Margary in Mangyun. I saw him several times. He was going about the town, sometimes accompanied by Chinamen, and sometimes alone. Two officials, Lyo Tsheng-tsheng and Shoon Tsheng-tsheng, came down from Tengyue. It was said they had a force of between 3,000 and 4,000 men. The men were not allowed inside the town, but we heard the noise made by them outside the town at night.

On the evening of the 21st, I heard that Mr Margary and his men had all been killed. Mr Margary was said to have been asked to go and see some hot springs, and when he got on his pony they knocked him off and killed him. His men were killed in the khyoung [temple] *in which they were staying. The local chief was very angry at this being done. It was done, not by any local Shans or Chinese, but by orders of the men from Tengyue. One of Mr Margary's men – a cook – is said to have escaped; they did not spare him, but I heard that he managed to escape.*

We Burmans were concealed by the people of the place. On 23rd Feb one of the Chinese officers said "These Burmans have joined the English, and have cut off the head of one of our officers. Many Chinamen and Kachins have been killed by them, and they have danced in front of the English when they opposed us. They ought to be killed". The Shans advised us to fly, so I fled at night... I heard that the heads of Mr Margary and the Chinamen who were killed were taken up to Tengyue after being exposed in the town".

With the rest of the expedition safe, Browne suggested sending out scouts to gather news about Elias and Moung Yu, but was advised that the less he drew attention to them the safer they would probably be. And much to everyone's relief, Elias reappeared at Bhamo on March 2, having raced back along a little-used track after hearing of the assault on the expedition. He and Cooke had reached the border town of Mengmao unhindered, but at Mengmao's ruinous courthouse they found Li Zhenguo. Li was welcoming, disarmingly frank and personally approved their travel permits, but advised against continuing into China as there was trouble on the road between Mengmao and the next town, Sehfan. Mengmao's chief, clearly under Li's thumb, also refused to help them; then their maps and surveying equipment were stolen. On February 17 Cooke decided to return to Bhamo, leaving Elias to negotiate his onwards passage alone; but both Li and the chief firmly stuck to their story, so after a few days – by the 20th or 21st – Elias was forced to head back too.

The British realised that, as the expedition had originally planned to follow the southern route, Li Zhenguo must have travelled there to stop them. But Li was clearly a skilled tactician, quite capable of confounding their plans without resorting to violence. And Elias's account proved that Li was far away at Mengmao on February 21, and could not possibly have been directly involved in either Margary's death or the attack on Browne's party.

With no more intelligence left to gather at Bhamo, the defeated expedition steamed downriver to Mandalay.

Reaction

So, according to accounts collected immediately afterwards, this was the story so far: Margary and at least four of his five servants had been killed by Chinese at Mangyun on February 21, and Browne's party had been attacked outside Seray the following morning by several hundred Chinese soldiers sent down from Tengyue, allied with local Kachin and Shan forces under a man named Li Shouk-goon.

The British wanted to know who was ultimately responsible for the attack. Given that apparently four thousand soldiers had been mobilised to oppose the expedition (even if only a few hundred of them had actually taken part) the ambush must have had the sanction of Chinese officials. But was it an entirely local decision, arranged between Li Zhenguo and Tengyue's authorities – presumably Wu Qiliang and Jiang Zonghan – or were their superiors involved? Browne pondered the possibilities:

> "*It still remains for us to discover the origin of the general order to stop us, issued in defiance of the Imperial passport. Did the Peking Government at the very time it issued the passport send secret orders that we were to be opposed... Or did the Viceroy of Yunnan* [Cen Yuying], *who Mr. Wade describes as an anti-foreign official, take it upon himself to disregard the orders from Peking?*"

And why had the attack taken place at all, given that Margary had experienced nothing but goodwill at Mangyun and Tengyue on his way towards Burma? Here, there were rather too many possible reasons: the appearance of a large, heavily armed foreign expedition making their way through a region which was still volatile after decades of civil war; the unfortunate fact that Sladen's previous expedition had befriended the hated rebel Muslim leadership at Tengyue; the belief that the British had come to build a railway, and its likely negative effect on local business; the Chinese administration's ingrained distrust of foreigners and their alien religion – all might all have contributed to what was soon labelled as "The Yunnan Outrage".

There was also the question of Burmese involvement. King Mindon might have had plenty of valid reasons for wishing the British to fail, but had he really connived with the Chinese authorities to slaughter the expedition? And had the Burmese elephant envoys been used to spread lies about the British, to encourage a rising against them? Browne believed that they might: "the Governor of Tengyue... received Margary civilly, but after Margary left, the Burmese Embassy passed through. What perfidious suggestions these Burmans may have whispered into the Governor's ear we can [only] imagine." British suspicions were further reinforced by Father Lecomte's story of that xenophobic monk and his supposed letter from the Burmese king.

Browne concisely summed up what was needed to answer these questions: "A local inquiry under the protection of an armed force seems to be the only possible method of getting at the bottom of the matter and exacting reparation." Yet over the following months attempts to arrange this seemingly direct, pragmatic solution were undermined, both by politics and how the small store of fact and informed speculation about the affair became distorted, enlarged, and finally bent into bold theories about what had "really" happened and who was "really" responsible – all whipped up by a storm of righteous letters and newspaper editorials.

*

On 3 March 1875, just ten days after the attack, a telegram reached Britain from India. As *The Guardian* reported the following day, "The Burmo-Chinese Expedition Attacked. An Englishman Murdered. Sad intelligence has reached us concerning the Burmo-Chinese expedition under Colonel Browne. A private telegram from Calcutta states that the members of the expedition have been attacked by natives, and Mr Margary, son of General Margary, Royal Marines, murdered." The paper tactfully left out that the original telegram also claimed that Margary's head, along with those of his five Chinese companions, had been hung up on Mangyun's walls. The news was broken to the House of Commons by the Under-Secretary of State for India, Lord George Hamilton:

> "*I regret to state that a telegram has been received from the India office informing us that the expedition which started from Burmah to China was on the 22nd of February, at a place called Mangyun, attacked by several hundred Chinese, together with a large number of hill tribes. The main part of the expedition got off with three wounded, but I am afraid they have lost the greater part, if not the whole, of their baggage. I regret to add that a distinguished serving officer, Mr Margary, who was making his way overland to join the expedition, got separated from the party, and that he, along with five Chinese, was surrounded and killed.*"

The Times led the British papers in speculating as to who was responsible. "It may be safely assumed... that the attack was made by regular Chinese troops [under orders of the Governor of Tengyue]... strong suspicion will rest on the Burmese Embassy, which preceded the English Mission, of having encouraged the local Chinese authorities to attack the English expedition", despite having official passports issued by Beijing. Britain's regional journals agreed, adding "There has already been sufficient evidence of the covert desire of the King of Burmah to oppose obstacles to any efforts of the British to open a trade route across the borders from Burmah to China."

On March 7 a "correspondent in Rangoon" – almost certainly a combined effort by Elias and Anderson – wrote a detailed account of the attack to *The Times*. But unlike many other reports to follow, it urged caution before doling out blame: "It is hardly possible to conceive that the Chinese Government has in any way been implicated in this... It is premature to arrive at any conclusion until further advice throws more light on this matter. It is to be remembered that the town in which this happened has but lately been on the confines of the area of the great struggle between the Panthays and the Chinese, and years of war naturally beget lawlessness and contempt for human life."

The Times also printed an understandably sad, indignant letter from Major-General Henry Joshua Margary, the murdered man's father. The general had served in India during the Mutiny of 1857, and his letter echoed beliefs honed in the aftermath: that the only way to deal with resistance to British rule was to retaliate with maximum force. Having quoted the original telegrams announcing the attack – including the claims that Chinese forces, commanded by Li Zhenguo's nephew, were responsible, and that Margary's head had been exposed on Mangyun's walls – he asked:

> *"Will our present noble Government and the British nation allow this most outrageous insult and defiance of it to pass unavenged? I trow not. If it did, our hold on India would be imperilled. As it is, no doubt exaggerated rumours of a large force of English "foreign devils" being easily defeated will spread through China and elsewhere like wildfire, and what may be the effects of it if we do not act promptly? Mangyun should be razed to the ground and Tengyue occupied by us – two feats easy to be accomplished; and then there would be sufficient protection, both moral and physical, for a commercial route through Burmah into China open to all countries."*

This letter gave a foretaste of the difficulties which were to entangle identification of the culprits behind Margary's murder. Li is an extremely common family name in China (there are at least half a dozen involved in Margary's story) and the telegram confused Li Zhenguo's nephew Moung Yu – the inoffensive merchant-interpreter left behind at Seray by Browne, whose Chinese name was Li Tongshi – with Li Shouk-goon, who the tribesmen attacking Browne's party had claimed was leading them.

*

Meanwhile Browne had arrived back in Mandalay, where he was told that the planned ambush had been common knowledge at the Burmese court on February 16, five days before Margary was killed. This convinced him that the Burmese embassy had played a part in the affair and, avoiding an awkward meeting with King Mindon, Browne hurried down to the British headquarters at Rangoon. Here he found Hassan, son of the late Panthay leader Du Wenxiu, living in exile after his mission to Britain. The Chinese had since learned all about Hassan's travels, adding to their suspicions about the real motives behind Browne's expedition.

Hassan passed on what he had heard from his contacts in Yunnan about the attack. While the British were still planning their expedition the previous year, King Mindon had asked Chinese merchants at Mandalay what the reaction in China was likely to be. The merchants wrote to the Tengyue gentry, who in turn wrote a letter to Cen Yuying, stating that the province had only just recovered from the Muslim rebellion and were worried about the British expedition causing trouble for the town. Cen understood their concerns and suggested chasing the British away; but as they were carrying official passports and couldn't be stopped once they entered Chinese territory, they must be prevented from reaching it in the first place. This explained the choice of the ambush site: although the Sino-Burmese border was technically marked by the Tapeng river, which the expedition had already crossed, local opinion held that Mangyun town marked the frontier.

*

Inflammatory letters, repeating and enlarging what had already been said, poured into *The Times* throughout March: "The murder of Mr Margary in Yunnan appears to have been so deliberately committed that it is to be hoped that the British Government will not in this case be content with the expression of deep regret and offers of pecuniary recompense to the relatives on the part of the Chinese Government, which have on occasions been held sufficient reparation for outrages perpetrated on foreigners in China." The writer suggested that demands follow the Chinese model: to hold the local officials responsible for acts committed in the jurisdiction, and, once they had arrested the perpetrators, have the officials demoted and the criminals executed. This was assuming, of course, that it wasn't the officials themselves who were responsible.

Another letter demanded that enquiries be made in Mandalay to discover whether the Burmese were in any way involved; the author was possibly informed by Elias, who had become convinced that King Mindon was behind the attack.

> "*Some days ago Lord George Hamilton stated that the attacking force was composed partly of Chinese and partly of Hill men... the Hill tribes concerned must have been Kachin, who are Burmese subjects...* [Not only that, but] *Li Zhenguo would naturally view with displeasure the approach of a party of British officers, whose predecessors* [Sladen's expedition] *had made friends with his bitter enemies, the Mussulmans.*"

The letter concluded, without having given the least bit of evidence, "The Government of the King of Burmah is at least as much, and probably more responsible [for the attack] than that of the Emperor of China." Other letters agreed, adding that the apparent politeness shown to the mission inside Burmese territory "is no indication of the real feelings of the King or his advisors, and the general impression is that there is nothing short of an actual invasion he dreads more than the extension of British influence or trade beyond his capital [Mandalay] in the direction of China."

Meanwhile the British government was hoping that their representative in China, Thomas Wade, would somehow resolve the matter without involving them. In parliament, prime minister Benjamin Disraeli managed to praise Wade and deplore Margary's murder, while refusing to commit to any action:

> *"We sent instructions to Mr Wade, her Majesty's minister at Pekin – and her Majesty's most able Minister at Pekin, for it would be impossible to speak too highly of his qualifications – to call upon the Chinese government to make a strict investigation into all the circumstances connected with this deplorable affair, and until we receive his report it will of course be out of our power to decide upon the steps we will take. The death of Mr Margary is a public calamity (hear, hear)... he was a young man of great promise and ability, who had displayed all those qualities which were suitable to the eminent career which I have no doubt awaited him had his life been spared."*

Disraeli finished up by pointing out that the assault had occurred in the vague borderlands between China and Burma, in a district inhabited by a mixed population where it was doubtful whether China's Imperial government had any real power. *The Guardian* leapt on these remarks. "Mr Disraeli seems to have said a little too much in reply to the question as to the melancholy fate of Mr Margary and his servants. It is of course quite proper to wait for an explanation from Pekin; but it was scarcely necessary to suggest to the Chinese an excuse [that they had no control of this border region] of which probably they will not be slow to avail themselves... [However,] The most recently published letters of the late Mr Margary show that his safe conduct from the Central Government secured him every mark of respect from the chief military commander at Mangyun, where he was afterwards killed, and, as seems beyond doubt, by a military force."

Back in China, on March 12 Wade wrote to Prince Gong Yixin of the Zongli Yamen, the Chinese Ministry of Foreign Affairs, informing him of Margary's death and the attack on the expedition. It was unfortunate that Wade pinned blame for the attack on "a nephew of Li Zhenguo", again confusing Li Tongshi – the interpreter Moung Yu – with the mysterious Li Shouk-goon.

Prince Gong immediately replied to Wade, acknowledging that "Her Britannic Majesty's Government is not likely to be satisfied with the mere assurance that orders to institute an enquiry have been sent by express to a Provincial Government, from which no answer can be expected in less than half a year's time", and so dispatched an express message to Yunnan ordering the authorities to begin their investigations immediately. His commands were sent by a relay team of Imperial couriers who were said to cover about three hundred kilometres per day; these riders were punished if they failed to complete their section in the allotted time, and it was illegal to delay them in any way.

Even so, it took Prince Gong until March 21 to pass the news on to the throne and request that the Yunnan authorities immediately appoint "judicious officials" to find out what had happened. This delay wasn't routine bureaucratic sloth: until now the palace had been fully occupied with the complex consequences of the death that January of the dissolute Tongzhi emperor – officially from smallpox, though others suspected syphilis. Only recently married, Tongzhi had died leaving no male heir, a crisis resolved in late February by his infant cousin Guangxu being adopted as the new emperor. *The Times* mused that the political ramifications of this succession remained unclear, but that Britain should still assert its rights over the death of Margary. "If the news of this murder spread through China without the sequel that reparation has been demanded and made, those [Chinese] hostile to the foreigner will be able to record a success very prejudicial to a good understanding between Europeans and the new Government."

*

By the time the throne had been informed, Wade had already made his first demands for settling the affair: the crime must be investigated immediately by a special Commission which must include at least one

British officer; fresh passports should be issued for a new British trade expedition between Burma and China; and an indemnity of 150,000 *taels* (ounces of silver) must be paid by the Chinese government. All these were reasonable enough, though – considering the widespread belief that Burma was in some way involved – China was being asked to admit its guilt before any investigation had even taken place.

The Chinese authorities responded in good diplomatic style; Wade had not explained the reasoning behind his demands, and this allowed Prince Gong to muddy the waters. In his view, as the attacks had taken place on Chinese soil it was for the local officials to investigate the affair and judge any suspects, "whether the British Government should appoint officials (to be present) or not". This led to a barrage of messages between Wade and Prince Gong, who "in view of the extremely grave nature of the present case" – and the fact that Wade essentially warned him that if he didn't accept this point, Britain would declare war on China – eventually consented not to allow anyone arrested in connection with the affair to be put on trial without British observers being present.

But Wade's second point was calmly fended off by quoting Britain's own wording as laid out in its treaties with China: any passports for a new expedition would have to be applied for through the usual channels. As for the indemnity, the amount awarded would depend on the value of property lost as a result of the incident, and surely couldn't be set in advance of an investigation.

Wade had also taken advantage of the situation to demand that the Chinese government resolve several outstanding issues which had nothing to do with Margary, concessions promised to Britain under the various "Unequal Treaties" but which China had so far managed to avoid implementing. These included items concerning diplomatic privilege, transport taxes, trade and outstanding grievances against specific Chinese officials. Prince Gong refused to consider these extra demands however, stipulating that "other claims unconnected to the Yunnan affair should be dealt with on their own merits... separation is necessary in order that the threads of current business be kept distinct".

Wade countered that the attack on Browne's expedition was the outcome of wider Chinese policy: "So long as the representative of foreign powers are treated as vassals... and so long as treaty obligations are studiously kept from the knowledge of people by careful exclusion of these matters in the *Peking Gazette*, so long will outrages occur." Here Wade made a fair point. The *Peking Gazette*, which published Imperial edicts and reported on court affairs, refused to mention any situations involving foreigners. (For example, regarding the investigation of the Margary Affair, it only reported that officials had been sent to Yunnan to investigate trouble, without mentioning the foreign aspects of the case.) This meant that the Chinese public were only informed of these matters by rumour and speculation, making foreign actions in China appear completely arbitrary, stripped of any context and distorted as they passed around the country by word-of-mouth.

These issues were all debated with vigour over the coming months, the Chinese writing increasingly lengthy, complex letters picking apart the minutiae of British claims, demanding that the British justify everything in terms of their various "Unequal Treaties"; while Wade, growing ever more fractious, made equally detailed rebuttals while doggedly pushing his original demands.

And it wasn't just the Chinese authorities who were nettling Wade. When Britain's Foreign Secretary, the Earl of Derby, questioned whether Mangyun was even within China's jurisdiction, Wade could barely conceal his irritation as he pointed out that China had long claimed authority over this entire border region with Burma. (Even so, Wade himself admitted later that he'd had trouble identifying Mangyun amongst the tangle of local names used in Chinese records.)

*

On March 25 Dr Anderson and the expedition's fifteen Sikh soldiers returned to Calcutta, where they were mobbed by the press and foreign residents, all eager to hear first-hand accounts of the attack. The Viceroy of

India, Lord Northbrook, visited the soldiers to express his appreciation of their "gallant behaviour" in defending the expedition, and local English-language papers reiterated the belief that the Burmese elephant envoy had probably had a hand in the affair – though they pointed out that as the British government in India had no diplomatic relations with China, it would be up to the British Foreign Office to settle the matter.

This highlights another problem bogging down progress in the affair: the involvement of three separate strands of British bureaucracy. First there was the Home Government in London, which had approved Browne's expedition but which, as Disraeli had made clear, wanted somebody else to settle its troublesome aftermath. Then there was the British Government of India at Calcutta which had proposed and organised the expedition; individual employees such as Browne were doing their best to keep interest in the affair alive, but overall the administration had enough problems governing India and Lower Burma without getting involved in a dispute with China as well. And finally there was Thomas Wade at Beijing, who had been dragged in by the murder of one of his administrative staff but was having a tough time convincing the Chinese – on whose territory the incident had occurred, and whose officials might well be involved – to approve any kind of external investigation.

Meanwhile Li Zhenguo was detained at Tengyue by Wu Qiliang, who opportunistically blamed him for the attack on Browne's party. Shortly afterwards, the Yunnan governor Cen Yuying – the very man that the British were beginning to suspect was in fact responsible – was ordered to investigate Margary's murder by the Chinese government. Cen duly received a report from Li Zhenguo, which included letters to the Tengyue Gentry in which Li (to calm their fears of unrest at the approach of Browne's expedition) promised that he was "taking vigorous and active precautionary measures, with the view of stoutly defending the region under his care".

*

April 8 saw details of the Margary Affair appearing for the first time in China's English-language press, though – given that by this point it was widely known about in Britain and India, not to mention by the Chinese authorities – it must surely have already been public knowledge. The authoritative *North-China Herald* at Shanghai ran a headline announcing "The Murder of Mr. Margary", and seems to have drawn its copy from sources telegraphed from India, padded out with local information. "Few men who have lately passed through the Shanghai Consulate have been better known than Mr Margary, and every one who knew him esteemed him. We can say with all sincerity that the Service has sustained a great loss by his death, and that very many people have lost a valued friend".

This first report was concise and stuck to known facts: "the outrage appears of the most painful and brutal character. It is said that Mr Margary was enticed into one of the yamens [government offices] at Mangyun, with three of his Chinese servants, and was there killed while the rest of the party were attacked but escaped with the loss of all their effects, three Europeans of their number being wounded. It is further stated that Mr Margary's head was placed on the city wall". An editorial added "As the expedition was provided with passports from the Chinese Government this attack is inexplicable". The paper demanded full reparations and went on to bang drums about retribution, suggesting using spare regiments from India to storm southwestern China.

By this time Wade had succeeded in one of his demands and obtained passports from Prince Gong allowing two British Commissioners, accompanied by a Chinese official, to travel to Yunnan and investigate Margary's murder first-hand. These passports read:

> *MR WADE, Her Britannic Majesty's Minister in Peking, issues the following passport to ———, British officers proceeding by his desire to Yunnan for the purposes of being present at the trial of persons charged with the murder of a British officer in that province:-*
>
> *This is to request the Governor-General of Yunnan, and the High Authorities of any other provinces through which the officers above*

mentioned may have to pass, to give orders to their subordinates in charge of the frontier passes or elsewhere to treat them with civility, and to assist them on their way with all speed.

Stamped with the Seals of Her Britannic Majesty's Minister at Peking and of the Yamen of Foreign Affairs.

The wording only mentioned Margary's murder and not the attack on the rest of the expedition – an omission that the Chinese authorities were to exploit later. At any rate, Prince Gong confirmed that "no one accused of participation in the outrage shall be sentenced, until the officers sent by Mr Wade shall have had an opportunity of hearing the evidence against them. This at least ensures that a strict enquiry will be made on the spot, by persons interested in arriving at, rather than disguising, the truth." It seemed that the investigation into the Yunnan Outrage would shortly begin, and Wade believed the two British observers could be on their way to Yunnan by May.

*

Over in India, Browne had travelled to the cool hills of Simla, the British administration's summer headquarters, where he recorded cynically:

"I have been sent to supply the [Indian] Government with information so that it may decide on the next move to be made. I find I might have been spared the journey, for before my arrival the Government had adopted the plan of making no move at all, and of leaving everything in the hands of Mr. Wade at Peking... A local enquiry made by Consular officials under the protection of Indian bayonets would be much more likely to elicit the truth than a host of Chinese mandarins sent from Peking, supposing even that the Chinese Government is blameless in this matter, which is very doubtful."

Browne was duly ordered to Beijing to assist Wade in his negotiations, but before leaving India he requested some form of government recognition be given to the fifteen Sikh soldiers who had defended his expedition so bravely.

While disappointed by the Indian government's reluctance to get involved, Browne did appreciate that they were also trying to resolve a particularly fractious territorial boundary dispute with King Mindon, and until the matter was settled it would be provocative to send an armed British force through Burmese territory into China to avenge Margary's murder. This dispute dated back to 1852, when it was decided that the border between British and Burmese parts of the country, "after crossing the Irrawaddy, was to run due east along a line nearly corresponding to the eighteenth parallel, until it struck the course of the Salween." The problem here was that this line would bisect territory of the Karen ethnic minority, which the British considered independent. So they left Karen lands intact, drawing the Burmese boundary around them to the north and their own line to the south. But King Mindon considered the Karen to be his subjects, and his maps absorbed their territory and drew the southern line as his own frontier with British Burma – thereby angering the British.

And now British tempers were fraying further as belief of Burmese involvement in Margary's murder grew. In London, *The Pall Mall Gazette* accused the Burmese court of:

> *"arrogance and duplicity... From Mandalay every letter brings tidings of defiant preparation* [for war with Britain]. *All the ironworks of the King are in ceaseless activity turning out arms; steamers are getting ready for service, shipping guns and stores; troops – or hordes of armed rabble if you prefer it – closing in upon the frontier; trade at a standstill, and the Burmah officials more insolent than ever."*

Despite admitting that these reports were probably overblown, the paper went on to say that local "experts" were "unanimous in fearing that the King may anticipate [the British envoy] Sir D. Forsayth by making some desperate raid upon our districts, such as was predicted some months ago in the local papers... It is understood that Sir D. Forsayth carries an ultimatum to Mandalay [to comply with the border issue], and if it should be rejected by the Burmese Court it is difficult to see any other issue out of the difficulty than war."

Not wasting the opportunity, the *Gazette* also rehashed the story that King Mindon had written to the tribes at Bhamo ordering them to attack the Browne's expedition, but again admitted that as this rumour had come from the Indian press, it probably had no foundation in reality. Considering the rest of the article they then concluded in a strangely conciliatory tone, "We cannot go to war on the grounds of conjecture" and pointed out that the attack had occurred inside Chinese territory, that the Chinese had never been tolerant of foreign incursions, and that there might be no need to look for Burmese involvement.

In Burma, a *Rangoon Gazette* editorial, leaning heavily on innuendo and rumour, elaborated on the believed malevolence of the Burmese king. Though outwardly supporting Browne's expedition, it was "well-known" that Mindon had actively tried to obstruct it by forcing the British to take the route followed by the elephant embassy, and became angry when he heard that Margary had managed to meet the expedition safely at Bhamo. "It will greatly confirm our suspicions if we find that, between Margary's first visit to Mangyun, where he was so well received, and the second when he was treacherously murdered, the Burmese embassy had passed through that town." The paper didn't feel it was necessary to qualify any of their inflammatory assertions, and either was ignorant or didn't care that Browne had in fact taken the northern route, not the one followed by the embassy.

The *North-China Herald* agreed that both Mindon Min and his elephant tribute were deeply involved in the attack, but continued that "however the King is implicated, this will not lessen the responsibility of the Chinese Government for the acts of its officers, nor will it lessen the criminality of the official by whom Margary was murdered, and who instigated the attack on Colonel Brown's party". The paper also demanded that punishing the perpetrators should be the driving force behind any enquiry, and insisted, reasonably enough, that in order to be taken seriously the British investigators must be high-ranking officials. "The Outrage in Yunnan" editorial berated the Chinese authorities because, even if it were proved that they had no direct involvement in Margary's death, the Imperial government at Beijing was still responsible: it was their lacklustre rule which had created a state of lawlessness along China's "semi-savage" frontiers and allowed the attack to occur.

By now *The Times* also wanted to blame everybody. "There seems really no doubt that the whole affair was instigated and carried out by the officials [at Mangyun], and there seems reason to suppose collusion on the part of Burma." The Chinese hadn't leg to stand on: Margary carried a passport issued by Beijing, was killed in a Chinese town within the jurisdiction of Tengyue, and that Chinese soldiers, under orders from the local authorities, were probably involved. The paper hoped that the Burmese king would be implicated, providing an excuse for the British to advance their frontier in Burma right up to Bhamo – and the sooner this happened the better, because the French were clearly planning to annexe Vietnam, and Britain needed to keep up with their own territorial acquisitions in the region. With Britain on the Burmese border, France to the south in Vietnam and Russia along China's northern frontier, foreign powers would be better able to pressure China into accepting any future demands.

*

Despite all the colonial sabre-rattling, the British government in London was still refusing to take any responsibility for organising a commission into Margary's death. Questioned in late April about how things were progressing, Disraeli replied that "Mr Wade has been instructed by telegraph to ask the Chinese Government to make a strict investigation into all the circumstances of this unfortunate case" though, despite a flurry of correspondence between Wade and Whitehall over the previous month covering this exact issue, Disraeli claimed that he didn't know whether Wade had asked Beijing yet, or what their response had been.

In fact, as reported in the *North-China Herald*, the Chinese had just appointed an official named Song Baohua to accompany a British commission – if one ever managed to actually leave for Yunnan. Song was from the eastern port of Ningbo and had once been employed by the Yangjitang trading house at Shanghai, where he had learned a little English. Since then he had become a protege of Li Hongzhang, China's premier statesman, but his most recent posting had been as a maritime sub-prefect to the obscure river town of Gegu, downstream from Tianjin. Though Wade had "a good opinion of his intelligence", other British commentators were concerned – some would say insulted – by the selection of such a minor official to the commission. It suggested that the Chinese authorities were hardly serious about the investigation; though a seemingly decent man, Song would doubtless be intimidated by the higher-ranking officials he would be expected to cross-examine at Tengyue, and – if these same officials had been involved in Margary's murder – he would be unlikely to persuade them to incriminate themselves.

*

On April 30 *The Times* published a more detailed account of Margary's murder which had apparently originated with the Burmese Resident at Mangyun:

> "*Mr Margary entered the town on the 19th or 20th of February, and during that and the following day walked about the place chatting familiarly with the inhabitants. On the evening of the 21st some Chinese civilly invited Margary to accompany them to some hot springs a few miles off, which they wished to show him, and while in the act of mounting his pony he was cut down from behind, and dispatched with their swords and spears. Two of his servants*

> *were afterwards murdered in the house they had occupied in the town, and the others on their way to draw water. The cook, it is said, escaped."*

The *North-China Herald* favoured a slightly different version supplied by Doctor Jones Lamprey of the 67th Regiment, stationed in middle Burma at Thayetmyo. The paper claimed that this account had come from the sole survivor of the attack, Margary's groom (not his cook), though didn't explain how this man had suddenly appeared in Burma, nor why the British authorities hadn't immediately interviewed him as an eyewitness. At any rate, it confirmed that Margary was speared while mounting his horse, having been invited by a local chieftain to visit some hot springs. His head and those of his Chinese servants killed alongside were later displayed on the walls of Tengyue (not Mangyun). An outraged editorial imagined Margary's head hanging in a basket, ogled by curious peasants and merchants as they passed through the city gates, and laid blame for the attack on a mixed group of Chinese soldiers and local Kachin bandits.

The Pall Mall Gazette stuck to safer ground by quoting *The Times'* correspondent at Rangoon (probably Elias again): "So many rumours have been circulating regarding the King of Burmah's acts and intentions that it is difficult to elucidate the truth" and that trade in Burma had consequently ground to a standstill. At Bhamo, Captain Cooke had been protecting a large band of former Panthay rebels who had fled persecution in China; after a stand-off with the Burmese authorities, who also wanted to arrest them, Cooke managed to escort the Muslims safely to the British at Rangoon. This hadn't improved British business prospects at Bhamo; nor did it it help that local China-Burma trade was flourishing despite Margary's murder, or to be told by merchants there that the death of a mere foreigner was not something that should get in the way of business.

The *Gazette* continued that the Burmese king, despite protesting his goodwill towards the British, was "diligently arming, laying in warlike stores, and has a force collected of about 40,000 undrilled and undisciplined men. He has mounted guns on his river steamers, and is building forts to guard the approaches to Mandalay." At the same time, "it is astonishing to notice the sudden good feeling and attachment the King has shown lately for the Chinese." While admitting that the King was an astute politician, the paper continued that British forces in Burma could easily depose him and destroy his palace at Mandalay if he attempted a direct attack on them. Knowing this, the King was soon expected to agree to the British-drawn Karen boundary, and to "express regret at poor Margary's death, and throw the onus of that murder on the Chinese".

Considering the question of why Margary was treated well on his journey towards Burma but attacked on his return, the *Gazette* conveniently ignored the possibility that Margary on his own posed no threat to anyone, but as part of Browne's large armed party could have been feared as the forerunner of an invading force. Instead, the paper suggested that, as there had been no time for the Chinese authorities at Mangyun to communicate with Beijing, this change of heart must have been ordered by the Burmese authorities, who were so much closer. According to this theory, everything pointed "strongly to the King of Burmah as the instigator of all the opposition to the expedition and the subsequent murder of Margary", reminding readers that if the guilty parties avoided justice then British prestige across Asia would be undermined.

*

In late May the British authorities at the central Yangzi port of Wuhan made a startling announcement: a young Chinese named Wang Xiushuang, who had travelled with Margary all the way to Burma, had just turned up in the city. From his statement it seems that after reaching Bhamo he had left the main expedition and instead accompanied Cooke and Elias during their attempt on the southern route. Having been turned back from Mengmao by Li Zhenguo, a messenger from Browne arrived alerting them to the attack on the expedition and Margary's murder. Wang, who was a nephew of Margary's murdered troubleshooter, Lu Dalin, returned to Mengmao where he begged a travel permit from Li Zhenguo so he could get through to Mangyun and bury his uncle's corpse.

Along the road Wang met a horse dealer who told him how Margary, Lu and the cook (Zhou Yuding) had gone to bathe in the springs outside Mangyun when they were attacked and killed "under a tree bearing yellow fruit, not more than a hundred yards from the town walls. Their ears were cut off and the bodies thrown in the water. The clerk [Yu Dujian, aka "Goggles"] and the servant [Zhang Yongqiang, "Bombazine"] were inside the town where, from the Tou-tsung hill, the servant fired off Mr. Margary's five-barrelled revolver. He fired five shots without hitting anybody... the clerk and servant escaped into a temple where they were killed". The horse dealer said that Margary's luggage had been found to be stuffed with arms, as had (rather inexplicably) the two Australian horses brought along as gifts; clearly, the British had been planning an invasion.

Wang was unable to confirm any of these details or recover to his uncle's remains, as Chinese soldiers prevented him from entering Mangyun. In fact everyone was fleeing the surrounding countryside for the security of Tengyue's lava-block walls, convinced that the British would return with a vast army and slaughter them all. Wu Qiliang had applied for military reinforcements, there were roadblocks everywhere, and soldiers were ransacking inns looking for spies and suspects. Wang, protected by Li Zhenguo's pass but travelling at night whenever possible to avoid trouble, spent the next few months making his way overland into Sichuan province, where he found work on boats heading eastwards down the Yangzi, and so escaped to Wuhan.

Wang's account of the murder was the first to reach the British from a Chinese source; while it failed to suggest who was responsible, it did add some plausible details, later confirmed. But Wade – always convinced of the superiority of his own ideas and methods – was largely unimpressed by Wang's testimony, stating "I should trust little or anything that fell from him, unless it were supported by the evidence of others". For their part, the English-language papers managed to embellish Wang's story, while getting all the details wrong. The *North-China Herald* quoted the rival *Shanghai Courier*:

> *"One of Mr. Margary's Chinese attendants has arrived at Hankou, having escaped death himself through being absent from Mangyun on an errand at the time of the murder. 'He was told that the two Chinese with Mr. Margary at the time (his cook and a man he had brought with him from the Shanghai Consulate) fought desperately; the latter killing several of his opponents before he himself was overpowered. Margary was killed before he had time to strike a blow. After dispatching him and his two attendants, the crowd proceeded to his lodgings, where they found the teacher and the boy, whom they literally cut in pieces. Of course they stole everything they could lay their hands on.... But we hear that* [Wang] *is half silly from privation and suffering, and is as yet unable to give a very coherent account of his proceedings.' He had begged all his way to Hankou, hiding all through the day and travelling only at night".*

Meanwhile the *Hongkong Times* uncovered a completely different tale, apparently from a foreigner who had overheard two Chinese officials discussing the affair. This "described how poor Mr Margary was massacred whilst at dinner with the officials and at a given signal viz., two claps of the hand, the first to seize him, the second clap to behead him, and it is now beyond all doubt an arranged plan was made by the officials to kill him, and this has been corroborated by a priest (French), who arrived here from Yunnan on Saturday night; this gentleman was in Mr Margary's company". Presumably, this priest was Father Fenouil, who had seen Margary pass through Kunming the previous year and predicted his demise.

*

So, while newspapers in Britain, India and China loudly pushed around their jumble of fact and speculation, only occasionally introducing any fresh information, the first genuine step towards resolving the Margary Affair had been made. On May 11, sources at Beijing announced that Thomas Grosvenor, the second secretary to the British legation, along with one Edward Colborne Baber, would accompany the Chinese commissioner Song Baohua to Yunnan and investigate Margary's death.

Born into an aristocratic family in London in 1842, Grosvenor was a career diplomat who had joined the corps in 1861 and served at Berlin, Washington, Madrid and Vienna before being transferred to China. Predictably, the idea of his heading the British mission failed to impress Browne: "The selection of Mr Grosvenor seems open to criticism. One would have thought that an intimate knowledge of the language, the people, and the country would have been indispensable qualifications for the head of such a mission. Mr Grosvenor does not claim to be possessed of any of these qualifications."

As for Baber, the announcement printed a question mark after his name; obviously nobody had heard of him. This young Cambridge graduate had arrived at Beijing as a student interpreter in 1867 where he staggered his employers by mastering an extraordinary three thousand Chinese characters in just three months. Appointed as a first-class assistant interpreter in 1872, Baber – like Margary – had also served briefly in Taiwan.

The Chinese had begun their investigations too. Cen Yuying now memorialised the throne, reporting the despatch to Mangyun of Yang Yuke (the vigorous Bai general who Margary had met at Dali) and an official named Chen Xichen to confirm that the assault had happened on Chinese soil, in which case he would order an appropriate response.

The British were not impressed that it had taken Cen three months to begin looking into the case, concerned that the Tengyue officials responsible might quietly have been moved elsewhere in the meantime. They also disbelieved outright Chinese claims that Yunnan was too distant for concrete information about the affair to have reached them yet: it only took ninety days for commercial post – far slower than Imperial communications – to travel between Kunming and Shanghai. Indeed, details of the incident seemed to be public knowledge all over China: wall posters mentioning the attack on Browne's party had appeared both at Beijing and in Sichuan province, while in Hunan province a British missionary applying for a travel permit was warned by the magistrate not to proceed in case he met with the same fate as Margary.

*

By now it was early June. Wade was keeping details of his negotiations with the Chinese government secret, frustrating Shanghai's gossipy foreign population. The *North-China Herald* tried to stir things up, sulking that "Everyone is asking what is being done in regard to the Yunnan outrage, and everyone is driven to conclude – nothing." The longer that Grosvenor's Mission delayed their departure, the more time the Chinese authorities would have to invent some ridiculous alternative story – that Margary killed himself, or was eaten by a tiger (which had, of course, nearly happened) – and concoct the evidence to back it up.

Meanwhile the British in India were agitating for King Mindon's removal and the annexation of Upper Burma, and Chinese traders there, believing war was about to break out, were apparently leaving the country in huge numbers. Perhaps there would be an invasion of China too. Colonel Browne was even now on his way to Beijing to meet Wade and, thought the *Herald*, to force the Chinese government to "promptly punish the murderers of Mr. Margary. In the event of all reparation being refused for the catastrophe at Mangyun, it is possible we may enter on another Chinese war."

Browne was indeed on his way to China, but not to start a conflict; he spent the sea journey bringing himself up to speed with the "long and acrimonious correspondence" between Wade and Prince Gong of China's Ministry of Foreign Affairs. Recalling Wade's original demands to the Chinese government, Browne noted glumly that only the first one – that a diplomatic mission would be sent to investigate – had been agreed to. But he realised that Wade's progress was probably being hampered by lack of overt support from the British government in London, who were more concerned about the immediate threat of being dragged into a war brewing between Turkey and Bosnia-Herzegovina, an event which was far closer to home on the edge of Europe.

It also seemed certain that the Grosvenor Mission would need to cooperate with the Yunnan governor, Cen Yuying, and Browne thought this might be a problem. At the very least he believed that Cen, along with Li Zhenguo and the military officials at Tengyue, Wu Qiliang and Jiang Zonghan, shared responsibility for not preventing the attack on his expedition and Margary's death, and felt that all four should be stripped of their ranks until the actual perpetrators were brought to justice. But in his private journals Browne doubted the real culprits would ever be charged; instead some innocent scapegoats would likely be executed in their place. He concluded sarcastically "What a farce! ... However, I suppose that Mr. Wade, with his unequalled experience and knowledge of China and its people, knows best."

The *North-China Herald* went further, accusing Cen of direct involvement in the affair: "We now hear it is reported in well-informed native quarters, that the Governor [Cen Yuying] has also written a memorial to the Emperor, telling of his own prowess in beating back Col. Browne's expedition, and offering to keep the frontier clear of all foreigners, no matter of what nation". The paper later concluded that "The murder of poor Margary in Yunnan seems to the ordinary Chinese official an act of bravery worthy of high reward. The delay of the British Government in exacting redress, will only seem an acknowledgement of Chinese prowess."

*

Back in Britain it was reported in the House of Commons how Li Zhenguo had fled to Burma and been welcomed at Mindon's court.

When the British asked why a prime suspect in the Margary Affair was being honoured by the king, they were told that "Li had been sent as Ambassador from China with the Proclamation announcing the accession of the [new] Emperor of China." The British authorities in India, already bogged down in various border issues with Burma, were prepared to accept this excuse; not so in London, where Lord Hamilton saw the matter as a deliberate snub to British political power and further proof of Burmese complicity in the case. The London *Standard* added to the tension, commenting grimly that a war with Burma "is, we fear, no longer a remote contingency."

Arriving in China, Browne caught up with Wade at Shanghai and found him "more undecided and pessimistic than ever". There was still no date for the mission's departure – Grosvenor and Baber were kicking their heels upstream at Wuhan, sweltering in the city's notoriously humid summer weather and waiting for permission to leave. Wade was even doubting the value of sending them to Yunnan at all to take part in what would no doubt be a staged trial, their presence only adding legitimacy to the farce.

And now the powerful politician Li Hongzhang had nominated his own older brother – confusingly named Li Hanzhang – as chief commissioner for the Chinese investigation. Born in 1821, Hanzhang had led a solid administrative career, serving as a magistrate before his current posting to governorship of the central Chinese provinces of Hunan and Hubei. But as the brother of so influential a bureaucrat, the British doubted that he could remain impartial at a trial whose defendants would include his own fellow officials. The court duly approved his appointment in the *Peking Gazette*: "We, the Imperial Regents, command Li Hanzhang, the Governor-General of the Huguang provinces, to proceed, post haste, to Yunnan, to enquire into and settle a certain affair which has taken place in that province. Respect this!" The edict's wording typically managed to hide any mention of the key foreign aspects of the case behind the bland phrase, "a certain affair".

While at Wuhan Grosvenor and Baber met with Li Hanzhang, who despite the imperial command to depart immediately showed no signs of setting out for Yunnan. Li also proved completely uninformed over the circumstances of Margary's murder and refused to investigate the attack on Browne's party at all, claiming to have no prior knowledge of it. An angry Wade wrote to Prince Gong demanding an explanation, though Li Hanzhang's ignorance was partly Wade's own fault: when applying for passports, he had only mentioned Margary's murder as the cause of the mission, and not the assault on the rest of the expedition.

By mid-July Wade's glacial progress had even been noticed in London, where the Foreign Secretary, the Earl of Derby, was quizzed on when the mission to investigate Margary's death would actually set off. Derby replied with a rambling speech: an attack on Margary and Browne, as government employees, was an attack on the government itself, and "we owe it to the honour of the country, and we owe it to our officers, who in the performance of their duty have the right to all the protection that the power of England can give, and that this outrage shall not remain unavenged." He also repeated gossip that the Chinese government had planned the whole incident long in advance, and managed to implicate the Burmese king as a likely accomplice. Buried amongst this inflammatory oratory Derby did vaguely answer the question, hoping that the Grosvenor Mission might set off for Yunnan by the end of August.

*

At Beijing, Wade now made an effort to move events forward, threatening to close the British consulate unless Cen Yuying was publicly censured for failing to investigate Margary's murder. He also demanded proof that the Chinese government fulfil the obligations of the three Unequal Treaties, that they regularly informed the general population of their dealings with foreign nations by publishing accounts in the *Peking Gazette*, and that a minister be despatched to Britain to apologise for the whole affair.

But as Browne again pointed out, Wade was still making essentially the same demands as five months earlier, having achieved almost nothing in that time. Wade himself admitted privately that sending an armed mission from Burma to occupy Mangyun or Tengyue would be the only way to get China to take the matter seriously – but declined to explain why he wouldn't adopt this plan. "That is his secret" sniped Browne, who believed that the reasons were entirely political: an invasion from Burma would place the whole affair in the British Government of India's hands, while Wade clearly wanted to control things himself in order to gain additional concessions from China which had nothing to do with the Margary affair.

By late July Browne had heard enough. He made his goodbyes and headed back to India, ashamed to have been in any way connected to the negotiations and utterly disillusioned with Wade's handling of them: "His scheme for deluding the public with the idea that good will result from sending a couple of officers to be spectators at the farce of a trial, is repugnant to my ideas of what is right."

*

It was now decided that, should Grosvenor's mission ever leave for Yunnan to investigate the affair, the British would send an armed party to meet it on the Sino-Burma frontier near Mangyun and escort them safely through the Kachin Hills to Bhamo. But, as a lever in the ongoing negotiations over the Karen border, King Mindon was refusing to allow British troops to move through his Upper Burma territories – a lack of co-operations interpreted by Britain as yet more evidence of Burmese complicity in Margary's murder.

Here the Burmese stood up for themselves, rejecting any implication that they were involved in the attack on Browne's party. As reported by *The Times*:

> "*his Excellency in Council carefully investigated every statement bearing on the subject... no evidence whatever has either then or subsequently been brought forward to show that the Burmese Government officials were concerned in the attack, excepting a Burmese anonymous letter which had been sent to some Kachin chiefs on the lower route between Burmah and China (which was not the route taken by the mission), desiring them to have no friendly intercourse with the foreigners... This letter has subsequently been reported to have been written by a Burmese priest, who has been punished for his act.*"

However, the paper repeated the rumour that Burma's elephant embassy must have stirred up the Chinese population: "Not a word is said regarding the well-known fact that an Embassy from Mandalay to Pekin had passed through Yunnan a few weeks before the unfortunate party arrived there. No reason is assigned for setting aside the opinion universally entertained throughout India and British Burmah... that the King was really responsible." But the writer offered no evidence supporting this "universally entertained" opinion, also ignoring that the whole idea of Burma's direct involvement began with the defrocked priest and his discredited letter.

*

The Pall Mall Gazette in London warned that Britain's prestige had been so damaged by Wade's inaction that China was beginning to flex its muscles. Reprinting a letter from Hong Kong, they reported that "Some of the Chinese papers have even threatened that the English ships of war which have gone up the Yangtze to Hankow will be shot down by the guns of the newly-armed Yangtze forts. English sportsmen from Shanghai had been attacked by a mob and only saved themselves by flight, and the house of the American mission at Jinjiang, on the Yangtze, had been plundered."

In fact these incidents weren't uncommon: foreigners out hunting game along the Yangzi valley often got in to trouble with villagers by trampling crops or even accidentally peppering farmers with shot, while mission property was always considered an easy target by xenophobic agitators. More reasonably, the letter continued that the Chinese papers "express surprise at so much noise having been made about the death of a single European", when no compensation or responsibility was being offered for sixty Chinese who had perished recently in the shipwreck of the foreign-owned vessel *Fusing*.

Given the urgent need to clarify what happened to Margary, questions were asked in Parliament why the Grosvenor Mission was still sitting idle in eastern China instead of making its way to Yunnan – was it really just waiting for the torrid summer rains to end or was there some political reason? The government replied that they had no idea when Grosvenor's expedition would set out either:

> "*no doubt the heat of the weather in China had been one reason for deferring the inquiry referred to, and it was the first duty of Mr. Wade to consider the health of the persons under him. The mission would probably start before long; but there were other causes besides the hot weather which prevented it from starting – causes which related to the state of the country both on the side of Burmah and of China, as well as other considerations concerning political complications.*"

*

At the end of the month it finally became clear that Wade had delayed pressing his demands until the Chinese announced the results of their own investigations. On 31 July Prince Gong forwarded China's official report:

> *"The Governor of Yunnan* [Cen Yuying] *has recently addressed a memorial to His Majesty in which he states that Brigadier-General Yang Yuke and Taotai Chen Xichen ... went themselves to Mangyun and there discovered that, in the 11th moon of last year (December 1874) a foreigner called Margary, on his way from Tengyue (Momien) to Burma had passed through Mangyun, and again, when in company with some foreign officers and soldiers from India, whom he had met by appointment, and who came for the first time, the whole party reaching Yunnan in the month of February. ... Moved by the sight of their property, savages forthwith mustered in a large force, barred the road and robbed and plundered the foreigners, first killing the foreign official Margary, who was acting as guide to the party."*

Prince Gong went on to warn the British not to send their own investigators to such a wild and remote region, as the local authorities wouldn't be able to guarantee their safety.

Having risked his own reputation in order to allow the Chinese to have first say, Wade was furious: after a delay of six months, was Prince Gong really condoning so superficial an investigation, one that avoided any possibility that China's own troops and officials were involved in the affair? Even worse, they were blatantly trying to scare off any first-hand enquiry by Britain as well. His reply to Prince Gong was undiplomatically blunt, utterly rejecting Cen Yuying's story that a band of savages had attacked the expedition and warning that "the transmission of so idle an explanation at this juncture is calculated seriously to impair any confidence that might have been felt in the good faith of the Chinese Government". As for the idea that the attackers had been simply after plunder, in that case how had the infinitely wealthier Burmese elephant embassy managed to pass unmolested just shortly before?

Wade repeated Browne's version of the affair at length to Prince Gong, quoting eye-witness testimony and intercepted letters and identifying the attackers as local tribes incited and supported by several hundred Chinese troops led by "Li Shouk-goon". He underlined that as the expedition carried passports issued by the Beijing government it was therefore China's responsibility to protect the expedition from harm, and Britain could only conclude that local officials – and here Wade particularly singled out Cen Yuying – had at best been grossly negligent of their duty both before and after the attack. "The first question to which Her Majesty's Government is looking for an answer is – upon whom is the responsibility for this act to be laid?"

Though all this was still being kept secret, Wade's rage was leaked to the press, who drew their own conclusions. The *China Mail* decided that "The ultimatum to Peking on the Margary case appears to be even more stringent than we supposed" and that the Chinese would have just twenty-four hours to agree to handing over "ten *lakhs* [one million] of dollars, and the heads of the officials responsible at Tengyue" in compensation. The *Times* warned of "the absurdity of treating the Chinese as if they are a civilized people who can be expected and relied on to do right of their conscience. Their impulse is to encroach as far as foreigners will let them, and to evade any responsibility they can escape."

*

And yet, as verbal fireworks died down, the situation still coasted on unresolved for the next month, Wade pitching his demands, Prince Gong fending them off, newspaper editorials complaining how the British authorities were keeping the public in the dark. But at least one point was cleared up while all this was going on: over in Burma, King Mindon had surrendered to British demands over boundaries, withdrawn his claim to Karen territory and accepted their independence. Apparently as part of the deal, the chief British negotiator, Sir Douglas Forsayth, now accepted Burmese protestations that there was absolutely no evidence to link the Burmese king with the attack on Browne's expedition. Even though the London *Standard* thought Forsayth too moderate for accepting this view, they admitted that the only other option would be to mobilise forces and attack Mandalay – which even the *Times* thought might be an overreaction.

At the beginning of September Wade's temper was still smouldering and he was describing the attack on Browne's expedition as "an act of war", the only question being whether or not it was deliberate. And there were signs that this new, bellicose approach was finally forcing the Chinese government to take the situation seriously, or at least to admit how slowly they had been moving – though of course, the blame for this was shifted away from Prince Gong and towards lesser officials. An edict declared that:

> *"...it was the duty of Cen Yuying, in his capacity as head of the Provincial Government, to make a prompt investigation into the minutest details of the occurrence, in fulfilment of the demands of justice. That, on the contrary, six months should have elapsed without his having proved able to make effectual inquiry and to report the result to the Throne, is assuredly a serious dereliction of duty. ... If* [investigator] *Li Hanzhang, and the others concerned, indulge in any further dilatoriness, or allow their conduct to partake in the slightest degree of an attempt at evasion,* [let them ask themselves] *whether they are capable of facing the consequences of so grave an offence."*

In fact Li Hanzhang, first ordered to Yunnan two months previously, had only recently set out on his mission. The government now sent him an assistant, a retired former governor of Shanghai named Xue Huan, who was dispatched to Yunnan with all speed.

Suddenly it seemed that China had agreed to all Wade's demands. A correspondent for *The Times* at Shanghai sent a telegraph to London outlining these concessions: China would send an ambassador to Britain to apologise, would punish those responsible for Margary's murder and the attack on Browne's expedition, pay an indemnity to Margary's family, and open a Burma–Yunnan trade route. Although the paper described the negotiations as "impeded by the mingled arrogance and cunning of the Chinese officials", it at least backed the by now official view that Burma's king had nothing to do with the Margary Affair – or at least, if he did, it was politically astute at this stage to ignore it. However, Britain ruled its empire by prestige, and it would be dangerous to accept anything that lessened it; political settlement was all very well if it worked, but if not, the troops should go in. They summed up complacently, "This arrangement... may be regarded as satisfactory and closes for the present a threatening chapter of Eastern politics."

The *North-China Herald* at Shanghai was less certain, pointing out that Grosvenor's mission – Britain's own investigation – had yet to depart, delayed because:

> *"it was thought better to negotiate terms of settlement first, and investigate the case afterwards. And this appears to us an error of judgement... Now, eight months after the event, the murderers of Margary and the assailants of Colonel Browne remain undisturbed, and may have emigrated to the borders of Thibet or the plains of Manchuria... The presence all this while of a strong British force in Yunnan would have lent weight to the negotiations at Peking."*

*

In any case, it turned out that news of any agreement was exaggerated. Within days the Chinese were back-pedalling on the deal, but Wade had finally had enough. On September 17 he threatened to disband the British legation, warning Prince Gong that he saw no point in continuing negotiations and "could place no confidence whatever in the purpose of the Chinese Government to do justice in the matter of the Yunnan outrage". And so, continued Wade, "if the dignity of the [British] Government is to be respected in China, and due protection insured to the persons and interests of British subjects, Her Majesty's Government must reckon on other means than Treaties." Wade's move to close down the legation and his "other means than Treaties" suggested that Britain was about to declare war on China.

The Chinese caved in at last, and the Imperial throne published memorials accepting all the British proposals concerning Margary. Aside from guaranteeing the safety of Grosvenor's mission to Yunnan, China would dispatch an embassy to Britain to apologise for Margary's murder and the attack on Browne's party. British and Chinese diplomats would now meet as equals and be able to negotiate directly with each other, instead of solely through Beijing's Ministry of Foreign Affairs; and these concessions and all future official dealings with foreigners would be published in full by the *Peking Gazette*, so that the Chinese public could be properly informed about them.

But it seemed the Chinese were still holding back on approving Wade's other demands, the ones that concerned commercial agreements stemming from the Unequal Treaties, which China had ignored to date. Again Wade threatened to close the legation, the English-language press predicted war with China and the invasion of Yunnan through Burma, and finally the Chinese gave in. On October 7 China's Ministry of Foreign Affairs memorialised the throne, requesting that a "prompt and efficient" investigation into Margary's death be carried out, criticising the shallowness of Cen Yuying's earlier report, admitting that the attack on Browne's party had been made by "troops in the service of the Chinese Government" – a major concession – and again commanding Li Hanzhang to reach Yunnan as soon as possible.

The British government was delighted, the Foreign Secretary, the Earl of Derby, writing to congratulate Wade: "I have great pleasure in conveying to you the entire approval of your conduct by Her Majesty's Government, and their high appreciation of the ability and perseverance with which you have conducted the recent negotiations." Others were far less impressed. Margary's father, clearly disgusted by the lack of concrete action, wrote another letter to *The Times*:

"I heard through the political agent at Bhamo that the Chinese (no others) speared my son to death, and then cut off his head for exposure, and threw the rest of his body into a stream to be eaten by fishes, birds, and dogs... I demand of my Government that the cruel massacre be avenged according to the laws of God and man; and that there remains the outrageous insult to Great Britain to be wiped out... the murder and attack were known in London on the 2nd of March last, and up to this time there appears to have been nothing done but talk."

*

On October 10 Wade was shown a draft for the *Peking Gazette*, announcing that foreigners with approved passports travelling in the interior were to be assisted by all local officials and not molested in any way. There was also a decree announcing the murder of Margary and the launching of an official investigation, and a warning to the officials involved to present the true facts of the case to the throne. This reporting of foreign affairs by the Chinese-language press satisfied Wade that Beijing was going to act on his demands, and he gave the Grosvenor Mission permission to leave for Yunnan.

But despite these pronouncements in the *Gazette*, China's population were still sticking to their own view of events. The *North-China Herald* translated comments in the Chinese-language paper *Yi Bao*:

"The general feeling of the people is unfriendly to foreigners, and the tendency of the latter to go up-country can only lead to quarrelling and trouble. It would be better therefore that foreigners should be asked to refrain from going up country for three years; but if they are determined obstinately to go, and will not yield, then the Chinese officials should withhold travelling passes. If, then, foreigners, not being willing to give in, and having no passports, get into trouble, it will not be the concern of our officials. Our officials having every

day a great pressure of public business, how can they follow foreigners and protect them? If foreigners will obstinately go up country having no passports, then if the people in the country kill every one of them it will be only the foreigners themselves seeking death. China would be right, and the Westerners would be wrong."

Another *Yi Bao* editorial took things further, promoting Li Zhenguo as a hero and stopping just short of urging a popular uprising against the British:

"Will it be necessary to wait until Li Hanzhang arrives at Tengyue to discern the right and wrong of England and China, and the merit or guilt of Li Zhenguo? If Margary was guilty of leading Indian soldiers and surreptitiously attacking our country, and Li Zhenguo killed him, then truly Li is a loyal subject, truly he is a meritorious subject. He is without fault, and although Margary has died, he died in guilt. China and the West being at peace, the Sovereign and Government of England and the Envoy of England would certainly not instruct Margary to treacherously attack us. By treacherously attacking us without the authority of the Sovereign or the Government, although he dies for it he carries the guilt with him. If, after he has been killed, China also kills a loyal subject and meritorious officer as compensation for his life, it will not only be unreasonable in China, but it will be held contrary to reason in all Western countries. ... If Margary surreptitiously attacked us and was killed in consequence, then Li Zhenguo's merits should be largely rewarded. If by chance China is at peace with all other nations, and only England displays enmity and wants to fight, then Li Zhenguo should be chosen out as a great general to conduct the war. Then, the more he can kill, the more should he be rewarded, in order that all the people under the heavens may hear of it, and be desirous of dying to serve their country. This should also be a warning to those

who rely on coercion: they are very few, we are numerous. What is there to fear?"

*

On October 23 members of the Grosvenor Mission, nominated back in May and waiting patiently for the past few weeks at Shanghai, were finally given permission to depart for Yunnan. The mission already comprised Grosvenor, Baber and the Chinese official Song Baohua; in addition Wade now sent them vice-consul Arthur Davenport, who was fluent in Chinese and had long experience of both the British and Chinese justice systems.

Wade also issued the mission their final instructions: they should travel to Kunming as quickly as possible, and there meet up with Li Hanzhang and the other Chinese investigators. It was expected that by this point the Tengyue authorities would have rounded up various suspects for the attacks on Browne and Margary and sent them to Kunming for trial. Grosvenor should uphold the British version of events, and reject attempts by the Chinese to blame "savages", bandits or rebels disguised as Chinese troops, unless it was also admitted that they were acting under the orders of local officials. As far as possible Grosvenor should stay in the background and let Baber and Davenport observe at the trial. Under Chinese law Tengyue's civil and military governors were at the very least guilty of dereliction of duty for allowing the attacks to happen within their jurisdiction, but Grosvenor should not expect a serious sentence to be imposed even in the event of their conviction.

Whether or not the Mission were satisfied by the trial's outcome, afterwards they should continue right through to Bhamo in Burma, stopping at Mangyun to retrieve Margary's body. Throughout its journey, the Mission should collect as much practical information as possible about the trade, industry, towns, cities and landscapes along the route.

On the following day, 24 October 1875, almost exactly eight months after Margary's murder, the Grosvenor Mission departed Shanghai aboard the steamship *Fychow*.

Investigations

Of the many possible ways of travelling across China between Shanghai and Yunnan, Grosvenor had decided to follow the Yangzi river upstream for 1,700 kilometres to Chongqing in Sichuan province, from where they would head southwest overland for the final nine hundred kilometres to Kunming. Possibly this was simply to pioneer a new route (Margary had travelled further south through Guizhou province), but more likely was dictated by the sheer quantity of luggage, porters, secretaries and general staff amassed by such an important official expedition. Given the state of China's roads, it was far easier to ship such a large entourage as far as possible by boat, even if this meant fighting upstream through the fearsome Three Gorges between the Sichuanese border and Chongqing.

Along the road Grosvenor proved to be fairly tolerant of Chinese attitudes, though apt to be abrupt when he felt he was being lied to or manipulated – understandable given that his mission's whole purpose was to investigate a serious blow to British prestige.

*

It took the mission just three days by steamer to reach Hankou, Wuhan's north-bank settlement, where they were entertained at the foreign concession by the British consul. Here they also met Father Pouriat, a Roman Catholic missionary who had travelled briefly with Margary on his way to Yunnan the previous year. According to Pouriat, news of Margary's murder first caused panic at Kunming, the citizens believing that a vengeful British force would soon be at the gates; also that Lei Yingshan, one of governor Cen Yuying's own staff, had said that Cen had wanted to kill Margary when he was at Kunming, but was afraid of reprisals. And although Cen was now laying all the blame on Li Zhenguo, Lei Yingshan insisted that it was Cen himself who had ordered troops to Tengyue to repulse Browne's party and murder Margary.

The mission departed Hankou on November 5, heading upstream along the kilometre-wide Yangzi in a large junk escorted by two Chinese gunboats. Progress was ploddingly slow; they were moving against a seasonal northerly breeze and the ribbed sails of Chinese vessels prevented them from sailing close to the wind. These middle reaches of the Yangzi also formed such huge loops across the plains that you could spend all day under sail and at dark still find yourself only a mile further west towards your destination. Grosvenor's diary became a long list of wildfowl, game birds and hares slaughtered as he dispelled boredom by going ashore to shoot every afternoon. Song Baohua, however, took no exercise and with nothing else to distract him – "not being a literary man", as Grosvenor put it – he became increasingly depressed and dishevelled.

Still, at this pace there was time to take in scenes of daily life along the river. Yangzi river dolphins – now extinct – were then a common sight, while Davenport noted that locals harvested the thick reed beds growing in the shallows for constructing their thatched wattle and daub houses. Farmers planted beans and cereals in winter, with summer crops of rice and cotton; Davenport was surprised at the "slovenly and unscientific" way seeds were sowed broadcast, rather than using a drill. The cotton was woven into a coarse tough cloth held to be cheaper, more durable and warmer than the imported foreign product, dispelling the dreams of entrepreneurs hoping to make their fortune by selling finer British textiles in China's interior.

And so passed the three weeks it took their sluggish, windbound, heavily-laden junk to reach the port of Shashi, a journey which would have taken just five days by road from Hankou. Shashi comprised an unappealingly "long, straggling, dirty, unwalled" community and the residents appeared "turbulent and troublesome", being under the thumb of a tyrannical warlord named Xu. Three miles away lay the historic city

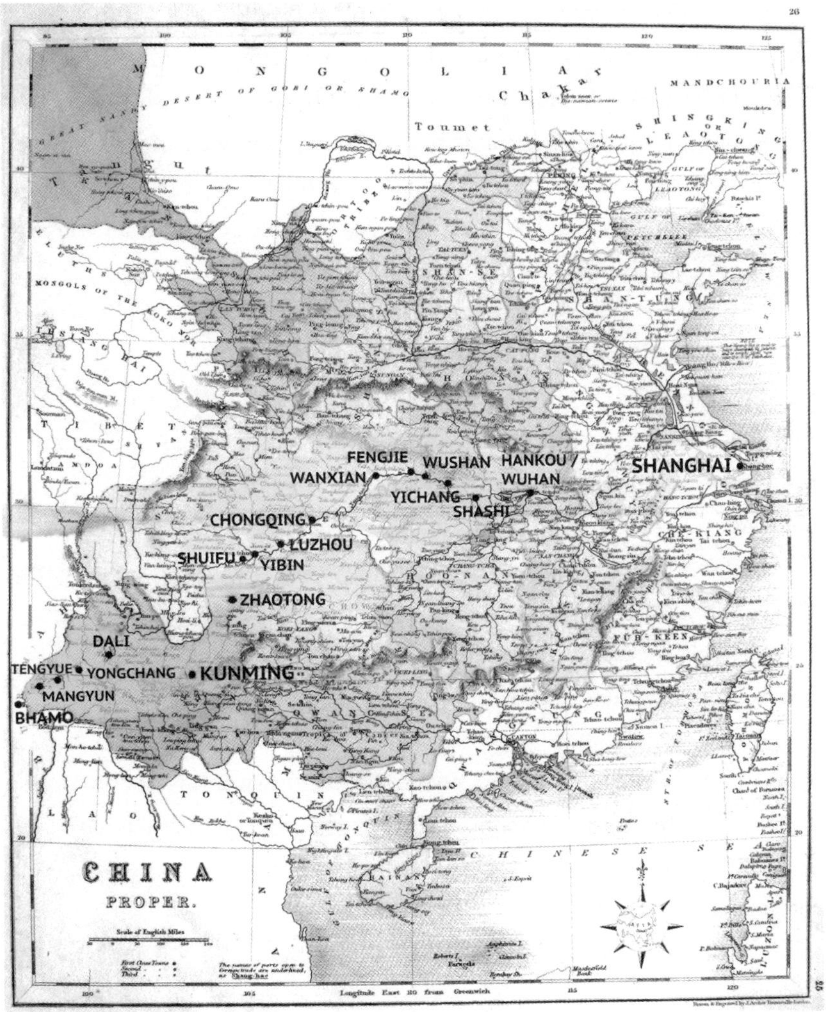

Grosvenor's route across China

of Jingzhou, ringed by a high stone wall and enormous moat which had protected the city during the Taiping Uprising, when Jingzhou was one of the few major settlements along the middle Yangzi not to be captured by rebels.

The mission toured Shashi's sights, climbing an octagonal, six-storied stone pagoda; the crowds of curious townsfolk which inevitably followed foreigners about were kept at a respectful distance by courthouse staff with staves and whips. Davenport felt that Shashi would make a good Treaty Port: Chinese merchants were already well established here and it was one of the busiest marketplaces along this section of the river, also being close to the Taiping Canal which offered a direct route to the vast Dongting Lake and a maze of river systems reaching all the way south into distant Guangdong province. Attempting to collect data on the amount of taxable trade passing through the town, Davenport interviewed Shashi's transit revenue officers but – not surprisingly – only got vague answers to his questions. Most Chinese officials were so badly paid that they had to skim their accounts and solicit bribes just to get by, and the last thing any of them wanted was an audit.

In fact the main reason for Shashi's existence was as docks where heavy Sichuanese junks from Chongqing, strongly built to survive the rigours of the Three Gorges upstream, disgorged their cargo into the lighter, faster vessels used along the middle Yangzi. As described by Davenport, "These junks, some of them capable of carrying upwards of 150 tons of cargo, line the river face of the town for nearly two miles, and average from 500 to 600 in number." They were too clumsy and rode too high in the water to be useful further downstream, besides which paying wages for the large number of crew they required made hiring these vessels a very expensive option.

*

Meanwhile, after months of inaction it seemed the Chinese investigations in Yunnan were firing up. Li Hanzhang had finally arrived at Kunming, where he was soon joined by his assistant Xue Huan, the former Shanghai governor. Not long afterwards the *North-China Herald* reported that "Fourteen unhappy wretches have been brought from the district where Mr Margary was murdered to the prisons of the Capital [Kunming]. Two among them died on the road. The twelve others, who do not speak Chinese, are very probably ignorant of why they were arrested. ... an inventory is being made of baggage which has been collected at the place where Mr. Margary was murdered."

A similar letter from a well-informed French source at Dali – probably the Father Leguilcher who had met Lagrée's expedition back in 1868 – put the number of those arrested and sent to trial at sixteen, adding however that everyone knew the guilty parties were in fact soldiers under the command of Wu Qiliang and Jiang Zonghan at Tengyue. A third version of this story reported to Wade in Beijing added that the suspects had all had their fingers cut off. Wade was also shocked to read a decree announcing that the Yunnan governor Cen Yuying was to join the Chinese investigation at Kunming, instead of being put on trial himself as the British had wanted.

*

On December 1 the mission docked below the walls of Yichang at the mouth of the Three Gorges. As usual they announced their arrival to local officials, though in a rare moment of bad humour Grosvenor refused to accept the card of a senior naval officer because he didn't like the sloppy, "grotesquely large" handwriting, and sent back the messenger who had delivered it with instructions to have it written out neatly. This minor insult didn't go down well; Yichang's magistrate brought gifts for all, including a welcome pair of chickens, but the senior town prefect, though he made a point of greeting Song Baohua, ignored Grosvenor completely. Otherwise Yichang seemed prosperous enough with a well-to-do population, the main streets lined with busy shops and elaborate guildhalls, which acted as hotels and business venues for merchants from other provinces. Davenport saw room for improvement however, and felt that steam navigation, when it arrived this far upstream along the Yangzi, would open trade up considerably and perhaps allow the port to one day outcompete Shashi.

Now was the time to transfer all their belongings into two sturdier Sichuanese junks needed to travel upstream; Grosvenor and Davenport took a roomier vessel, leaving Baber and Song Baohua to make do with a rather more cramped option. The following day, accompanied by a fresh pair of gunboats, the mission departed Yichang and headed into the Three Gorges – despite the reluctance of the crew, who were having trouble organising themselves properly.

The Three Gorges were a notoriously hazardous section of the Yangzi, over two hundred kilometres of high perpendicular cliffs channelling the river past rapids, submerged shoals, dangerous mid-stream rocks and treacherous undertows. In summer the river was swollen by seasonal rains and snowmelt upstream, currents were at their worst and the numbers of shipwrecks far higher, even though the deeper water carried you safely over some of the obstructions. In winter – when the mission was passing through – the water ran low and some channels were almost completely blocked by exposed reefs, which could tear the bottom out of any lightly-constructed hull. Especially rough sections of the gorges needed "trackers" – teams of men harnessed together along the banks – to haul the boat upstream against the current. Grosvenor soon came to admire the skill, discipline and hard work that the Sichuanese crew displayed in managing their junk, especially the way they fended the vessel off obstructions with iron-shod poles, though the men had no time to keep themselves clean and he found their smell oppressive. As they struggled upstream an unseasonal westerly wind made the journey even tougher going than usual; the boats were simply too heavy to fight both this and the currents. Grosvenor dreamed again of the day that steamships would make the journey right through to Chongqing – a feat not achieved until 1898.

Ten days of this brought them to Wushan town in the middle reaches of the gorges, whose bright, eager governor seemed to have had exposure to foreigners before in the way that he smoked a cigar. Davenport gathered information on local coal deposits and the gushing Daning salt springs to the north (which remained in use until the 1960s). Next came Qutang gorge, the shortest and narrowest of the three, and on the other side Fengjie, "a picturesque city built on the side of hills on the left bank of the river. It contains several handsome buildings, and is a clean town, being supplied with fresh spring water carried over the walls by means of hollow bamboo pipes... Unfortunately, the lower part of the city is too near the high summer level of the river, and almost the whole of two faces of the wall had recently been destroyed [by floods]". During an earlier inundation in 1870 the veteran general Bao Chao, a native of Fengjie, had donated a million *taels* of silver to help rebuild the town.

Fengjie had very little trade and its revenue came from a customs inspection station which milked all river traffic for transit taxes on commercial goods. This alarmed Song Baohua, who was rumoured to be smuggling silk in his junk. Resident French missionaries told the British that Fengjie's customs collected at least a million in silver annually, but that after the town's officials had taken their cut less than a third of this windfall ever found its way to the Imperial coffers. One of the missionaries, Father Pons, passed on a rumour that Cen Yuying had been summoned to Beijing to explain his role in the Margary Affair, and that many Chinese believed he was behind the whole thing.

Departure from Fengjie was delayed by an obscure but loud and aggravated argument between the junk master and a drunken courthouse runner, probably over an unpaid bribe. They paused briefly at next major town, Wanxian, but clearly not for as long as the junk's crew, always keen for entertainment ashore, had been hoping for: they wasted the rest of the day tacking unnecessarily from one bank to the other, and evening found them moored only a mile or two upstream, still within easy reach of Wanxian's pleasures. Davenport commented dryly, "For some reason or another the main body of the crew disappears when we reach a place of any size, and is never recoverable until the next day".

By now they were through the last of the gorges and inside the eastern reaches of Sichuan province, a densely-populated part of China where every possible inch of fertile ground was under cultivation. Hillsides were contoured with irrigated terraces and every village held a market at least once a week. Opium was clearly a major crop, along with sugar cane, tea, tobacco, mulberry for silk, fruit and the usual staples of rice, beans and peas. Farmers lived amongst their fields, guarding their winter vegetables with packs of half-starved dogs. The whitewashed, timber-framed houses appeared unusually large and tidy, and overall the area exuded a sense of sufficiency and contentment rarely seen elsewhere in China.

*

In mid-December the *North-China Herald* reprinted an article from the London *Times*, in which the British government finally unveiled the outcome of negotiations between Wade and the Chinese. The accompanying editorial expressed relief that Shanghai's foreign residents now had answers to why negotiations had taken so long, and seemed fairly positive at the outcome, noting that Wade "has not been contented with simply demanding reparation for the particular outrage in question; he has taken the opportunity to obtain valuable concessions on the principal points of importance in our relations with China."

A week later, the *Peking Gazette* published the first official report by the Chinese investigators Li Hanzhang and Xue Huan at Kunming, who had now "enquired the general features of the case, and caused to be brought before them all the documents constituting the record of the affair, upon which they have with all despatch commissioned competent officials to arraign the prisoners charged with the crime of murder, who have already been apprehended and brought up for trial, and to elicit by means of rigorous investigation the actual facts, which shall be laid in a memorial before the throne."

The report went on to say that Tengyue's citizens, worried at the thought of a large armed body of foreigners approaching from Burma, had organised a militia to defend the city. Used across China at the local level, these civil forces or train bands were raised by the gentry, and while they might have included numbers of professional swordsmen and martial artists, mostly they comprised ordinary townsfolk, freebooters and even known bandits. Often poorly trained and badly led, they were notoriously unreliable in battle, difficult to control, and frequently abandoned their missions to simply pillage the countryside.

Which was exactly what had happened, according to the report: taking advantage of general unrest, certain "lawless offenders" had teamed up and attempted to plunder the British. Though Tengyue's military officials Wu Qiliang and Jiang Zonghan were not directly to blame, they should have kept their district in better order and had been unforgivably slow at reporting and then investigating the affair, and so both should be "removed from their posts and provisionally stripped of their rank, and arraigned with the other parties for trial." Meanwhile Cen Yuying, in his own report to the throne, deflected blame for the attack onto Li Zhenguo and requested his imprisonment at Kunming under "rigorous examination", even though he admitted that Li himself had intended only to obstruct Browne's expedition, not to kill anyone.

It was now revealed that the Chinese commissioner Li Hanzhang, far from spending months lying idle in eastern China after being ordered to Yunnan, had in fact sent a secret agent to the region to gather information. Brigadier-General Li Sheng had disguised himself as a cloth merchant and spent a month undercover at Tengyue, before travelling back to meet Li Hanzhang at Kunming and deliver his report, which echoed those of his superiors: that Margary was murdered by bandits after he resisted their attempts to rob him, and that orders for gathering bands of "lawless savages" to prevent the British from entering China had come from Li Zhenguo – who, however, was not involved in Margary's murder. Li Sheng concluded his report by emphasising that at no time were any Chinese soldiers involved in the affair.

So despite earlier admissions that their military were responsible, the Chinese investigators were now reverting to the story that "savages" and outlaws were behind the actual attacks, under orders from Li Zhenguo – though as a sop to British demands they were also blaming the relatively minor local officials Wu Qiliang and Jiang Zonghan. Meanwhile Li Hongzhang, Li Hanzhang's powerful younger brother, had met with Wade in Beijing and completely exonerated Cen Yuying from any blame in the affair – except that, as governor of the province where the offence occurred, Cen was guilty of negligence under Chinese law. Li therefore suggested that the loss of three degrees of rank with no dismissal from his post would be punishment enough. Wade countered with the British suspicion that Cen had, in fact, ordered that the expedition be repulsed. Li Hongzhang admitted that if this were true Cen indeed deserved to be executed, but that he would need firm proof.

*

By Christmas the Grosvenor Mission had arrived at Chongqing, Sichuan's imposingly walled second city, which occupied a long, hilly peninsula at the confluence of the Yangzi and Jialing rivers. Despite living up to their expectations as "the emporium of western China" – shops displayed goods from everywhere between Tibet and Shanghai – high taxation had forced so many merchants away that the majority of Chongqing's fine mansions lay empty, while the flotillas of junks moored up for miles around languished on the low-water mudbanks for want of business.

Here they also found a community of polite and helpful French missionaries; one Father Vinçot showed a letter from a colleague at Kunming airing the rumour that Cen Yuying had paid Li Hanzhang a bribe of thirty thousand silver *taels* to make a favourable report on him to the throne. But Cen had also declared that if summoned to Beijing to answer for the affair he would rather rebel and execute the British commissioners. Some Chinese Christians confirmed the story, adding that Cen Yuying initially refused to meet with Li Hanzhang at Kunming; that Li Zhenguo had managed to get a substitute to pretend to be him, and that this man was now in prison in his place; and that a two-hundred strong militia were waiting to ambush the mission on the Sichuan-Yunnan border, led or at least organised by the Bai warlord Yang Yuke. They were advised to send a body of scouts disguised as traders ahead, to report back if they heard of any anti-foreign agitation.

Two weeks later and with the New Year behind them, the Grosvenor Mission docked at Luzhou, whose separate old and new sections faced each other from opposite banks. From the outside a fine-looking place on a hill overlooking the river, almost the entire old city inside the walls had been abandoned and turned into fields: during the eighteenth century a local woman had murdered her husband's grandmother, a case which so incensed the moralistic emperor Qianlong that he ordered the original city razed to the ground and the population relocated. The entire naval force of the upper Yangzi – comprising just two fishing punts – was moored a short distance away: the vessels were armed with unreliable popguns but the neatly-dressed crew were clearly too afraid to actually fire them in case they exploded.

New Luzhou was a port for salt mined to the north-west at Zigong, whose brine wells were the most extensive in China. A large poster on the city walls referred to Margary's murder and ordered people to treat foreigners with civility, and the mission later obtained a copy of this "Margary Proclamation" from the courthouse. But Luzhou's authorities seemed under the impression that the whole affair had been settled already, and that the negotiations at Kunming were to discuss the opening up of a trade route between China and Burma, and that a proper road to facilitate this was already under construction. Luzhou's general public were far better informed, fully aware that the mission was on its way to the Burmese border, and why.

On 22 January 1876 Grosvenor's party reached Yibin, at the junction of the Yangzi and Min rivers, the latter bringing traffic down from the Sichuanese provincial capital, Chengdu. Though small, Yibin sported a number of bookshops, something very rarely found outside a major city and proof that the town was unusually prosperous and hosted a cultured elite. A short way upstream they settled in for a few days of enforced rest over post-New-Year celebrations at Shuifu, beyond which the Yangzi became unnavigable and they would have to continue overland to Kunming.

This looked as if it would take some planning. Festivities aside, a time which Chinese prefer to spend at home with their families rather than travel, the country to the west of Shuifu was the mountainous territory of the Yi, a proud, aristocratic, horse-riding ethnic minority known locally as the Lolo. Chinese officials said that the Yi caused no end of trouble; they were self-sufficient and utterly fearless, men fighting with swords and the equally tough women wielding clubs. They lived in the highest mountains well away from any roads, though occasionally a few turned up at lowland village markets to trade medicinal plants and firewood for salt. Notorious as slavers, parties of Yi frequently raided these borderlands looking for captives, and porters the mission tried to recruit for their travels were reluctant to move beyond the safety of the town. And yet when the British managed to interview several captive Yi in the local jail they found them obliging and articulate, not at all the picture of wild savages painted by the Chinese.

Shuifu's officials also filled the mission in on some local history. Eastern Sichuan had enjoyed prosperity until the end of the Ming dynasty in 1644, but then came the violent, despotic rule of the warlord "Yellow Tiger" Zhang Xianzhong, and the region was depopulated. Resettlement from other provinces since the early eighteenth century had been so successful that it now seemed as if the area was becoming overcrowded, and for the first time ever Sichuan had begun importing rice from elsewhere in China. But Davenport believed that rather than a population boom, the reason for this was a recent change to growing profitable cash crops such as opium instead of foodstuffs.

*

Back at Beijing, Wade was trying to persuade the British Admiralty to beef up its fleet in China, in order to put pressure on the Chinese government. At the same time, the *North-China Herald* reported that British troops were on the march through Burma to Bhamo; this was probably to provide an escort for Grosvenor's mission when it arrived at the border, but there were fears that the Chinese would see it as an invading army and mass their own forces in the region. Wade also heard from Li Hanzhang in Kunming, confirming that the culprits who killed

Margary and attacked Browne's party had been caught, but that they wouldn't be punished before Grosvenor's mission arrived.

British hopes for the mission's outcome had been expressed by Queen Victoria herself, in an address to Parliament in early February:

> *"The representations which I addressed to the Chinese Government, as to the attack made in the course of last year on the Expedition sent from Burmah to the Western Provinces of China, have been received in a friendly spirit. The circumstances of that lamentable outrage are now the subject of an inquiry, in which I have thought it right to request that a Member of my Diplomatic Service should take part. I await the result of this inquiry in the firm conviction that it will be so conducted as to lead to the discovery and punishment of the offenders."*

In India, Browne felt that the Queen's speech would at last force the Chinese government to take the matter seriously, but that if the British government really believed the Grosvenor Mission's investigations would "lead to the discovery and punishment of the offenders", it was either extremely naive or had been badly misinformed.

*

Porters and travelling arrangements finally organised, the mission left Shuifu on foot on February 4, their heavily-laden "army of baggage, chairs, braves and coolies" extending for over a mile as they followed the banks of the Hengjiang south-west towards the Yunnan border. As they trudged steadily on, the sense of prosperity slowly drained out of the landscape, "the houses become gradually inferior, ruins appear, the condition of the people falls off, the land is no longer so carefully cultivated, and we gradually found ourselves on the outskirts of a region which had been devastated by [the Muslim] rebellion". Chinese they met provided more rumours surrounding the circumstances of Margary's death: that he was murdered on the orders of the Tengyue military officer Wu Qiliang, and that Yang Yuke – now with five thousand men – was gearing up to prevent them from entering Yunnan. Song Baohua developed a fever and had to be dosed with quinine.

And then came a strange meeting. In a humble farmer's cottage, dressed in plain cotton clothing and surrounded by farm animals, they were greeted by one of the Chinese investigators, Xue Huan. Born locally, as a young man Xue had been appointed as a minor magistrate over in eastern China and then risen rapidly to become a provincial inspector for salt, a notoriously rapid route to enrichment through the vast bribes offered by merchants eager to secure the limited supply of trading licenses. He defended the port of Tianjin against British warships at the end of the Opium Wars, and deflected rebel attempts to capture Shanghai during the Taiping Uprising by hiring American and Filipino mercenaries. Later promoted to the Imperial court, Wade reported that he proved unpopular with his colleagues and by 1868 had retired back to Sichuan.

Davenport seemed completely unaware of Xue's identity, though this wasn't his fault; Wade had only been told of Xue's participation in mid-December, and there had been no time since to get a message from Beijing to the mission. Wade described Xue as deaf, senile (in fact he was barely sixty years old) and "notoriously anti-foreign", and believed he had been sent to Yunnan simply to obstruct the British investigations. Presumably Xue was spending time at home with his family, but the expedition was to meet him again a few weeks later at Kunming.

As they neared Zhaotong, the first major town in northern Yunnan, the expedition emerged from the flurry of foggy hills that had characterised their last few weeks of travel, and found themselves on a dry, sunny plateau "South of the Clouds" in Yunnan. They came across flocks of Brahminy ducks eating poppies, and easily rounded up the drug-addled birds without the trouble of having to shoot them first.

The road became crowded with porters carrying all sorts of goods: blocks of tin, medicinal plants, coal, copper, opium, tea from Pu'er in southern Yunnan, salt, cloth and cotton. Another local product was rare and durable *nanmu* timber, in high demand for making coffins and the supporting pillars used in temples and imperial buildings: the sixteenth-century emperors Jiajing and Wanli had imported over twenty-one thousand giant logs of this timber for buildings in Beijing's Forbidden City, employing an army of woodcutters, engineers, stonemasons, blacksmiths, ropemakers and carriers to fell the trees and transport them to the capital. Davenport noted that ordinary planks of *nanmu* sold at Shanghai for $200 each, a coffin could cost as much as $800 and even small offcuts were gathered up and sold by weight. Later on he saw the trees growing all through the China–Burma borderlands, seemingly unappreciated by the local Chinese.

Contrary to predictions that they would be ambushed on entering Yunnan the mission enjoyed a promising welcome at Zhaotong, where a huge crowd of citizens and officials came out to greet them. It was an attractive place, on a rise in the middle of a valley, with many temples and backed by snowy mountains – though like all of northern Yunnan, Zhaotong still bore scars of the recent rebellion in its barely cultivated fields and a visibly undernourished, ragged population. Zhaotong's magistrate had just returned from suppressing another uprising at Bijie, east in neighbouring Guizhou province, but the town's military commander proved friendly and astute, questioning them closely about modern firearms, and without even being asked provided three big ponies for the British to ride. Davenport was pleased to find British cloth for sale at the market, alongside foreign clocks, watches and buttons.

*

On March 6, after passing a succession of war-ravaged hamlets, abandoned villages and wasted countryside, the Grosvenor Mission arrived at Kunming, having taken over four months to travel here from Shanghai. Almost immediately Grosvenor was received by Li Hanzhang and Xue Huan (last encountered on his farm in northern Yunnan), who again reassured him that no suspects would be summarily executed for Margary's death.

Grosvenor also received a petition from Li Zhenguo, who was in prison at Kunming along with his "nephew" Moung Yu (alias Li Tongshi, the man who had accompanied Browne from Burma as an interpreter). Li Zhenguo had heard that the British believed that "Li Shouk-goon" – the mystery man accused of leading the attack on Browne's party – was also his nephew, and denied the connection. Zhenguo offered his own life story as proof of steady conduct: how he had raised militias to fight against the Muslim Uprising, how this led to him losing his property and family, but despite this had never raised taxes or looted but always used his own funds. He had faithfully and fairly carried out official duties, as anyone at Tengyue could confirm. He received official approval for his conduct, and in November 1874 was sent to Mengmao to deal with a band of troublesome outlaws led by a son of the former Muslim governor at Tengyue, Li Guolun. On January 12 he had met Margary and gave him every assistance. The following month he met Elias at Mengmao, who could therefore vouch for the fact that he couldn't possibly have taken part in Margary's murder or the attack on Browne. He finished by asking the British to ensure he received a fair trial.

Grosvenor uncharitably believed Li Zhenguo's story had been cooked up by his superiors to support their own version of events. He also met with Cen Yuying and wrote a vivid description of the contentious, war-hardened provincial governor.

> "*Cen is a thick-set man of 48 years, a very dark complexion, stolid but outspoken in manner, and evidently of pronounced temper. He is descended, at two generations, from [an ethnic minority] family in Guangxi. States that in his youth he could walk, when not engaged in military affairs, 30 or more miles a day. He now prefers a horse. Does not smoke or drink wine. Has been in Guizhou and S. Sichuan, and throughout Yunnan. Is apparently not liked by the officials of the province on account of his temper. Has never seen*

> *foreigners before.*" (In fact Cen had met the French adventurer Jean Dupuis here at Kunming in 1869.)

Typically outspoken, for his part Cen depicted Yunnan's rural population as rebellious savages, only fit for execution. Grosvenor countered that he had met with nothing but courtesy along the road; Cen pointed out that this was probably only because the mission was armed, and that Browne's expedition was attacked because locals believed that it was spearheading a British invasion. Grosvenor asserted that the British had enough trouble holding on to India, and had no intention of getting themselves tangled up in another enormous country by invading Yunnan. This must have sounded utterly unconvincing – even insulting – to any Chinese who had lived through the past thirty-five years of Britain imposing their unwanted attentions on China.

A few days later Li Hanzhang invited the British to a banquet. Despite enjoying themselves, Grosvenor couldn't help noting that it was common knowledge that Li Hanzhang had been heavily bribed by Cen, who had in fact paid for the feast. Both the British and Chinese spent the meal politely spouting platitudes and dodging each others' questions.

The mission needed to be able to gather information from anyone who wanted to supply it, so Grosvenor was understandably peeved on discovering that their quarters were being spied on by a gatekeeper who recorded the name of everyone who dropped round to see them, and even turned away people he felt had no right to enter. Grosvenor had him removed. There was certainly no shortage of gossip and street talk: a merchant from Fujian province, right across the other side of China, confirmed that Cen Yuying was paying Li Hanzhang fifty *taels* of silver a day as a retainer, in addition to other bribes; that Li Hanzhang's spies had reported the truth to him about exactly what happened to Margary and Browne; that Cen Yuying feared being summoned to Beijing and had sworn he would rebel rather than go; and that Yang Yuke had been ordered to a new post in Guangxi province to get him out of the way, but was refusing to leave his power base at Dali.

Meanwhile Davenport was getting a feel for the city, walking around and chatting to minor officials. They complained that Kunming was so remote from the rest of China that it was impossible to find people with enough education to serve as government clerks. The southern half of the city was well populated and thriving, but the northern end had fallen into disuse, becoming mostly "cultivated fields, a fine parade ground and a large swamp". The once-extensive suburbs outside the southern wall, almost totally destroyed during the Muslim Uprising, were being slowly rebuilt. A broad canal connecting the city to southerly Lake Dian had become clogged with vegetation, and Kunming's western outskirts were now fringed by pungent marshes, the locals complaining that the stench was blown into their homes by prevailing winds. The Salt Commissioner believed that nine tenths of the city's former population had "run away", which Davenport considered was a polite way of saying that they had died, either during the uprising or the subsequent outbreak of plague. This was endemic in southwestern China but had flared regularly since the end of the Muslim Uprising, killing everything from vermin to domestic pets and people. Anyone infected was quarantined in their rooms with water, and prodded once a day with a long pole from any convenient windows to see if they were still alive. The general feeling was that plague had killed more people than the war.

On March 14, Li Hanzhang finally presented his official version of the affair, drawn from his own investigations. If Grosvenor was expecting any dramatic about-turns in the Chinese position – some eyewitness evidence, an admission that the Chinese military were involved, perhaps even that they acted on Cen Yuying's express orders – he would have been extremely disappointed. Not only did Li Hanzhang paint his own delay in reaching Yunnan in the best possible light, he also praised Cen's involvement:

"At the time of receiving his present appointment, Commissioner Li Hanzhang was furnished with no information, and the hearsay statements which had reached him were conflicting; he feared

moreover that a mere residence in the capital of Yunnan would not enlighten him much on the circumstances. He would hear and see nothing. Accordingly, on his journey to Yunnan, he instituted private enquiries all along the route and further dispatched a [military officer named Li Sheng, from Suijing town in Hunan], *disguised as a cloth dealer, to proceed to Dali, Tengyue and Mangyun, and acquire secret information.*

Five months having elapsed since the outrage, it was to be feared that the criminals would leave the neighbourhood; the Commissioner therefore wrote to the local officials to lull the offenders into a sense of security, so that they might be apprehended at a convenient moment. This difficulty was, however, much simplified by the activity of Cen Yuying, the Futai [provincial governor], *who arrested the guilty parties before the Commissioner's arrival...*

[On the matter of who masterminded the incidents, several of the local Tengyue gentry were questioned, and they named Li Zhenguo, who was duly arrested and interrogated]. *That he refuses to confess is not surprising; nor in view of the gravity of the crime can we proceed to torture, as he might afterwards retract and assert that the confession was wrung from him by pain. ... Such is his obstinacy that three months' examination has only elicited from him three words: "I know nothing" (bu zhi dao), doubtless in the hope that if he does not confess he cannot be punished...*

It was after crossing the Husong River, fifteen li *from Mangyun, that Margary encountered the bandits who, in accordance with their usual practice* [intended to rob him or kidnap him for ransom]. *They were a mixture of wild men, Chinese renegades, and Chinese kidnapped when young, but included no Muslims amongst them. Margary refused their demands and shot one of them, thinking to disperse them, whereupon they surrounded him. He dismounted to engage them, and was murdered, along with four men who accompanied him. Margary was killed with their swords; they had no firearms. Another Chinese who was with Margary had remained at the temple (Mianfo Si) from where Margary had just set out, to attend the baggage; immediately after the massacre the robbers hurried to the temple to plunder, but the man escaped.*

... Colonel Browne afterwards dispatched Li [Tongshi, alias Moung Yu], *his linguist, and Shi Yutian to go forward, to enquire about the security of the road and to look for Margary. On advancing several* li *they met several people leading Margary's pony. These were the* [robbers who had killed Margary] *and the two men, recognising the pony, fled in different directions. Shi Yutian, who was employed by* [Clement Allen], *not by Margary, appears to have made good his escape. Not so Li, the linguist; he was seized by the robbers, bound, and taken to a cave. His captors then went off to plunder and Li got away, but was recaptured and bound by the ankles for some ten days, after which he was informed that they did not propose to feed him for nothing. So he performed menial services for them, and in ten days more managed to escape to Tengyue. ...*

On receiving the Imperial command, and hearing from Commissioner Li, Cen Yuying dispatched a force which captured twelve of the robbers, and killed or wounded six. The soldiers also suffered some loss. They succeeded in recovering two ponies and a quantity of Margary's baggage; among other articles a gun in a case, which has not yet been opened.

... Li Zhenguo was neither involved with the murder of Margary, nor did he instigate it; his sole object was to stop Colonel Browne and had no idea that Margary had gone on ahead of the party and met his fate at the hands of the robbers. Nor was Li Zhenguo present at the "stopping" of Colonel Browne, for [Elias] *saw him at Mengmao on 18th February.*

The number of the band was probably about 2000, armed with a few gingals, swords etc. They did not fire a single shot. Colonel Browne seeing he was beset opened fire and wounded a few of them, and paid the head man of his coolies to go round and set fire to the jungle. Li Zhenguo's band, seeing the jungle fired and fearing they had to engage a large body of troops then dispersed, and Colonel Browne returned to Burma.

We consider the above to be a thoroughly trustworthy account of the affair."

*

Assuming that if they lied in one thing they lied throughout, Grosvenor ridiculed the Chinese account, in particular the claim that no shots were fired by the force that attacked Browne, and that out of two thousand people said to be involved, only eleven tribesmen had been brought to court. But to an impartial observer Li Hanzhang's report seems plausible enough, if undermined by the Chinese commissioners' reluctance to travel beyond Kunming in order to check their facts. The account is also clearly slanted – if not engineered outright – towards denying any official responsibility.

At any rate, Grosvenor concluded:

"The Chinese text of the evidence... contains nothing but a wearisome repetition of lying asservations together with flat contradictions (entirely unsupported) of the evidence obtained by Colonel Browne from Burmese on the spot of the attack and subsequently at Bhamo... Not a single witness, in the English sense of the word, has been produced, and not a soul concerned in the attack on Colonel Browne (if I except the eleven savages at present in custody), although [governor] *Ting admits the attacking party to have been nearly 2,000 strong."*

*

One week after receiving Li Hanzhang's report, the Grosvenor Mission were invited to witness the suspects being cross-examined in court about their roles in the affair. Having read transcripts of the previous three sessions, Grosvenor dismissed them as being simple verbal confessions from the accused and, unimpressed with the idea of participating in what he described as a "burlesque of a trial", sent along the mission's linguists, Davenport and Baber.

Despite many foreigners believing that China had no laws worth speaking about the country's justice system was well-developed and (in theory at least) had a good deal to recommend it. The official Qing legal code was published in 1740, and listed all crimes – including different degrees of killing, robbery or simply disobedience – alongside their punishments, which ranged from ten strokes of a light bamboo pole to execution by strangulation, beheading or slow slicing.

Courts were largely open to the public, who were therefore fully aware of how the authorities had acted in each case; the local magistrate served as detective, judge and jury, organising all investigations, interrogating witnesses, and weighing up expert reports from coroners and the like. One weak point was that the accused had to admit their guilt before being convicted, because here the magistrate was allowed to use a certain amount of force to gain a confession, including beatings with bamboo and other limited forms of torture. Many innocent people must have pleaded guilty rather than face having thumbscrews applied or their fingernails pulled out, but if the accused died while being interrogated, the magistrate himself might face execution. Any sentence resulting in one of the higher levels of punishment – including all death penalties – had to be confirmed by a higher court before being carried out.

Under this system cases involving either murder or robbery were expected to be solved within six months, or the investigating officials would again be penalised by the Imperial court. Obviously the Margary Affair had exceeded this time limit, but then the Chinese authorities could have argued that their laws were intended for the Chinese only; there were no established rules for cases involving foreign victims.

*

By the time Davenport and Baber arrived, the prisoners had taken their stand inside the doorway to the courthouse, clearly visible to the crowds of spectators in the yard outside. The centre of the hall was flanked by court police holding heavy bamboo poles, ready to step forward and hold the prisoners down for a beating if ordered. On a dais at the back of the hall, facing the prisoners, sat the officials: governors Ting and Jiang, acting governor Cen Yuying, treasurer Pan, judge Cang and prefect Xiong. Davenport and Baber were at first crammed into a back corner, where they could see and hear nothing, but on protesting were moved to better seats amongst the Chinese officials at the front.

The court stood and saluted as the eleven heavily-fettered "savages", described as Kachin, were brought forward and allowed to squat on their haunches before the officials. They looked fairly relaxed and comfortable and, to the British, seemed to have no idea why they were being interrogated, or that they faced a death sentence. According to the court there were originally twenty of them, but the others were either killed during capture or had escaped; their names were given in Chinese as Er Tong Ao, La Dou, Er Lagan, Er Gan, Lu Landang, Er Gan, Er La (aka Wei Tongba), Er Ganggan, Er Paila, Er Yangshuang and Shi Nai. But as they only spoke their own languages, their statements had to be translated by a court interpreter.

In trying to make sense of what follows, it's worth noting that the interpreter himself was later identified as Li Shouk-goon, the very man who might have led the Shan and Kachin factions that attacked Browne's party. If this is true he'd have good reason to muddle the evidence, and it was farcical that he was cross-examining the stand-ins being blamed for his own actions, in front of British representatives who had no idea of his true identity.

In short, the story went that the bandit leaders Er Tong Ao and La Dou killed Margary and his four Chinese companions with the assistance of Er La, Er Paila and Er Yangshuang. Er Ganggan refused to speak but the court interpreter said he also joined in the killing. The others only helped with looting. They threw Margary's body into the river, took two horses, and divided the other spoils – clothes and personal possessions – between them. They didn't kill the man looking after the baggage, or cut off Margary's head. La Dou, Er Lagan and Er Gan also took part in the attack on Browne, describing how the foreigners fired at them, and that the battle lasted half a day.

First to testify was the shrill-voiced and excitable Er Tong Ao, who declared that he had no family and didn't know his own age. He heard that foreigners travelling between Burma and Yunnan were coming past his territory loaded with goods. He decided to gather La Dou his men, twenty-three in all, armed with spears and swords, and hold the travellers to ransom. On the same day, beside the Husong river under a yellow-fruiting tree, they saw Margary and tried to rob him. Margary, on horseback, immediately shot at them, so La Dou and one "Xiao Hong" attacked him with their swords. Margary dismounted and was felled by La Dou. The rest killed his Chinese companions. Er Tong Ao took one of the horses, La Dou and Xiao Hong went shares in the other, and the remaining booty was divided between everyone.

La Dou then set off to take part in the attack on Browne's party, but Er Tong Ao went back to his hideout in the hills. He later heard that La Dou and his men had fought with Browne; some of his men had been injured and they took no booty. Later, the Chinese came and took them prisoner, along with the horses and plunder taken from Margary. He ended his account with a standard formula, "This is true".

Next to speak was La Dou. He confirmed Er Tong Ao's statement about the murder of Margary and his men, holding up four fingers to confirm the number of people killed, adding that they threw the bodies into the Husong River. Hearing that Browne had over a hundred baggage animals, La Dou gathered more of his men from the hills, along with "Li Fa's Mahommedans, Chinese outlaws who live in the mountains" and they all set off to rob the British. They attacked Browne's party but were beaten back and, realising they were no match for them, fled. Later, the Chinese came and took them prisoner, along with the horses and plunder taken from Margary. "This is all true".

Davenport and Baber might not have been aware that the interpreter was possibly the man behind the attack on Browne – or that "Xiao Hong" was Shouk-goon's Chinese name – but they were sharp enough to realise that the accused could barely understand him, that his questions were leading and that he greatly expanded their replies, which were often little more than grunts or shrugs. The examining officer, Ting, also only demanded that the Kachin confirm a prepared version of events, rather than asking them for their own statements.

Inconsistencies also began to surface. One written account stated that Er Gan was shot by Margary, while another claimed that Margary stabbed him with a sword. Now somebody again asked which man was wounded and governor Jiang confirmed it was Er Gan. However, the interpreter immediately claimed that the wounded man was not in court. Er Gan was then asked directly, and vehemently denied that he was ever wounded by anyone. As Grosvenor later commented dryly, "It would seem scarcely possible to crowd so many contradictions into so few words."

As the prisoners were led off after their interrogation, the Chinese crowd outside pressed in close for a closer look. One of the Kachin, annoyed at the crush, bashed a rubber-necker over the head with his manacles.

*

Next to be called were the military officers from Tengyue, Jiang Zonghan and Wu Qiliang – both removed from office for allowing the affair to happen within their jurisdiction, but otherwise unmentioned in the official Chinese account. The British now suspected that Jiang and Wu were directly responsible for Margary's death and the attack on the expedition, or at the very least were taking the fall for their superior, Cen Yuying.

Jiang stated that Wu and Margary had exchanged gifts at Tengyue, but that Margary gave no notice of his intention to return from Burma. They sent no soldiers to stop Browne; indeed, no soldiers ever left their stations, even unofficially. Tengyue was five hundred *li* from Mangyun by local reckoning (in fact rather less than this, though estimated distances in China were extremely fluid). The city militias were often called out to deal with bandits and rebels; rumours were rife that foreign soldiers were marching on Tengyue, and it was feared that outlaws would attach themselves to their party and enter with them. Margary and his followers were killed by savages after refusing to pay them for safe passage; their heads were not cut off and exposed on a wall. Li Zhenguo had said nothing about planning to stop foreigners, but that anyway Li was at Mengmao when everything happened, looking into the case of Ma Er, a Muslim; however, local people reported that Li's men were responsible for blockading roads in the region. If Li Zhenguo was involved in the affair, he would certainly not have told them.

They had heard nothing about the incident for a month afterwards. They had no troops available to investigate at first, but later sent fifteen hundred soldiers to seize those responsible, killed over forty and captured fourteen men and fifty packages. Three of the prisoners later died. The Chinese lost fifty men and three officers during the operation.

Wu Qiliang's evidence was more precise. On 21 December 1874 he had been informed of Browne's expedition, and that Margary was on his way to meet them with all the correct passports and would shortly arrive at Tengyue. On 5 January 1875 Margary and his escort left Tengyue for the border. However, Tengyue's citizens were thoroughly unnerved at the thought of foreign troops coming to the town, and the heads of Tengyue's eighteen militia groups met to discuss the situation. Wu had never ordered them to stop the foreigners.

In February, Wu heard that Margary had been killed by robbers near Mangyun, and that Browne's party, along with two hundred Burmese soldiers, had been repulsed. Wu immediately informed his superiors, and two months later visited the region with a thousand men where he "ascertained beyond doubt that the murder was committed for the sake of plunder".

Next the Bai warlord Yang Yuke from Dali had come down to Tengyue with his men in mid-July. Working with local forces, they had eventually located the robbers, capturing nine at Wa-chiao Cave and eight more at Yun-yen Cave, along with stolen property. The twelve surviving robbers and the recovered property were sent to Kunming. Wu concluded that had Margary informed officials at Tengyue that he was returning from Burma, they could have arranged safe passage for him; "Margary did not do this, and met his fate by his own imprudence. We officials could not prevent it".

When Jiang and Wu left after giving their statements, the whole court stood to salute them, much to the disgust of the British observers.

*

The following witness was Browne's former interpreter Moung Yu, alias Li Tongshi. According to his statement he was about thirty-seven years old, and had a mother aged seventy, and a younger brother. As a youth he had moved to Burma, where he traded in jade and other goods at Rangoon and elsewhere. He then decided to return to Yunnan to see his mother, taking along three thousand *taels* worth of goods and five hundred *taels* in money – his profits from over ten years in business.

Moung Yu had met up with Browne at Bhamo and joined the expedition for protection as much as anything, as the British were guarded by fifteen Sikh soldiers and a Burmese military escort. Having reached their final camp, they heard through the Burmese that the area ahead around the Husong River was infested with bandits. Margary doubted this rumour and went on ahead to check with his five Chinese assistants, accompanied by Moung Yu. At Seray, the chieftain told Margary that Li Zhenguo was at Mengmao. Moung Yu was suspicious of the people here, especially after Seray's head declined to escort Margary to Mangyun, claiming he feared an ambush by savages. Margary went on to Mangyun anyway, ridiculing Moung Yu's timidity and leaving him at Seray to await instructions. The next day Browne arrived, but soon went back to the British camp to organise the luggage carriers, leaving Moung Yu and Shi Yutian to await news from Margary.

The next day the two men decided to continue to Mangyun, but having gone only eight *li* they met a party of twenty or thirty men armed with spears and swords – savages and bandits, not Chinese soldiers – who were leading Margary's pony. Realising what must have happened Shi Yutian ran away, but Moung Yu was captured. Finding he had no money, the bandits beat him, tied him up and held him captive in a cave. There were a few Chinese outlaws among them. At one point his guards drank themselves into a stupor and Li escaped but was recaptured; then about three weeks later he managed to get away a second time, while the bandits were all off hunting. He begged his way back to Tengyue, after which he fell ill for five or six months. By the time he had recovered the suspects had already been captured. Being separated from Browne's party, he had no idea of the circumstances of the attack on them. He hoped that someone would recover his property.

*

Last to be examined was Li Zhenguo; Grosvenor's notes succinctly described him as "an old-looking man, though his age is only 43. Has a long prominent upper lip. Pig-tail thin. Low stature". He met Margary at Mangyun and saw his passport, gave him a present and provisions, and appointed two men to escort him to Bhamo. Margary said he was on his way to meet British officials, but didn't know when he would be coming back, and would send a dispatch later notifying Li of their itinerary.

Afterwards, on the 15th of the 10th month, Li went to Mengmao, which he estimated to be six hundred *li* from Mangyun. Here he received a letter from Tengyue's civil militia, which was concerned that a foreign force was approaching and asked him to return to Tengyue to help protect the town. He was unable to go, but later heard that the militias had been called out on several occasions.

On February 19, Elias and Cooke arrived at Mengmao and asked Li to arrange an escort back to Burma for them as the road was unsafe. As they had official passports Li complied and Elias presented him with a gun in thanks. Li acknowledged this by sending Elias his card, dated February 24. Li didn't tell Elias that he had three hundred soldiers with him.

Li later heard of Margary's death and the attack on Browne's party. But he was clearly far from Mangyun at the time – which Elias could confirm – and denied having anything to do with the affair. He did, however, take part in capturing the accused and recovering Margary's property. "He never joined with the wild people to oppose foreigners, and all he asks is for justice. This is the truth".

When asked why, when he was later in Burma, he didn't call on the British resident, Li Zhenguo replied that he was only there for three days and had no time to make any official visits.

*

That night Grosvenor drew up a chart comparing British and Chinese views of the case. Based on intercepted letters and the reports of friendly Burmese in Mangyun at the time of the affair, the British believed that Margary had been killed by Chinese soldiers on his way to a hot spring outside town, his men had been killed in the town itself, and all their heads had been hung up on Mangyun's walls. Browne's party had been attacked by a force of up to two thousand men led by one Li Shouk-goon and including substantial numbers of Chinese soldiers, after the expedition's Burmese bodyguards had been sent a letter warning them to flee or die alongside the British. A Burmese scout had met Li Shouk-goon returning to Mangyun after the fight.

The Chinese maintained that Margary's killers had been bandits from the hills, a mix of local tribesmen and renegades. They agreed that he had been killed outside Mangyun – though no location was given – and had shot at one of his attackers before being cut down, along with four of his Chinese companions. A fifth member of Margary's staff had escaped. Li

Zhenguo had organised the attack on Browne, carried out by his forces along with villagers and Chinese outlaws. Li's aim was to repulse the British, not kill anyone, so none of his two thousand men had fired a shot.

Despite the British scorn for Chinese evidence, both views of the affair (which were not, on the whole, mutually exclusive) were built entirely on hearsay – it's just that the British decided that their informants were the ones telling the truth. Grosvenor also noted that although the Chinese themselves admitted that about two thousand people had attacked Browne, not one of them was brought to trial; and that except for the accused themselves, no witnesses were produced at all.

Before leaving Kunming, the mission again met with commissioners Li Hanzhang and Xue Huan, who invited them to witness the accused officially signing their statements. Grosvenor declined and tried to explain why he couldn't accept these confessions without any material evidence backing them up. Li and Xue, though exceptionally polite and attentive, clearly had no idea what he was talking about. Grosvenor then carefully went through what he saw as inconsistencies in the Chinese case one point at a time, to which the commissioners replied that each matter had been thoroughly investigated and that their account was therefore accurate. Having warned them that the British Government was unlikely to agree, Grosvenor turned the discussion to planning the next stage of his journey to Mangyun, where he would meet up with his British military escort and continue to Burma.

The mission also received the recovered property belonging to Margary and Browne, though some items – such as a watch whose mechanism had been skilfully removed, and Browne's sword-less sword belt – had clearly been tampered with along the way to Kunming. Grosvenor had them packed in preparation for sending to Margary's family.

One of Kunming's Roman Catholic fathers called to see the expedition, apparently with some fresh information about the affair, but proved too frightened of being denounced to the authorities to pass it on. They were also introduced to General Lei Yingshan, the gossipy official who father

Pouriat had mentioned way back east while they were at Hankou; Lei was an apostate Christian who was made responsible for organising their security as far as Mangyun. For no obvious reason Grosvenor disliked him at first and suspected Lei would cause trouble along the journey.

*

And so the Grosvenor Mission headed west out of Kunming on March 26, following the main post road towards Dali, Yongchang and Tengyue: the very route that both British expeditions had hoped to explore. The countryside improved at first, with the major towns of Chuxiong and Zhennan quietly regaining their prosperity on the back of local salt and copper mines, though a disproportionate number of people exhibited signs of leprosy or goitres. It seemed that many local farmers were in fact recent migrants from Hunan and Sichuan provinces, former soldiers who had been demobbed after the Muslim Uprising ended and took possession of vacant farmland abandoned during the war. At Zhennan they passed a hundred-strong mule train carrying Burmese cotton to Kunming, signs that cross-border trade was recovering too.

At one village along the way they met another central player in Margary's story: Yang Yuke, the general from Dali who, according to one of the accounts given in court, had led the force which recovered Margary's luggage, rounded up the bandits who killed him, and brought them to trial. He was now on his way to Kunming, and Grosvenor described him as a small man with wide-set eyes, moderately educated but of slightly rough manners and appearance. Yang told them that Cen Yuying's stepmother had just died, which would mean Cen retiring from office for a required mourning period. Despite having reported to the throne that he had travelled as far Mangyun to investigate the affair, Yang admitted to Grosvenor that he had never been further than Tengyue in all his life. If true this meant that the whole story about Yang capturing the bandits near Mangyun was a lie, but Yang might also have told the British this to minimise his apparent involvement in the affair.

Lei Yingshan now proved his worth, filling in Grosvenor with background rumour about Yang, most of it focused on his reputed avarice and lechery. Despite being an ethnic Bai "barbarian", Yang had now bought Chinese citizenship and purchased a concubine in Beijing, but later had her executed, or even killed her himself (a story later confirmed by one of his descendants). For his part, Lei regretted that Cen Yuying had to retire, as he admired Cen's firm grip on Yunnan and considered his replacement, Pan Dingxin, as ineffectual and not widely respected (though a decade later Pan would fight French forces to a standstill in Vietnam – admittedly after losing several battles).

At Yunnanyi – a town whose ancient cobbled main street survives today – a magistrate named Ming turned out to be an old friend of Baber's, and Grosvenor found him well-educated and sensible. Ming told them that it was common knowledge that Cen Yuying ordered the Tengyue officials Jiang Zonghan and Wu Qiliang to repulse the Browne expedition, of which Margary's death was an unforeseen consequence. In return, Grosvenor asked Ming if he knew anything about Li Shouk-goon, the bandit leader they were still trying to identify. Ming wasn't sure; he thought (incorrectly) that "Shouk-goon" might be Li Zhenguo's military name, but had no idea – whoever Shouk-goon actually was – whether he had been present at Margary's death or the attack on Browne.

One day they encountered a large herd of water buffalo, the first sight they'd had of these beasts for a long while – a sign that they were approaching the edge of the dry Yunnan plateau, and would soon descend into a wetter, lusher sub-tropical countryside. Then the long snow-capped ridge of the Cangshan range rose to the north, with Erhai Lake at its foot; they passed through the town of Xiaguan and rode up the lake shore to Dali, former seat of Du Wenxiu's rebel Panthay Sultanate. Entering through the south gate they found an annual fair in full swing, the streets seething with Tibetans, minority tribes from the Vietnam and Burmese borders and Chinese from almost every other province here to enjoy themselves and trade in jade, musk, precious stones, rare medicinal plants, silk, salt and copper. Adding to the scrum were hopeful scholars, at Dali to sit the first regional government exams to be held since the war. The British were extremely lucky to find a place to stay, basic though it was; it was later revealed to have been the scene of a huge slaughter at the end of the Muslim Uprising, and rumoured to be so infested with ghosts that no Chinese was willing to spend a night there.

But underneath this fairground atmosphere, Dali had barely recovered. The suburbs, which once extended far down the lake shore, were still a mass of ruins, while inside the walls the eastern side of town was almost abandoned and the western quarter, though crowded, showed signs of plague. One Chinese military officer happily recounted how he had taken part in the drowning of three thousand Muslim men, women and children in the lake; there were already so many unburied bodies in the town, and disease was so prevalent, that they had drowned these prisoners so that they wouldn't have to dig their graves. A civil official later confirmed the story, but was rather shame-faced about the incident. Of the forty thousand Muslim families once resident at Dali, barely a handful remained.

Grosvenor now sent a message to Captain Cooke at Bhamo to ask him to send stores ahead, as the expedition was running low on spirits and other essentials. He was told that there was only a slim chance that Chinese officials would let any supplies through, however, as the roads were rumoured to be thick with bandits and that the authorities would be blamed if the stores went missing. Grosvenor also met Dali's magistrate, a man named Chen, who had been part of the team reporting to the Chinese government about Margary's death but who, like Yang Yuke, admitted that he never went closer than Yongchang to investigate.

On April 15 the British left this unhappy town for the three week journey to Tengyue. Their road twisted all over the place – across valleys, plateaus and ridges, and through woodland and meadows of wildflowers and opium poppies. At one village Lei Yingshan heard that a band of outlaws under a rebel named Li Chao were plundering the roads on the far side of Yongchang, about halfway to Tengyue; they would have to assess the situation there and perhaps hire a bodyguard. This Li Chao was rumoured to have kicked off his criminal career by killing his wife and burning down the family home, though this was a hackneyed story told about outlaws right across China, to show how thoroughly they had cut all ties with civil society.

Ten days into their travels the mission descended sharply to cross the Lancang (Mekong) over an iron chain suspension bridge, about fifty metres long, "named Tsi-hung chiaou, or Rainbow bridge". The crossing had originally been over a bamboo rope bridge, but the huge span made it dangerously unstable and it had been replaced by a ferry, whose passengers pulled themselves over using a cable stretched across the river above them. After many capsizes and loss of life, the government had funded this substantial structure, complete with grand stone piers, in 1502.

On the far side was an immediate ascent into the hills, then down again into the next long, sub-tropically fertile valley and the infamous town of Yongchang, root of the Muslim Uprising back in 1856 and whose officials Margary described uncharacteristically as "brutes". As usual almost everything inside the city walls had fallen to rubble and vegetable plots, the few surviving buildings poorly maintained and the residents even more so. Baber's servant spoke to some villagers who had just returned from an abortive expedition to buy opium at Mangyun; they had turned back at Tengyue after hearing rumours of aggressive Shan groups operating in the hills beyond. Lei Yingshan advised holding up at Yongchang for a few days to check whether Li Chao's bandits were still a threat on the road ahead; Grosvenor doubted that caution was necessary but agreed to stay for two days.

In fact Grosvenor found himself warming towards Lei, partly because he was clearly eager to be seen doing his best to protect them, but also because he was completely unguarded about passing on what he suspected about the Margary affair: that Margary was indeed killed at Mangyun by Chinese, and not outside it by Shan bandits, and that Yang Yuke and Jiang Zonghan were heavily involved.

As it happened the first stage of the road beyond Yongchang was well-guarded by soldiers, so Li Chao's bandits didn't show – if they had ever really been a threat. There was another tough haul over mountains, then the mission found themselves "in a regular gutter between two high ranges of hills" at the Nü (Salween) crossing. The two-stage suspension bridge here extended eighty metres to a mid-river mole, and then perhaps another sixty metres to the far bank, though at this time of year the river ran dry under the shorter western stretch. The deep, narrow valley was stinking hot despite the time of year, and locals told the British that trade died off completely in summer because of the valley's bad reputation for fevers; even locals were forced to leave the valley and returned only in autumn. The poisonous miasma was said to glow like a rainbow, and infected travellers would bleed from their eyes, nose, mouth and ears. The mission stayed the night and for once their Chinese escort roused themselves early to cross the valley before sunrise and the heat of the day.

There followed another hard climb and difficult, steep descent to the Longchuan river, which they crossed over a simple twenty-metre-long bridge; and then it was back into foggy, humid hills once again, the horses slipping so badly on the road's worn, tilted flagstones that everyone had to walk.

*

On May 3, after a final near-sheer descent of six hundred metres into a "punch-bowl" of a valley, the Grosvenor Mission arrived at Tengyue, glad to have put the most severe stage of the journey behind them. Here they collected letters from Captain Cooke at Bhamo asking where the mission were planning to wait for them on the road, and to say that the stores Grosvenor requested had been sent on April 17. Grosvenor was annoyed to find that they hadn't arrived yet.

The British spent barely two days in town; perhaps there was no point. Any military officials who might have been involved in Margary's death and the attack on Browne's party had been moved on, either to jail in Kunming or to other posts, and it was at Mangyun that there was still a chance of picking up fresh information.

All the same, Lei Yingshan passed on some snippets he'd collected in town. These blamed Jiang Zonghan for the events leading to Margary's death, and again "named the individual who is actually responsible for the murder" as Li Xiaohong, in all probability the mysterious Li Shoukgoon – as his name might be pronounced locally – the man that Browne's attackers claimed was leading them, and possibly the interpreter at the trial in Kunming. Lei described Li Xiaohong as "neither a robber by profession nor a 'wild man', nor a 'Chinese renegade', nor a 'Chinese kidnapped when young'. By the Burmese he appears to have been looked upon as a minor Chinese official, but he is in all probability nothing more than a *protégé* of Li Zhenguo. His presence at the murder and implication in the act as asserted in the depositions, summarily dispose of the statement that the affair was a mere fracas with savages arising out of a demand for blackmail."

Lei Yingshan further believed that Li Xiaohong was sent to Mangyun by Jiang Zonghan expressly to plan the murder of Margary, and revealed that he was himself under instructions from the Chinese commissioners at Kunming to arrest Li if possible – proof, said Grosvenor, that Li Hanzhang was perfectly aware that the trial at Kunming was a sham. The British also tried to discover whether Margary's head was ever exposed on Tengyue's walls, but nobody admitted to ever having seen it – Grosvenor believed that Tengyue's citizens had been threatened with execution if they told the mission anything at all.

And so they set out for Mangyun, by this time immune to the inevitable warnings of bandits thronging the road ahead. As Davenport wrote in his journal, "Robbers were reported to be spread over the whole country from Shandong to Momein [Tengyue], but we saw none" adding, almost with disappointment, "and only passed by one murdered body during the whole journey".

There was one long stage through a thunderstorm, but on the whole the going was easy, Davenport pleased to find that this section was just about the only level road that the mission had encountered since stepping ashore in Sichuan back at the end of January. And the next day their stores sent up from Bhamo finally arrived, after taking a long sixteen days over what should have been just four stages – probably, thought Grosvenor, because the porters had spent the extra time gambling at Mangyun. The fresh supplies of coffee, brandy and beer were especially welcome.

On May 8, just three days out from Tengyue, the British crossed the Nanbeng river in dug-out canoes supported by thick bamboo tubes either side, their baggage and bodyguard using a ford lower down, and not long after arrived at Mangyun. As was often the case out in the countryside, they were put up in a temple "which is not badly situated, being rather above the general level of the village".

Straight away, they sent out Baber's Chinese servant – sadly never named in Grosvenor's reports – to make discreet enquiries about Margary's murder. He returned with the news that two petty officials had come down from Tengyue and were spreading the word that anyone caught talking to the mission would be carted off back to the city and executed. Unsurprisingly the villagers, though willing to chat about anything else, ceased speaking the moment Margary's name was mentioned, doggedly insisting that not one foreigner had passed through town the previous year.

Grosvenor heard that their military escort was on the way from Burma border to meet the mission, and began looking for somewhere to accommodate them. Having examined a couple of other temples to see if they were suitable, he heard that the local authorities had fled town (most likely so there could be no chance of their meeting the British) and that the courthouse was therefore available. But here Grosvenor found Mangyun's female chieftain in residence, who was completely ignorant as to mission's presence and purpose. Their fixer Lei Yingshan apologised for allowing this breach of etiquette – the British should have visited her immediately after arriving at Mangyun – and began negotiations to hire mules and pack animals for their journey to the border. Grosvenor also asked Lei to warn her of their escort's imminent arrival, emphasising that although armed they were peaceful. But the presence of a Chinese military official overawed the chieftain, and it was left to Grosvenor to sort everything out. Captain Cooke and the escort arrived at Mangyun the next day.

*

Baber's servant now went undercover again to try and discover which one of Mangyun's three temples was the "Mianfo Si" where Margary stayed, and from which the killers apparently plundered his possessions afterwards. Unfortunately, it turned out that "Mianfo Si" was a generic term for any Burmese Buddhist temple, though he did confirm that the only ones in the area were at Mangyun itself. For the British, this undermined another aspect of the official Chinese accounts: having murdered Margary, surely a pack of bandits would never have been able to stroll through Mangyun in broad daylight and kill his men inside a temple. All Shan men carried long, machete-like *dha*, and would hardly have allowed a temple to be desecrated in this manner without retaliating.

Then a monk let on that Margary stayed in town at the house of a man named Wang, so Baber's servant went there, pretending to be one of Margary's former travelling companions who had managed to escape the slaughter. Wang and his family thought they recognised him and asked how he got away; he convinced them with an impromptu story and they all congratulated him on his good fortune. Baber's servant pretended that, in his panic and hurry to escape, he had forgotten the exact location of the killing, but that it was only a couple of *li* outside town, just a brief walk. Wang corrected him: "It is not surprising that you should not recollect, but the ford of the Husong River is really seven *li* from here."

The next day Baber's servant went back to Wang's house with gifts and, though the husband was out, gathered more information from the family and their friends. He also found that the monk who had named Wang was willing to talk about the murder himself:

> *"He said that first a letter had come down from the prefect at Tengyue, which was followed by a body of soldiers. That Margary had gone to the ford of the Husong River, with what purpose the priest did not know; that whilst Margary was there some wild men crossed the ford of the Husong and joined the Chinese soldiers in attacking and murdering Margary in a rice field by the river below the "banyan tree or trees". After his death, the attacking party cut off his head, and having nearly smashed it with stones, they brought it and hung it up on a tree not more than one hundred yards from the town as a warning to all travellers. Some people of Mangyun, fearing that if the head remained where it was, they would be implicated in the murder, went to the tree at night and taking the head down, threw it into a well. The priest did not know what well.*
>
> *Margary's body was either thrown into the Husong River or left on the spot where he was murdered. The priest added that 600 taels were paid to the wild men for their share of the work. The expression "banyan trees" is important as being a local denomination for a certain spot. (Baber got a temporary bridge made for* [Captain Cooke's] *troops to cross the Husong River, and upon asking where it had been erected was told "below the banyan trees".) The priest said, moreover, that there was not a man in Mangyun who did not know the story of the murder as he had told it."*

*

Grosvenor also interviewed the local gentry, six in all, but as with the townsfolk none of them admitted to knowing anything about the murder; one claimed he wasn't even in Mangyun at the time.

According to Chinese officials, keen to insist that Margary was killed by savage tribes way out in uncharted territory, there were ranges of hills bursting with bandits of all descriptions between Mangyun and the murder site. Grosvenor now visited the place and found it "distant 1 1/4 miles from Mangyun", exactly tallying with the monk's description. There were no hills or savage tribes; a clear path led out from town to a spot amongst flat paddy fields overlooked by three large banyan trees; halfway along were the bubbling hot springs which, according to that first report of the murder heard by Colonel Browne, were used as a ruse to lure Margary out here. Captain Cooke's Chinese interpreter had also independently named the location, having pointed it out on their journey to Mangyun a few days earlier, and described how Margary was attacked at the spring and then ran off towards yellow-fruiting banyan trees growing on a knoll, where he was cut down. This suggested that Margary was killed only just outside the town, not ten miles away, up in remote hills or even in Burmese territory, as claimed by various Chinese accounts.

Cooke's interpreter now gave his own version of what happened. He confirmed that Li Shouk-goon was indeed Li Xiaohong, a rapacious minor official and an understudy of Li Zhenguo's, who was not involved with Margary's murder but did take part in the attack on Colonel Browne. He also revealed that the eleven men on trial at Kunming, far from being bandits captured after a fierce struggle, were in fact innocent tribesmen from the Sanda district who had come down from the hills to sell amber and, not knowing what was happening, were rounded up as scapegoats by Chinese forces and carted off to Kunming. The people who actually killed Margary were a mixed mob of Kachin, Shan and Chinese vagabonds; they speared Margary while he was bathing at the springs and made off with his property. The attack on Browne was made by about four hundred men, comprising Kachin, Shan and civil militias from Tengyue. Though responsible for assembling and dispatching this force, neither Wu Qiliang nor Jiang Zonghan had actually left the city.

That evening there was trouble organising mule drivers for the next day's departure; none of the muleteers wanted to load any heavy gear, and it got left it in a heap on the ground in favour of all the lighter items.

And in the morning the men proved reluctant to get going without their missing boss (who was eventually unearthed in a drunken stupor).

On May 17 the Grosvenor Mission crossed the nominal border into Burma, to be met by an armed bodyguard of several hundred men sent by the Burmese king. In their following journey across the Kachin Hills, where the bandits who stood trial for Margary's killing were apparently from, Davenport interviewed the son of the Sanda's chief, who denied that the Chinese ever captured the eleven accused men in his territory.

Three days later the party reached Bhamo where of all people Grosvenor found Li Zhenguo's seventy-eight-year-old mother, Li Fanshi, who presented the British with a petition to save her son. She confirmed that during the murder of Margary and attack on Browne Li Zhenguo had been at Mengmao, "eight days journey from both places", as witnessed by Elias and Cooke. The Chinese investigators had at first accepted his alibi, but later Wu Qiliang, "in an access of rage and without listening to any explanation, perversely laid the blame for the stoppage of Colonel Browne upon him", and had Li tortured and imprisoned. Moung Yu could testify about the attack on Browne, and the monks at Mangyun's Mianfo Si could testify that Margary was killed at the town.

In her opinion, it was Tengyue's gentry and Wu Qiliang himself who were ultimately responsible for the actions of the town's militia, but they were blaming Li Zhenguo to conceal their own involvement. The militias who attacked Colonel Browne were sent by one of the Tengyue gentry and were led by three commanders, including Li Xiaohong/Shouk-goon, with over five hundred men. She also confirmed that Xiaohong had been the interpreter during the trial at Kunming. The high authorities believed Wu Qiliang's accusations, and so blamed Li Zhenguo for the whole affair; she begged the British to write to the Ministry of Foreign Affairs in Beijing that her son was innocent.

Li Fanshi's heartfelt plea was the final piece of evidence gathered by Grosvenor, who shortly afterwards departed aboard the river steamer *Chindwin* for the five-day cruise down to Mandalay. A sense of confused anti-climax hung over his mission's whole investigation.

The Aftermath

Grosvenor's departure from Bhamo in May 1876 pretty well ended all investigation by both the British and Chinese into Margary's murder and the attack on Browne's expedition. But of course that wasn't the end of the affair.

*

The Chinese view of the case was summed up in commissioner Li Hanzhang's initial report, later expanded by Beijing's Ministry of Foreign Affairs. The final version confirmed that Margary carried an official passport and had treated everyone politely, and so the provincial governor Cen Yuying had instructed Jiang Zonghan and Wu Qiliang at Tengyue to see to his safety. But with the border area in chaos after the Muslim Uprising, banditry was rife and many local people feared that the British expedition in fact heralded another invasion.

Tengyue's gentry asked Li Zhenguo to suppress banditry while at the same time allowing the British through. But Li's "curiosity and greed were aroused... he gathered together soldiers to stop the foreigners, but without intending to kill them. His plan was to repulse Colonel Browne's expedition and then ask for a reward from the central government." Tengyue's gentry, however, were completely against this idea.

Coming on ahead, Margary and his four companions were attacked by outlaws who tried to rob them. Margary shot one of the bandits, so the others killed him and his men. His body was thrown into the Husong river and could not be recovered, even after an extensive search and a reward being offered by the local authorities.

Two days later, Browne and the rest of the expedition "was stopped by a mob, made up of local bandits and some of Li Zhenguo's soldiers, along with the son of bandit Li Guolun [the Muslim governor at Tengchong who Sladen had befriended in 1868] and his men. Li Guolun's son had been imprisoned and later escaped to the hills, living there by robbery... They were not commanded by Li Zhenguo."

Meanwhile Moung Yu – Browne's interpreter and Li Zhenguo's distant relative – had been captured by the bandits. He eventually escaped and begged his way to Kunming, after which he helped the provincial government's investigations by cross-examining suspects in the affair. "The higher authorities sent a letter to Moung Yu, praising his behaviour and his achievement in gathering together sufficient evidence in the case. Since it was a matter between China and Burma, the higher authorities asked Moung Yu to send his reports to the British government to help support their conclusions."

Li Zhenguo, while far away at Mengmao and so not directly involved in either the attack on Browne nor Margary's murder, had nonetheless done nothing to protect the British, and had even employed the bandits who killed Margary. As Li had been appointed by Jiang Zonghan and Wu Qiliang, they were as much to blame.

While saying nothing about how they were captured, the report named the eleven tribesmen who had been on trial at Kunming and declared that they had "confessed to killing Interpreter Margary and his three companions, and to robbing Colonel Browne. They also reported that many other bandits were lying in wait to rob the travellers."

The Chinese account concluded with a statement that their report had been audited by Grosvenor and that:

> *"British officials were satisfied with the investigation. Jiang Zonghan and Wu Qiliang were stripped of their ranks and imprisoned. As for Li Zhenguo, he was stripped of his rank and imprisoned too, pending further interrogation and action by the Yunnan-Guizhou*

government. Margary's luggage and horse (fifty-one items in all) were handed over to British officials to take back with them."

*

But naturally the British were not satisfied with the Chinese version of events, and cared little about the demotion of three minor officials. Back at Rangoon in June 1876, Grosvenor wrote a long account to Wade in Beijing, dissecting the Chinese case and concluding that it was complete fiction, designed to frame local ethnic minorities and protect any Chinese officials involved. He accused Li Hanzhang's commission of a "careless disregard of fact and truth", their version of events nothing but a "long list of falsehoods and inconsistencies", and closed his report with "The total absence of anything like truth or even plausibility in the Chinese statement of the circumstances connected with the Yunnan outrage is really remarkable."

Wade in turn sent an even longer message to his superiors in London, admitting that despite the best efforts of Grosvenor, Davenport and Baber there was still no proof supporting any of the many different accounts of the affair – indeed, without a body to examine there was not even direct evidence that Margary had been murdered at all. He later described the Grosvenor Mission as a "fool's errand", nothing more than a sop to public opinion in Britain; after months of frustrating and heated wrangling with an obstructive Chinese government, he had only insisted the mission went ahead a matter of principle, not because he expected justice to be done. From the first he had believed China's government was complicit in the affair or was, at the very least, an accessory after the fact. "Our efforts, I admit" Wade wrote dejectedly, "have not secured to us the legal conviction of any person or persons that we can believe to be really responsible either for the attack on Colonel Browne or for the murder of Mr. Margary."

If Wade personally held anyone to blame it was Yunnan's provincial governor, Cen Yuying, whom he described as "one of the most ruthlessly severe officials that ever trampled out a rebellion... Governor Cen is stated to have broken faith with rebels, to have massacred numbers who were guiltless of rebellion. From papers in my possession, I know that he was in danger of impeachment for his cruelty." But even so, would Cen have dared to ignore an imperial command to protect the expedition, embodied in the passports that they carried? Not, thought Wade, unless he had received additional instructions, though doubtless these would have been couched in the most indirect terms – for instance that Cen should simply "protect the empire" against an invasion by foreigners. Then if Cen ever quoted them in his defence the government could say there was nothing specifically ordering him to attack the expedition.

Browne later met Grosvenor in London and read his private reports, agreeing afterwards that the whole mission had been a waste of time. He was also disgusted to discover that Moung Yu, his own interpreter, had been called as witness for the Chinese case. He noted two letters that Wade had collected, apparently communications between Li Zhenguo and a militia captain at Tengyue, in which Li had ultimately turned down the gentry's offer to lead an attack on the foreigners. Like the Chinese, the British were to conclude that, though committed to preventing Browne's party from entering China, Li Zhenguo played no direct role in either Margary's murder or the assault on the expedition.

Grosvenor himself was later appointed chargé d'affaires at Beijing, then secretary to the British legation at St Petersburg in Russia. He died there suddenly in 1886 "of paralysis of the lungs", aged just 44.

*

Despite his own personal doubts Wade did well out of the affair, his "energy and resource" in dealing with the Chinese government winning him a knighthood. This was met with derision amongst China's British population, who felt that Wade had responded to the murder of one of their own community with nothing but political posturing and empty promises. Nor had he restored honour to British India, which had organised the luckless expedition. Browne, scathing to the last, commented that the only people happy with this outcome – and that simply because the whole affair was finally over – were the home government in London.

But in fact the settlement with Britain over Margary's death cost China dearly. The Chefoo Convention of 1876 included a fine of 200,000 ounces of silver – up from the original demand of 150,000 – the opening of four more Chinese cities to foreign trade as Treaty Ports, a guarantee that foreigners could travel unmolested through the interior of China (known informally as "The Margary Proclamation"), and an official mission of apology to Britain in 1877. Other concessions governed the terms of official exchanges and had nothing to do with the affair, covering topics such as tax evasion in the opium trade, whether foreigners and Chinese could be tried under each other's laws (no), and preventing interference in Hong Kong's shipping industry.

Not that the Margary Proclamation was of much value: its terms were a recapitulation of the earlier Treaty of Tientsin, under which Margary should have been protected when he was killed. The four new Treaty Ports – Yichang and Wuhu on the Yangzi, and coastal Wenzhou and Beihai – proved similarly underwhelming, and none of them ever became central to British interests in China. One minor victory was the opening up of the massive Sichuanese city of Chongqing, not as a Treaty Port (in fact under the Chefoo Convention foreign merchants were explicitly forbidden from setting up shop there) but with a Resident to look after British interests in China's vast southwestern interior.

Two of the convention's most tangible outcomes were the mission of apology to Britain, which became China's first overseas embassy, housed then as now at Portland Place in London; and the reporting for the first time of foreign affairs in official Chinese proclamations, so that the Chinese public would know the real reasons for British actions – whether or not they approved of them.

All these were subtle, diplomatic concessions, and those who had agitated for firm action were disappointed; there was no razing of Mangyun to the ground, no military occupation of Tengyue. With such a tangled web of responsibility, nobody ever managed to prove who the perpetrators behind the attack on the expedition had been, let alone was able to punish them: the *North-China Herald* later commented half-heartedly that "It is still freely argued that the crime should have been traced up to its instigators at any cost, and that their exposure and degradation should at the least been insisted on".

Yet those believing that Britain had lost prestige by not physically avenging Margary's death completely missed the point. Britain had got its hooks into China through the shameful opium trade, had introduced a divisive foreign religion, had destabilised the country to the point that civil wars broke out causing the deaths of millions, had forced China to sign humiliating trade treaties, had almost bankrupted the nation through extortionate war indemnities, and had occupied sovereign territory. In Chinese eyes they were villainous bullies with no prestige to lose. Browne understood this by refusing to describe Li Zhenguo as a bandit; in his opinion Li's resistance to the 1868 expedition was simply the action of a loyal Chinese general doing his duty.

In addition, Tengyue had only just emerged from eighteen years of warfare in 1875, and the townsfolk clearly believed that Browne's expedition had come to stir up further trouble. Had British troops subsequently invaded the area to avenge Margary's death, the locals would certainly have fought back, and their slaughter would have added to the long catalogue of grievances that China could hold against the British empire.

*

In the end, the eleven Kachin prisoners were found guilty and condemned to death, though the British authorities – convinced they were innocent – negotiated an Imperial pardon for them.

As stated in the Chinese accounts, Li Zhenguo, Wu Qiliang and Jiang Zonghan were all cashiered. Wu seems to have vanished from the record soon afterwards – he appeared briefly the following year, bemoaning the loss of position and income – but Li Zhenguo soon returned to Mangyun, where he remained a powerful figure. In 1877 he was interviewed by the British explorers Mesny and Gill, who were passing through on their way into Burma, and Li later helped to recapture Bhamo after Kachins took it in 1884. He died five years later. His family home, now a private residence, sits in the whitewashed mud-brick back lanes of Qiluo village, a southern suburb of modern Tengchong city.

Jiang Zonghan also resumed his military career and by July 1876 was even back at Tengyue suppressing a violent uprising led by a disgruntled officer, a vagabond priest and a large mob of "bandits from Sanda". The same year he founded the Fu Chunheng small goods trading company with two merchants named Ming Zengguang (a Muslim) and Dong Yisan.

In 1885 France invaded northern Vietnam, which China considered to be a client state. Jiang followed his mentor, the Bai warlord Yang Yuke, to fight the French occupation; Yang was killed but Jiang survived and was promoted to a first rank military official. He later served as supreme military commander for Guizhou province, and donated ten thousand ounces of silver towards building the Jinlong suspension bridge over the Yangzi in northern Yunnan, now the oldest surviving bridge across the river. While his motives were probably financial – improving his own business by developing local infrastructure – legend has it that Jiang had been trapped at this very spot while fighting against the Muslim insurgency, and had sworn to build a bridge here if he survived. Whichever is true, the Imperial court took note of the expense and rewarded Jiang by having memorial arches built in honour of his parents. He similarly funded the Huajiang suspension bridge in neighbouring Guizhou, and a college in his home town – all high achievements for a man born into rural obscurity.

Jiang died in 1903, but there's a memorial hall to him at Dali and the company he founded thrived for another thirty years with branches in south-west China, Hong Kong and Burma, and held a supply contract for the Sichuan Army. Their one-time Kunming headquarters, complete with traditional galleried courtyards and carved mouldings, now serves as the *Silver Chest Boutique Hotel.*

In August 1876 the tough, unlikeable Yunnan governor Cen Yuying retired for a mandatory two-year period of mourning for his stepmother, allowing the Chinese government to quietly shelve investigations into any role he might have played in the Margary Affair. No further action was taken against Cen, despite attempts by Wade to have him arraigned for complicity and irate British editorials in China's foreign-language press branding him "The Cruel Viceroy". Indeed, Cen was later promoted to governor of Yungui, the combined territory of Yunnan and Guizhou provinces.

Four years later the British adventurer William Mesny was nearly killed by a mob in Guizhou province, in circumstances which echoed Margary's murder. Mesny became convinced that Cen – Guizhou's provincial governor at the time – had tried to have him assassinated too, and spent the next decade writing vindictive newspaper articles about him, even accusing his son Cen Chunxuan of cannibalism.

Cen Yuying contracted malaria while fighting the French in northern Vietnam and died in 1889, just after his sixtieth birthday. His low stone tomb looks southwards from the grassy slopes of Yao Shan, a hill to the east of of Guilin city, in his home province of Guangxi.

*

Another plausible version of what happened in February 1875 came from a surprising source. On 10 June 1877, Browne – by then back at Rangoon – was overjoyed at the unexpected reappearance of his interpreter Moung Yu, alias Li Tongshi, left behind at Seray with Dr Allen's Chinese secretary, Shi Yutian, and last seen by Grosvenor giving evidence at the trial in Kunming.

Moung Yu told Browne a very different story from the one he had been forced to recite at the trial. He and Shi Yutian had been robbed and held captive by Seray's chief, and had heard Chinese soldiers tramping through the village on their way to ambush Browne. The next afternoon several Kachin fighters turned up with bullet wounds and burns, and Moung Yu heard that the expedition had escaped.

That evening two Tengyue officers, Wang Binzhong and Li Shouk-goon – leader of the Shan and Kachin forces who attacked Browne, the "interpreter" at the trial, and ironically the same man that the British had constantly confused with Moung Yu – arrived to arrange compensation with Kachin families whose relatives had been killed. They tied up Moung Yu and Shi Yutian and took them to Mangyun, where they were tortured for refusing to denounce the British; Moung Yu's arms were dislocated after he was hung up with weights tied to his feet, and Shi Yutian was beaten to death. Moung Yu only escaped the same fate after his mother at Tengyue – who he had been on his way to see – bribed Wang Binzhong to protect him, but he was left chained up by his neck to a post for four months. He was finally taken to Mangyun and released on bail though warned to stay indoors, as officials had reported that all of Margary's companions, including himself, had been killed.

About a month later Yang Yuke appeared at Tengyue with two thousand men to take Wu Qiliang, Jiang Zonghan and Li Zhenguo into custody. Li had escaped to Burma – it was at this point that the British had accused the Burmese king of protecting him – but came back after his brothers were taken hostage. Along the way to recover Margary's luggage and horse at Mangyun, Yang Yuke rounded up thirty Kachin as prisoners. Yang kept fifteen of these who seemed unable to speak Chinese and sent them, along with Wu, Jiang and Li Zhenguo, to stand trial at Kunming. After four of the prisoners were found to understand Chinese, Yang had them murdered.

At Li Zhenguo's request Moung Yu went with him to Kunming, where he was told he would serve as a witness against the surviving Kachin. He refused until Cen threatened to put him on trial as a murder suspect too, after which he was coached in what he was expected to say.

Moung Yu confirmed that Li Shouk-goon, as the court interpreter, manipulated things so that the accused men appeared to condemn themselves. For instance, he translated the question "Why do you hate the English so much that you murdered Margary?" as "Do you cultivate rice, or what, in your fields?", and then reported the accused's innocuous answer as "The English are always taking other people's lands, so we hate them and killed Margary".

At Li Zhenguo's urging, Moung Yu sent a message to the Grosvenor Mission explaining what was really happening, which was intercepted by Cen Yuying. A furious Cen ordered them murdered in prison, but Li had powerful friends and the would-be killers were so intimidated that they refused to carry out their orders. Cen warned that if Moung Yu managed to contact to the Mission and told them the truth, then the British were to be killed immediately: "We may as well have a double as a single murder to answer for."

After Grosvenor had left and interest in the affair died down, Moung Yu and the other suspects were released from captivity. Back at Tengyue, there had been more trouble; half the soldiers brought down from Dali with Yang Yuke to escort the prisoners to Kunming had been left behind where, their wages unpaid, they staged an armed uprising. Five thousand people died in the rebellion's suppression; the leaders were executed and four barrels of rebel ears sent to Kunming as trophies. Wu Qiliang's successor was banished to Tibet for failing to stop the revolt.

At last Moung Yu finally had some luck: a friend from Kunming was appointed as Tengyue's new governor and looked after him until he recovered. He made his own enquiries into Margary's murder and came to the conclusion that Li Shouk-goon was the real culprit. Apparently, after Margary left Kunming on his way to the border, Cen Yuying ordered the governor of Dali to kill him, but not wanting to deal with the repercussions he passed on the order to the authorities at Yongchang, who in turn passed it on to Wu Qiliang and Jiang Zonghan at Tengyue.

Tengyue's friendly governor paid for an armed guard to escort Moung Yu back home to Burma, where he arrived after over two years in China, most of that time spent in custody. Browne sent his story to the British legation at Beijing, asking them to compensate Moung Yu for his ordeal, but the legation's penny-pinching bureaucrats refused, declaring that the Margary Affair was officially closed.

*

The British House of Commons finally exonerated Burma of any involvement in the "Yunnan Outrage" on 27 June 1876:

> *"As soon as intelligence of [Margary's murder] reached China, our countrymen there, in the absence of all authentic information, immediately rushed to the conclusion that it was owing to the treachery of the Burmese or Chinese Government, or a combination of both. Now there is abundant evidence to prove, especially that of Dr. Anderson, who was himself a member of the expedition, that there is no ground whatever for the accusation that either the Burmese Government or people were implicated in that matter."*

As for the elephants and their embassy, which had sparked so much suspicion for supposedly spreading slander about the British as they marched into China, their progress towards Beijing was tracked by the *Peking Gazette*, "bearing with reverence the address from the King of Burma to the Throne, and bringing with them articles of tribute". They reached Kunming on 1 April 1875 and a month later crossed into Guizhou province, arriving at the provincial capital, Guiyang, in mid-May, where the elephants were quartered outside the east gate in the grounds of Junzi Ting, the Gentleman's Pavilion, drawing large crowds.

Further east on the Guizhou-Hunan border at Zhenyuan – the attractive river town where Margary and his boatmen had been roughed up – the elephants' passage was recorded in verse by magistrate Wang Bing'ao, inside the Kuixing pavilion on Zhenyuan's arched Ming-dynasty bridge:

> *"Sweeping away the mist on Wuxi River, the Han envoy floated off by boat;*
> *Ploughing up the main post road, the Burmese rode across the bridge on an elephant".*

As elephants are associated with wisdom in China, and Kuixing was the patron deity of candidates sitting for the Imperial exams, the poem is doubly auspicious.

And so they continued through China, reaching Zhili, the area surrounding Beijing, on August 14 where they were provided with an escort by Governor-General Li Hongzhang, Li Hanzhang's more famous younger brother. As reported by the *North-China Herald*, the "tribute mission" – the name used in the Chinese press – arrived at Beijing in early September: "The [Burmese] envoys... have excited some contemptuous attention amongst the native population, who have never seen (in the present generation) anything more "outlandish" than these half-naked, turbaned and tattooed Southerners." The elephants themselves, going at their own, slower pace, rolled into Beijing at the end of the month.

In the spring of 1884 one of the elephants went berserk during a procession, smashing a carriage and hurling a eunuch into the walls of the Forbidden City before stampeding west down central Chang'an Avenue; Beijing's citizens had to hide indoors for the rest of the day until it was recaptured. The elephants were never taken out in public again. Some say they died of neglect, others that in the early twentieth century the final few were moved to the new Experimental Agricultural Station, now Beijing Zoo.

*

Partly in response to the French occupation of all Vietnam in 1885, Britain used a dispute over teak logging to provoke a third Anglo-Burmese war that same year and successfully annexed the rest of Burma, deposing King Thibaw Min, the late Mindon Min's son, in a campaign which lasted just fourteen days. The kingdom's final surrender was received by Colonel Sladen, making his final appearance in this story. Burma regained its independence from Britain in 1948, and was renamed Myanmar by the military government in 1989 – though for political reasons the name "Burma" is still used by some.

As the closest Chinese city to the Burmese border, Britain had Tengyue declared a free-trade Treaty Port in 1897, a notable achievement for a town over one hundred kilometres from the nearest navigable river, let alone the sea. In fact cross-border revenue never amounted to much, but Tengyue's British consulate later proved a haven for the handful of plant-collectors and eccentric travellers who passed through this remote corner of the country. In 1942 the Japanese captured the city, and Tengyue was destroyed once again by Chinese and US forces during its retaking in 1945 – as testified by the Confucian temple and British Consulate, both still scarred by wartime shell and shrapnel damage.

Rebuilt during the 1950s in a traditional timber-framed, balconied way, in recent years Tengchong, as it is now known, has fallen victim to China's relentless urge for modernization. Streets have been widened and metalled, old buildings and cobbled back-lanes demolished or gentrified as "new antique" districts, apartment blocks and shopping malls built. Short sections of the city's original lava-block walls survive, along with the reconstructed bell tower and a couple of temples – including the gourd-shaped Yaowang Gong, where Sladen's expedition stayed in 1868. The site of the nineteenth-century government offices and courthouse is now covered by a huge produce market, selling everything from Yunnanese ceramic steamers to fresh vegetables and livestock.

Tengchong opened its airport in 2009, connecting the city to the modern, sprawling metropolis of Shenzhen, over fifteen hundred kilometres to the south-east. This link capitalises on getting Myanmar jade and amber to one of their biggest markets – Hong Kong, just south across the border from Shenzhen – but in other ways Tengchong has again become something of a backwater. The main China-Myanmar expressway gives the town a wide berth, following the old Southern route to cross the frontier at Mengmao (now an ostentatious boom town known as Ruili), the very place that Li Zhenguo frustrated Elias and Cooke's attempts to enter China. Nor was Britain's Burma-China railway ever built, despite extensive surveying during the early twentieth century, though the French did complete a line from Vietnam to Kunming, following the gun-running route up the Red River valley pioneered by Jean Dupuis.

*

New details and versions of the circumstances behind Margary's death continued to crop up for decades afterwards. In the 1880s Lieutenant George Younghusband – elder brother of that quintessential Victorian man of action, Sir Francis Younghusband – wrote that in the Shan State of Kiang Tung "I came across a Hindu said to have been a servant of Margary's... He lived in great style at first, had lots of money, and married a Shan woman – all probably with Margary's money. He is now poor, and his wife keeps him by selling cigarettes".

Some sixty years later Rolla Rouse, British Commissioner at Tengyue, heard a story that Margary had been killed because he allowed his dog to travel in his sedan chair while he walked behind his entourage, and that a magistrate near Mangyun unwittingly bowed to the chair thinking that was Margary inside, only to be told that he had bowed to a dog. Furiously embarrassed at this loss of face he planned Margary's murder, later receiving a land grant from the government as a reward. The tale was told to Rouse by the magistrate's great-grandson.

In the Western legal sense, requiring conclusions drawn from concrete evidence and eye-witness statements, Margary's murder remains unsolved; his entry in the 1922 *Dictionary of National Biography* had to content itself with a vague "treacherously killed at Mangyun", without being able to say who was responsible. And without a body, headless or not, all theories about the circumstances behind the Margary Affair have to rely entirely on hearsay. Given how the British blustered and battled their way into India, Burma and China, the insecurity caused by the Muslim

Uprising in Yunnan and the fact that Sladen unfortunately negotiated with the rebel administration at Tengyue in 1868, it is unsurprising not only that Margary was murdered, but also that there was such a wide choice of likely suspects.

As for who was actually responsible, none of the contemporary investigators seemed interested in discovering the truth: the British authorities only wanted to find evidence of a carefully-planned conspiracy against them, which they could use as political leverage; while the Chinese hoped for a solution which excused their officials from any responsibility in the affair. In the end there were so many people with vested interests in promoting one version or another, so many armchair theorists, hostile witnesses, duplicitous civil servants and angry newspaper readers, that we will never know which of them, if any, was actually telling the truth.

Margary's father, Major-General Henry Joshua Margary, died in 1876 at the British seaside resort of Weston-Super-Mare "suddenly, of paralysis, through excessive grief at the loss of his dearly-loved and valued son". He was 65. Margary's own probate amounted to "effects under £200", which were sent to his mother Louisa as next of kin.

Margary had a nephew named in his memory, but this equally unlucky Augustus Raymond died even younger, aged just twelve. In 1880, a public subscription paid for a Margary Memorial on the riverfront in Shanghai's Foreign Concession area, which resembled a small version of London's Albert Memorial. It was removed by Japanese occupation forces during WWII and never replaced.

Today, Margary's sole surviving monument is a headstone-like marker on the roadside 1.5 kilometres west of Mangyun, whose Chinese inscription reads simply, "Site of the Margary Incident". A larger tablet opposite, erected in the 1990s in the shade of some old yellow-fruiting fig trees, provides one final interpretation of the events:

> *In the first year of the Guangxu emperor (1875), Browne and Margary followed the route from Burma and invaded the Yingjiang* [Sanda] *area at Mangyun. On the 21st of February, Margary*

encountered a group of local ethnic minorities. After he hastily killed one of them, the others were filled with righteous indignation. They killed Margary and his four companions, threw his body into the Husong River, and drove Browne and his military expedition out of the country.

After the incident, the corrupt and incompetent Qing government succumbed to foreign governments' demands and cruelly oppressed the patriotic people who had defended the borders of the motherland. They arrested those responsible for the massacre and signed the humiliating Chefoo Convention with the British government in the second year of Guangxu (1876). However, the feats of those soldiers and civilians who valiantly defended the frontier against the aggressors will never be forgotten.

Site of the Margary Incident

Glossary

Allen, Clement Francis Romilly (1844–1920). Allen joined the British administration in China in 1863 and was appointed backup interpreter to Browne's 1875 expedition. He later served in consular posts around the country and retired back to Britain in 1898. Despite long immersion in China he believed the Chinese had descended from ancient Babylonians.

Anderson, Dr John (1833–1900). Born into an Edinburgh banking family, he was appointed naturalist and medic to the 1868 and 1875 expeditions, making "a large collection of valuable specimens", and also authored the published accounts. He later explored Burma's Mergui archipelago, became professor of comparative anatomy at Calcutta, was a member of the Royal Society, Linnaean Society and Society of Antiquaries, and served as president of the London Zoological Society.

Arakan Modern Rakhine state in Myanmar. Originally an independent country between Bengal and Burma, annexed by Burma in the 1770s. Arguments over Arakan's borders led to the First Anglo-Burmese War of 1824.

Ava Former Burmese kingdom and intermittent capital city of the country from 1364 until the nineteenth century. Modern name Inwa.

Baber, Edward Colborne (1843–1890). Joined the China consular service in 1866 and accompanied Grosvenor's mission as interpreter; his notes and maps became the basis of the official report. Later explored Sichuan province, authoring *Travels and Researches in Western China* and *The Chinese Tea-trade with Tibet*, and served at Beijing, Shantou and Korea.

Beijing Chinese capital; historically transliterated as Peking and Pekin.

Bengal Northeastern region of India, covering modern Western Bengal and Bangladesh.

Bhamo Town on the Irrawaddy river in northern Myanmar, close to the border with China's Yunnan province. Used as a base by both Sladen's and Browne's expeditions. The Chinese name, Xinjie or "Newmarket", is pronounced "Xinkai" locally.

Bombazine, aka Zhang Yongqian. Margary's personal servant. Bombazine is a fabric, often used for mourning clothing, so perhaps he wore dark clothes or had a gloomy nature (though seems cheerful enough in Margary's accounts).

Browne, Colonel Horace Albert (1831–1914). Born in Lincolnshire, he was commissioned into the Indian Army in 1852. Leader of the abortive 1875 expedition to reopen trade routes between Burma and Yunnan, he also served as the last British Resident at the Burmese capital before Britain annexed the entire country in 1885. His acerbic *Reminiscences of the Court of Mandalay* is critical of just about everybody he had to deal with throughout his career.

Bulang Ethnic minority living along the China-Burma border regions.

Burma Modern name Myanmar. Buddhist kingdom between India and China, also bordering Thailand and Laos. In 1852 the British took control of coastal Lower Burma, leaving interior Upper Burma under the king's control. In 1885 Britain deposed the king and annexed the entire country; Burma regained its independence in 1948.

Calcutta Modern name Kolkata. Founded during the eighteenth century by the British East India Company on the site of a small fishing hamlet, the city grew to become capital of Bengal and seat of the British administration in India until 1911.

Cen Yuying, (1829–1889). Tough and abrasive Chinese general and administrator from rural Guangxi province, who rose to prominence after playing a key role in bringing the long-running and destructive Muslim Uprising in Yunnan to an end. As governor of Yunnan, the British held him responsible for Margary's death and some believed he had actually given the orders to attack the expedition. The higher Chinese authorities accepted Cen's reports that the attack had been carried out by a mix of bandits and ethnic minorities, and he escaped any censure over the affair.

Chongqing Important walled city on the Yangzi river, something of a trading hub for southwestern China and gateway into Sichuan province.

Cochinchina Southern Vietnam under the nineteenth-century French administration.

Cooke, Captain Crawford Boyd (1844–1925). Born in Madras to a British military family he served as the British Political Agent at Bhamo from 1874, and accompanied Elias to Mengmao the following year, as part of Browne's expedition.

Dai Thai-speaking ethnic group, also known as the Shan, along the China-Burma borderlands.

Dali Historically important city in western Yunnan, along the main road between the capital Kunming and the Burmese border. Du Wenxiu, leader of the Muslim Panthays, took Dali as his capital during his nineteenth-century uprising against the Chinese government. The French Lagrée Expedition managed to drop in during this time, and later both Margary and Grosvenor visited on their way to Tengyue.

Davenport, Arthur (1837–1916). Born in Gloucestershire, he began his China career as an interpreter and by 1875 was the British vice-consul at Beijing. After accompanying the Grosvenor Mission, he served as consul at Shanghai, Yantai and Tianjin before retiring to Devon around 1890. Author of *Upon the Trading Capabilities of the Country Traversed by the Yunnan Mission*, and *China from Within: a Study of the Opium Fallacies and Missionary Mistakes*.

dha Longsword carried by almost all adult men in the Burma-Chinese frontier regions.

Dupuis, Jean (1829–1912). French merchant and arms dealer resident in China from the early 1860s, who forged a route to Kunming from Vietnam in 1868 to supply the Chinese forces with modern weapons. In 1873 he was caught up in Francis Garnier's freelance attempt to capture Hanoi, dragged out by French forces, and deported back to France. He later wrote several books about his experiences but had faded into obscurity by the time of his death.

Dongting Lake Shallow but seasonally extensive lake on the Yangzi river between Wuhan and Yichang in Hubei province.

Du Wenxiu (1823–1872). Islamic scholar turned warlord from Yongchang, who in 1856 took Dali in Yunnan as the Panthay capital during his Muslim Uprising. After surrendering to Chinese forces at the end of the war, he committed suicide on his way to execution by taking an opium overdose. His son Hassan was on a diplomatic mission to Britain at the time, seeking support for the rebellion.

Elias, Ney (1844–1897). Educated in London, Paris and Dresden, Elias had travelled solo in China and Russia before joining Browne's expedition in 1875. His plans for an expedition to Tibet two years later were blocked by Thomas Wade and he was appointed joint-commissioner of Ladakh. Depressed by this settled life, he made an unsanctioned trip east across the Karakoram into Chinese Turkestan, and in the 1880s became political agent at Meshed in Iran. A modest man who turned down any recognition for his work, he retired in 1896 and died the following year from blood poisoning.

Embassy route The central trail between Bhamo and Tengyue, followed by Sladen on his way back to Burma in 1868. Also taken by the Burmese tribute embassy and their elephants in 1875.

Er Tong Ao One of the tribesmen put on trial at Kunming, accused by the Chinese of killing Margary.

Fenouil, Father. French priest at Kunming, who assisted the 1868 French Lagrée expedition, and after the event was quoted by the papers as having predicted Margary's death.

Garnier, Francis (1839–1873). Eventual leader of the 1866–68 French Lagrée Expedition to explore Vietnam, the Mekong region and China. In 1873 he returned to Vietnam to negotiate a trade agreement and was killed at Hanoi after attempting to seize the city.

Goggles aka Yu Dujian. Margary's Christian Chinese secretary, named after his enormous brass-rimmed spectacles. Killed at Mangyun.

Grosvenor, Thomas George (1842–1886). Second son of Lord Ebury, he joined the British diplomatic corps in 1861 and served at Berlin, Washington, Berne, Vienna and Copenhagen. As secretary to the British legation at Beijing, in 1875 he travelled from Shanghai to Burma investigating Margary's death. He died in Russia.

Guangxi South-western Chinese province where the Taiping Uprising began.

Guangzhou Capital of southern China's Guangdong province.

Guiyang Capital of Guizhou province.

Guizhou Southwestern Chinese province

Han Majority ethnic group in China, comprising over ninety percent of the population, and named after the Han dynasty (202 BC – 220 AD).

Hankou North-bank district of Wuhan, capital of Hubei province, on the Yangzi in central China.

Hassan aka Liu Daohong, adopted son of the Panthay leader Du Wenxiu. After the failure of his 1872 mission to London he arrived at Rangoon that December to hear that Dali was about to fall and he couldn't return home. Initially allowed to stay in Burma, he was later settled in India but received no further political help from the British government.

Hotha Important village on the central Embassy route between Bhamo and Tengyue, visited by Sladen's expedition on their return trip to Burma in 1868.

Hui A generic term for Chinese Muslims; also see Panthay.

Jiang Zonghan (1838–1903). Born into a lower-class ethnic Yi family, Jiang's soldiering skills were honed by Yang Yuke during the Muslim Uprising. As military commander at Tengyue, he met Margary in late 1874 and the two men seemed to get on well. Jiang received some of the blame for Margary's murder and was later demoted, but soon returned to his post, eventually establishing a successful trading house and becoming military governor of Guizhou province.

Jinghong City on the Mekong river near the Chinese-Lao border in Yunnan province, once the target of an ambitious British plan to build a railway from Rangoon to China.

Kachin Relatively recent arrivals to the Burma-China borderlands, they were divided into clans or tribes, lived in communal longhouses, kept slaves and believed in a spirit-world of *nats*. The British reported their having a bad reputation as troublemakers in Burma, but in China were treated with more consideration. Known in Chinese as Jingpo.

Kachin Hills Range of hills on the Northern route between Bhamo and Tengyue, home to several Kachin tribes.

Kunming Capital of China's Yunnan province.

La Dou Man blamed by the Chinese authorities for killing Margary and attacking Browne's party.

Lagrée Expedition French exploration of the Mekong river and adjacent regions in 1866–68. They managed to visit parts of Vietnam, Cambodia, Laos and Thailand before entering China's Yunnan province at Jinghong. From there they travelled to Kunming, Dali – where they attempted to meet Du Wenxiu, leader of the Muslim Uprising – before reaching the Yangzi river and following it all the way down to Shanghai. The expedition leader, Lagrée, died in Yunnan, and Francis Garnier led the final stages of the mission.

Laila, "Come Here", aka Lu Dalin. One of Margary's staff, a Chinese fixer lent him by a colleague at Shanghai. He was killed at Mangyun.

Lancang Chinese name for the Mekong river.

Lecomte, Father. French priest at Bhamo who tells Browne about a forged letter, supposedly written by the Burmese king, calling for locals to rise against the British.

Leguilcher, Father. French priest, long resident in China, whose help got the Lagrée Expedition into Dali in 1868, while the city was under Muslim occupation during the Panthay Uprising.

Lei Yingshan Apostate Christian general in charge of security for the Grosvenor Mission on their journey between Kunming and Mangyun. He works hard to protect the mission and lets drop plenty of background information which often contradicts the official Chinese version of events.

Li Guolun Muslim military governor of Tengyue during the Panthay Uprising, befriended by the British. He died at the end of the war, around 1874, but his son continued to stir up trouble along the border.

Li Hanzhang (1821–1899), Elder brother of the famous Chinese statesman Li Hongzhang. Ordered by the Emperor to investigate Margary's murder, he apparently delayed setting out, but in fact sent a spy ahead to Tengyue disguised as a cloth merchant to pick up news of what had happened. Eventually travelled to Kunming with fellow commissioner Xue Huan, where they worked with Cen Yuying.

Li Shouk-goon aka Li Xiaohong. Leader of the attack on Browne's party in 1875 and apparently the interpreter at the Kunming trial of the suspects arrested by the Chinese; possibly also the man who actually killed Margary. Described as a protege of Li Zhenguo.

Li Tongshi also known by his Burmese name, Moung Yu. Tengyue native and distant relative of Li Zhenguo, he fled to Burma at the start of the Muslim Uprising in Yunnan. Returning with Browne's expedition after the war, he was taken prisoner by the Chinese at Seray as an ally of the British; he later gave two completely different accounts of his time as a prisoner and witness at the trial in Kunming. His surname, Li, saw British reports confuse him with Li Shouk-goon, the man who led the attack on Browne's party.

Li Xiaohong See Li Shouk-goon

Li Zhenguo (died 1888), also known by his military title, Li Xietai. Warlord and general in the Chinese forces at Tengyue, Li fought the Muslim occupation of his hometown and later organised resistance against Sladen's party. Dismissed as little more than a bandit in some British accounts, people who met him – including Margary – were impressed by his obvious authority and intelligence. Although officially blamed for the attack on Browne's expedition, Li Zhenguo was several days' journey further south at the time, stopping Elias and Cooke from entering China along the Southern route from Bhamo.

Lin Zexu Chinese official who, by destroying British opium in 1839, was blamed for precipitating the Opium Wars and exiled to China's far west. He later investigated and suppressed Muslim-Han conflicts around Yongchang, disturbances which eventually escalated into the Muslim Uprising.

Lu Dalin, see Laila.

Ma Rulong (1832-1891). Born at Jianshui, southern Yunnan, he commanded the Hui forces which laid siege to Kunming in the early stages of the Muslim Uprising. He later defected to the Chinese cause and, awarded for bravery, served in Hunan and Sichuan. Heavily scarred from war wounds, Ma is believed to have died of complications from his injuries.

Manchu Horse-riding warriors from what is now northeastern China, who in 1644 broke through the Great Wall, captured Beijing and founded the Qing dynasty (1644–1912). Their rule was widely resented by China's ethnic Han majority.

Mandalay Burmese royal capital 1857–85.

Mangyun Small town with mixed Burmese-Shan-Chinese population, inside China but close to the Burmese border. It was a major staging post on the Bhamo–Tengyue road; Margary was killed just outside near some yellow-fruiting fig trees.

Margary Augustus Raymond (1846–1875; Chinese name 馬加里): Arrived in China 1867 and served as a British consular official at Beijing, Shanghai, Taiwan and Yantai. Awarded the Albert Medal in 1872 for rescuing shipwrecked sailors off Keelung. In 1874 appointed interpreter to Browne's expedition and travelled overland from Shanghai to Burma via Hankou, Guizhou and Yunnan provinces. Killed at Mangyun in malicious circumstances during the return journey into China.

Mekong Lengthy river in Southeast Asia, originating in China where it is called the Lancang.

Mengla Modern name Gan'ai. Settled district on the Tengyue–Mangyun road, divided into Xincheng ("New Town") north of the river, and Jiucheng ("Old Town") to the south.

Mengmao Modern name Ruili. A town on the southern route between Bhamo and Tengyue, right on the Burma border, where Li Zhenguo prevented Elias and Cooke from entering China in 1875.

Mindon Min (1808–1878). Burmese king ruling from 1854 and founder of the royal capital of Mandalay, whose reign was characterised by skilful juggling of British demands and Burmese interests. Initially suspected by the British for colluding with Chinese forces over Margary's killing and the attack on Browne's expedition.

Ming Chinese dynasty 1368–1644.

Momien Burmese/Shan name for Tengyue.

Moung Yu See Li Tongshi.

Muslim Uprising 1856–1873. Also known as the Panthay Uprising. A revolt against Chinese rule by Yunnan's ethnic Hui population. Though the origins were long-running racial frictions, the uprising itself had its roots at the town of Yongchang and successive eruptions of violence in rural copper mines and at the city of Kunming. Eventually led by a scholar-turned-warlord Du Wenxiu, who took the town of Dali as his capital and held loose authority over western areas of Yunnan. The uprising was systematically suppressed by Cen Yuying, working with the Bai warlord Yang Yuke and former Muslim rebel Ma Rulong, and ended with the Chinese capture of Dali and the death of Du Wenxiu, and subsequent campaigns to put down final pockets of resistance in Yunnan's far southwest.

Myanmar Modern name for Burma.

Nantin Modern name Lianghe. Valley and village on the Bhamo-Tengyue route.

nat Kachin nature spirits, taking many forms.

North-China Herald Authoritative English-language newspaper at Shanghai during the nineteenth century.

Northern route Track from Bhamo to Tengyue followed by the British expeditions in 1868 and 1875, which crossed the Kachin Hills to Mangyun.

Nü river Chinese name for the Salween.

Opium Wars 1840–1860. A series of conflicts precipitated by British attempts to force trade deals with China by importing opium against the Qing government's wishes. Defeated by modern weapons, the Chinese government was forced to sign "Unequal Treaties" opening up the country to foreign trade. The wars destabilised and discredited the Qing administration, whose loss of authority indirectly led to the massively destructive Taiping Uprising against their rule.

Panthay Uprising See Muslim Uprising.

Panthays Another name for Yunnan's rebel Muslims, from the Burmese word *pansee*.

Peking Former transliteration for the name of the Chinese capital, now written Beijing.

Peking Gazette Published official proclamations by the Qing court (a selection of which were translated in the *North-China Herald*). Announcements in the *Gazette* of all foreign dealings with the Chinese government was one of Wade's key demands for settling the Margary Affair; without these notices British actions in China appeared random and inexplicable to the general public, the source of much xenophobic resentment.

Ponline Village on the Northern route between Bhamo and Mangyun.

Ponsee Modern name Panxi. Village on the Northern route between Bhamo and Mangyun. Browne's expedition was attacked nearby in 1875.

Pouriat, Father. French missionary who travelled briefly with Margary in Yunnan.

Gong Yixin (1833–1898) Manchu prince who headed China's Ministry of Foreign Affairs and spent eight months jousting with the British representative Thomas Wade over the exact terms for the investigation into Margary's death.

Qing 1644–1912. Final Chinese dynasty, of Manchu origin.

Rangoon Now Yangon. Southern Burmese port city which became the capital of the British administration after 1852.

rupee Indian currency.

Salween Southeast Asian river originating in China, where it is known as the Nü.

Sanda Modern name Yingjiang. Large village on the Mangyun–Tengyue road.

Sawaddy First village on the Southern route between Bhamo and Tengyue.

Seray Modern name Xueli. A village in the hills southwest of Mangyun, visited by Browne the day before the ambush on his expedition, and where Moung Yu and Shi Yutian were left by the British, and later captured.

Shan See Dai.

Shanghai Major east-coast port on the Huangpu river, just up from the Yangzi's estuary. Originally an entirely Chinese city, after the 1850s different self-governing districts were built to accommodate various foreign populations.

Shi Yutian Dr Allen's Chinese secretary, left at Seray by the British the day before the attack on Browne's party and later captured – and apparently killed – by local militias.

Siam Nineteenth-century name for the region making up modern Thailand.

Sichuan South-western Chinese province bordering Yunnan.

Sladen, Sir Edward Bosc (1830–1890): British soldier and administrator. Born at Madras and educated in England, he later served in India and Burma. After leading the 1868 expedition to Tengyue, and taking part in Browne's 1875 attempt, he was appointed commissioner of Arakan and in 1885 received the submission of King Thebaw to British rule. Authored *Official Narrative of and Papers Connected with the Expedition to Explore Trade Routes to China via Bhamo*.

Song Baohua Chinese representative of the 1875 Grosvenor Mission to investigate Margary's death, who travelled with the mission from Shanghai to Kunming.

Southern route Longest of the three options between Bhamo and Tengyue, briefly explored by Sladen's scouts in 1868. The British hoped to follow it in 1875, until the chief of Sawaddy, first stop along the way, caused so much trouble they abandoned this plan – though Elias and Cooke, travelling independently of the main expedition, got as far as the Chinese border before being stopped by Li Zhenguo.

Sprye, Captain Richard Samuel Mare (1798–1878). Born in Devon, he served in the Madras Regiment in India and Burma until his support of an Indian prince against the British authorities saw him dismissed from office. He suffered a breakdown and retired to London, where he was bankrupted waiting six years before an appeal process fully acquitted him. He later inherited a considerable estate and began agitating for a trade route between Rangoon and Jinghong in China.

tael Chinese silver ingot currency, literally an ounce.

Taiping Uprising Mass peasant rebellion 1850–1864 against China's ruling Qing dynasty by failed government official Hong Xiuquan, which devastated eastern China and caused the deaths of an estimated twenty million people.

Talone Village on the Northern route between Bhamo and Mangyun.

Tengyue Modern name Tengchong. Last major settlement before the frontier on the road from Kunming to Burma, captured by Muslim forces during their uprising. The Muslim governor, Li Guolun, welcomed Sladen in 1868, which likely led to fears that the second British expedition in 1875 was coming to reinstate the rebel administration.

Tsitkaw First settlement on the Northern route between Bhamo and Tengchong.

Unequal Treaties Three treaties forced on the Chinese during the Opium Wars of 1840–1860, which opened the country to foreign trade and demanded huge financial indemnities.

Wade, Thomas Francis (1818–1895). Born in London and schooled in South Africa, Mauritius and Cambridge before being commissioned 1838. He went to China in 1842 as a lieutenant in the Opium Wars and in 1852 was appointed vice-consul at Shanghai, where he helped set up what became the Imperial Maritime Customs Service. By the time of Margary's murder he was British Minister at Beijing, and negotiated the terms of the

British investigation and China's apology. Accused of being too measured and slow, he was nonetheless knighted in 1875.

won Burmese official or minister.

Wu Qiliang Chinese general and administrator, previously posted to Yongchang where he helped arrange Burma's elephant envoy, Wu took part in recapturing Tengyue at the end of the Muslim Uprising, and was appointed acting Sub-Prefect there in 1874. He organised repairs to the city's bell tower and temples, before being blamed along with Jiang Zonghan for failing to prevent Margary's murder.

Wuhan Huge central Chinese city and capital of Hubei province, split into three parts by the Yangzi and Han rivers.

Xue Huan (1815–1880). Retired former governor at Shanghai, appointed Commissioner into the Yunnan affair alongside Li Hanzhang.

Yang Yuke (died 1885). Bai warlord at Dali mentored by Cen Yuying, widely mistrusted as a "barbarian" by the Chinese authorities, but who impressed some foreign observers with his courage and frank demeanour. His forces captured Dali at the end of the Muslim Uprising, and he later assisted the Tengyue authorities in rounding up suspects in Margary's killing – though he later told the Grosvenor Mission that he had never been to Tengyue. He died fighting against the French occupation of northern Vietnam.

Yangzi Also transliterated as Yangtze and Yangtse. China's longest river and major trade, transport and communications artery as it flows 6,300 kilometres eastwards from the Tibetan plateau across the centre of the country, to the coast near Shanghai.

Yichang Town on the middle Yangzi river, at the eastern gateway to the Three Gorges.

Yongchang Modern name Baoshan. Major town in western Yunnan on the post road between Kunming and the Burmese border. Violence between the Chinese and Muslim population here in 1845 sparked the widespread Muslim Uprising a decade later.

Yu Dujian see Goggles.

Yunnan China's most southwesterly province, bordering Tibet, Burma and Laos, and inhabited by multiple ethnic groups.

Zhang Yongqian See Bombazine.

Zhou Yuding Margary's cook, from Hunan. According to one source the sole survivor of the attack, though others reported him killed at Mangyun.

Select Bibliography

Alcock, Rutherford. *The Journey of Augustus Raymond Margary* (Macmillan 1876)

Anderson, John.

– *A Report on the Expedition to Western Yunnan via Bhamo* (Calcutta 1871)

– *Mandalay to Momien* (Macmillan 1876)

Andrews, Roy Chapman. *Camps and Trails in China* (D. Appleton 1919)

Atwill, David. *The Chinese Sultanate: Islam, Ethnicity, and the Panthay Rebellion in Southwest China* (Stanford University 2005)

Baber, E. Colborne. *Travels and Researches in Western China* (John Murray 1882)

Browne, Colonel Horace Albert. *Reminiscences of the Court of Mandalay* (1907)

Bruce, George. *The Burma Wars 1824–1886* (Harper Collins 1973)

Cause of the Riots in the Yangtse Valley: A "Complete Picture Gallery" (translation of 谨遵圣谕辟邪全图, *A Complete Picture of Obedience to the Sacred Mandate and Exorcising Evil*, Hankow 1891)

Chung-li Chang. *The Chinese Gentry: Studies on the Role in Nineteenth-century Chinese Society* (University of Washington Press 1955)

Cobden, Richard. *How Wars are Got Up in India* (William & Frederick Cash 1853)

Collis, Maurice. *Land of the Great Image* (Faber 1943)

Colquhoun, Archibald. *Across Chryse* (Sampson Low 1883)

Correspondence Respecting the Attack on the Indian Expedition to Western China and the Murder of Mr Margary, Presented to Both Houses of Parliament by Command of Her Majesty (Harrison and Sons 1876)

Coryton, J. *Trade Routes Between British Burma and Western China* (Royal Geographical Society 1875)

Cox, Hiram. *Journal of a Residence in the Burmhan Empire* (London 1821)

Dai, Yingcong. *Disguised Defeat: the Myanmar Campaign of the Qing Dynasty* (*Modern Asian Studies 38*, Cambridge University Press 2004)

Dalrymple, William. *The Anarchy* (Bloomsbury 2020)

Dautremer, Joseph. *Burma Under British Rule* (translated by Sir George Scott, Scribner 1913)

Davenport, Arthur. *Upon the Trading Capabilities of the Country Traversed by the Yunnan Mission* (Harrison and Sons, 1877)

Davies, Major Henry Randolph. *Yün-nan: The Link Between India and the Yangtze* (Cambridge University Press 1909)

Dictionary of National Biography

de Albuquerque, Afonso. *Commentaries of the Great Afonso Dalboquerque, Second Viceroy of India* (translated by Walter de Gray Birch, Hakluyt Society 1875)

de Carné, Louis. *Travels in Indo-China and the Chinese Empire* (Chapman & Hall 1872)

Dijk, Wil O. *The VOC in Burma 1634–1680* (Journal of Burma Studies Volume 6, 2001)

Dillon, Michael. *China's Muslims* (Oxford University Press 1996)

Dingle, Edwin. *Across China on Foot* (Henry Holt 1911)

Dupuis, Jean.

– *L'ouverture du Fleuve Rouge au Commerce et les Événements du Tong-Kin* (Challamel 1879)

– *Les Origines de la Question du Tong-Kin* (Challamel 1896)

Evans, Brian. *The Panthay Mission of 1872 and its Legacies* (*Journal of Southeast Asian Studies* Vol.16, No.1 Cambridge University Press 1985)

Ferguson, Niall. *Empire: How Britain Made the Modern World* (Penguin 2004)

Fletcher, H.G. *Tengyueh: Route Book of Travels in the Neighbourhood* (Shanghai 1927)

Fox, Pamela. *Causes of Han-Hui Conflicts of the 1840's in Yongchang, Western Yunnan* (University of British Columbia 1989)

Foster, William. *England's Quest of Eastern Trade* (A&C Black 1933)

Fraser, John Foster. *Round the World on a Wheel* (Methuen 1899)

Freeman, Michael and **Ahmed**, Selena. *Tea Horse Road: China's Ancient Road to Tibet* (River Books 2011)

Garnier, Francis. *Voyage D'Exploration en Indo-Chine* (Hachette 1873)

Geographical Journal, Vol. 10, No. 1 (Royal Geographical Society, July 1897)

Gilhodes, Charles. *The Kachins – Religion and Mythology* (Catholic Orphan Press 1922)

Gill, William John. *The River of Golden Sand* (John Murray 1880)

Grabowsky and **Turton**. *The Gold and Silver Road of Friendship: The McLeod and Richardson Diplomatic Missions to the Tai States in 1837* (Silkworm, Chiang Mai 2003)

Grosvenor, Thomas. *Diary of Mr Grosvenor's Mission* (National Archives FO17/742 – FO17/747)

Hahn, Emily. *China Only Yesterday 1850–1950* (Doubleday 1963)

Hanna, Willard Anderson. *Indonesian Banda* (c.1978; no publisher or date)

Hansard Parliamentary Records (http://hansard.parliament.uk)

Hickey, William. *The Memoirs of William Hickey* (4 vols; Blacket 1913–1925)

Hudson, Roger. *The Raj: An Eyewitness History* (Folio 1999)

Hummel, Arthur. *Eminent Chinese of the Ch'ing Period* (US Government Printing Office 1943)

Israeli, Raphael. *Muslims in China* (Cambridge University Press 1980)

Jack, Robert Logan. *The Backblocks of China* (Edward Arnold 1904)

Lamb, Alastair. *British Missions to Cochin China: 1788-1822* (Vol 34, parts 3 & 4, Malaysian Branch of the Royal Asiatic Society 1961)

Li Zhenguo and others. *Report of the Chinese Commissioners' Investigations and Findings* (National Archives FO 1080/177/1 – 1080/177/4)

Liang Chuyang *Research and Arrangement of "Cen Xiangqin's Chronicle"* ("岑襄勤公年谱"研究整理, published online at sohu.com, 2019)

Margary, Augustus Raymond. *Notes of a Journey from Hankow to Ta-Li Fu* (Shanghai 1875)

National Census (ancestry.co.uk)

Moon, Edward Penderel. *The British Conquest and Dominion of India* (Duckworth 1989)

Moorhouse, Geoffrey. *Calcutta: The City Revealed* (Penguin 1983)

Morgan, Gerald. *Ney Elias* (Allen & Unwin 1971)

North-China Herald (Shanghai 1850–86)

Osbourne, Milton. *River Road to China* (Readers Union 1976)

Pall Mall Gazette (London 1875–86)

Pemberton, Robert Boileau. *Abstract of the Journal of a Route Travelled by Captain S.F. Hannay* (*SOAS Bulletin of Burma Research Vol 3*, 2005).

Pigafetta, Antonio. *Magellan's Voyage: A Narrative Account of the First Circumnavigation* (Dover 1994)

Ramachandra, G. P. *Anglo-Burmese Relations 1795–1826* (University of Hull doctoral thesis, 1977)

Reid, Anthony. *Southeast Asia in the Age of Commerce, 1450–1680* (two volumes, Yale University Press 1988–95)

Rowe, William. *China's Last Empire: the Great Qing* (Belknap Press 2012)

Sangermano, Vincenzo. *The Burmese Empire a Hundred Years Ago* (Archibald Constable 1893)

Silberstein, Rachel. *A Fashionable Century: Textile Artistry and Commerce in the Late Qing* (University of Washington Press 2020)

Sladen, Edward Bosc. *Official Narrative of and Papers Connected with the Expedition to Explore Trade Routes to China via Bhamo* (Rangoon 1869)

Spear, Percival. *Master of Bengal: Clive and His India* (Thames & Hudson 1975)

Sprye, Richard. *Correspondence Between Captain Richard Sprye and the Rt Hon William-Ewert Gladstone on the Commercial Opening of the Shan States and Western Inland China by Railway Direct from Rangoon* (London 1865)

Staunton, George Thomas. *Ta Tsing Leu Lee, being The Fundamental Laws of the Penal Code of China* (translation of 大清律例重訂, London 1810)

Symes, Michael. *An Account of an Embassy to the Kingdom of Ava in the Year 1795* (2 vols; Edinburgh 1827)

Tagliacozzo, Eric and **Wen-Chin Chang** *Chinese Circulations* (Duke University Press, 2011)

Tarling, Nicholas. *Southeast Asia – A Modern History* (Oxford University Press 2001)

The Times (London 1875–86)

Tung-Tsu Ch'u. *Local Government in China Under the Ch'ing* (Stanford University Press 1969)

Vincent, Frank Jnr. *The Land of the White Elephant* (Harper & Brothers 1874)

Wang Shen-tsu. *The Margary Affair and the Chefoo Agreement* (Oxford University Press 1940)

Wei, Alice. *The Moslem Rebellion 1855–73* (University of Chicago thesis T24908; 1974)

Williamson, Alexander. *Journeys in North China* (Smith, Elder and Co. 1870)

Wilson, Horace Hayman. *Narrative of the Burmese War in 1824–26* (W.H. Allen 1852)

Woodman, Dorothy. *The Making of Burma* (Cresset Press 1962)

Younghusband, George John. *Eighteen Hundred Miles on a Burmese Tat* (W. H. Allen 1888)

Zhao Erxun *A Draft History of the Qing Dynasty* (赵尔巽，清史稿. 民国政府国史馆, 1929).

Also by David Leffman:

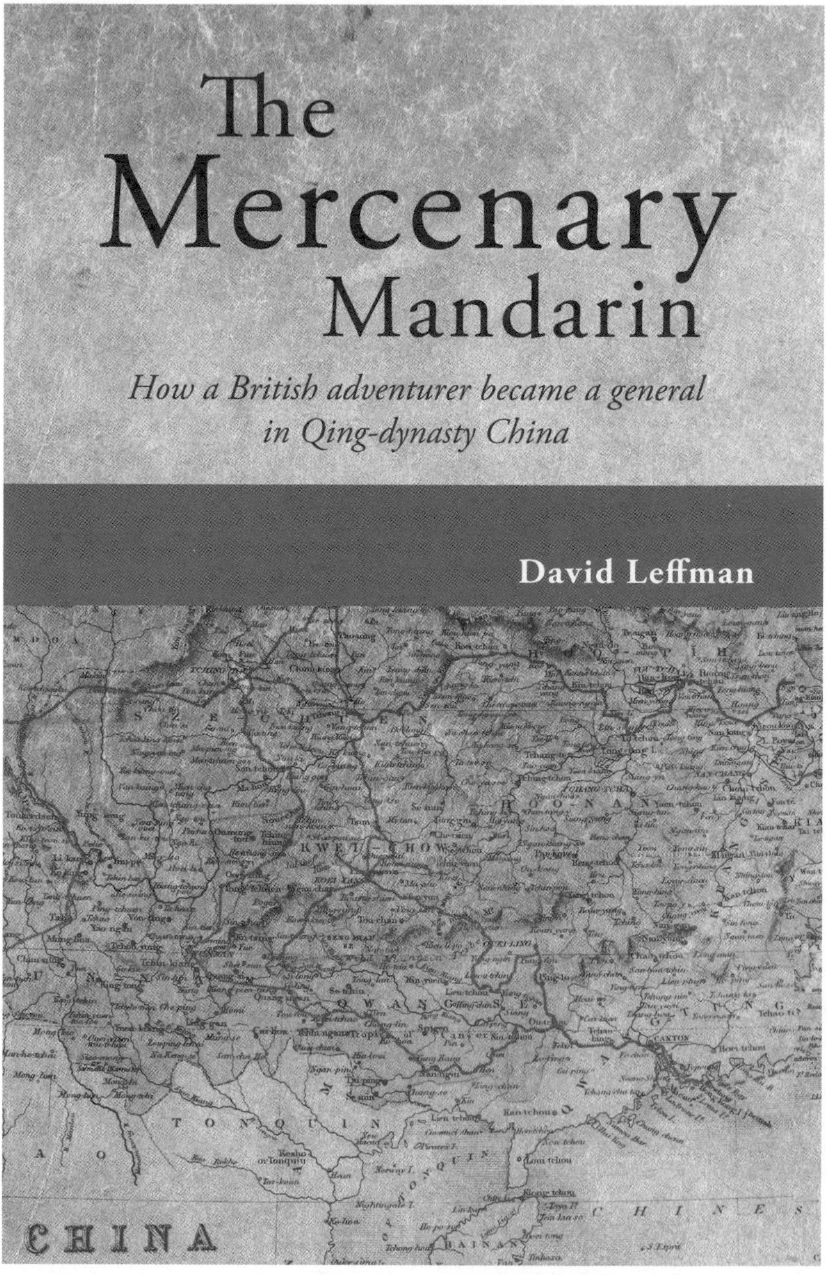

▲ "When you turn the pages of David Leffman's beautifully produced *Paper Horses*, you are tapping into [a] rich legacy. You're looking at something simple yet with profound cultural significance. It feels like reaching through time and touching history." – *Bookish Asia*

◀ "Scholarly in its approach, and clearly distilled from an immense amount of research… Leffman's telling of this tale is well-paced, his writing elegant and his knowledge of China impressive. The book is full of period detail, much of it showing just how remote inland China still was: in the 1860s the 800km journey up the Yangtze from the Three Gorges to Chongqing took six weeks, longer than a sea trip from Shanghai to London; while a Chinese general Mesny meets when he gets to Chongqing is amazed to discover that foreigners have knee joints."

– *South China Morning Post*